THE EARLY REPUBLIC,
1789-1828

Edited by
NOBLE E. CUNNINGHAM, JR.

HARPER TORCHBOOKS
Harper & Row, Publishers
New York and Evanston

FOR DANA

THE EARLY REPUBLIC, 1789–1828

Introduction, Editorial Notes, and compilation copyright
© 1968 by Noble E. Cunningham, Jr.

Printed in the United States of America.

First edition: HARPER TORCHBOOKS, 1968, Harper & Row,
Publishers, Incorporated, 49 East 33rd Street, New York,
N.Y. 10016.

Library of Congress Catalog Card Number: 68-65040.

Contents

III. INTERPRETING THE CONSTITUTION

IV. SHAPING NATIONAL ECONOMIC POLICY

V. Developing the Art of Politics

VI. Building a New Society

Introduction

On April 30, 1789, six years after the peace with Great Britain, George Washington stood on the balcony of Federal Hall at the corner of Wall and Broad Streets in New York City and took the oath of office as President of the United States. At that moment the future of the new republic whose leadership he was assuming was highly uncertain. Within the first decade after winning independence the young nation had overturned its initial constitutional system established under the Articles of Confederation, and in launching the new government under the Constitution its sponsors were well aware that a republican form of government never had been successfully extended over a large country. Four decades later, on March 4, 1829, Andrew Jackson stood outside the Capitol in Washington as Chief Justice John Marshall administered the same oath that Washington, and five successors, had taken. Although the Capitol was yet unfinished and the city had made but scant progress toward constructing L'Enfant's grand design, there was no longer any question in the minds of either Americans or the most skeptical European observers whether the new republic in America could survive. Though its future was still uncertain, the young nation and its new government under the Constitution had proved itself.

In the span of little more than one generation from the presidency of Washington to the presidency of Jackson, the growth of the nation in area and population and the movement of its people had altered immensely the map of America. In 1789 the population totaled slightly under four million, concentrated along the Atlantic coast. There were no states west of the mountains; the western boundary of the nation stopped at the Mississippi River, and to the south the territory of the United States nowhere touched the Gulf of Mexico. Virginia, the most populous state in the Union, had more than twice the population of fourth-ranked New York, and Philadelphia was the nation's largest and leading city.

By 1829 the thirteen original states had admitted eleven additional states to the Union, and most of the area east of the Mississippi had been organized into states. The population, now approaching thirteen million, had already poured across the Mississippi River into the vast area of the Louisiana Purchase secured from France in 1803. When Meriwether Lewis and William Clark set out from St. Louis in 1804, the great wilderness expanse between the Mississippi and the Columbia Rivers was, as Bernard DeVoto has written, "a blank, not only on the map but in human thought." With the Louisiana Purchase and the amazingly successful Lewis and Clark Expedition, this vast area, doubling the size of the United States, came suddenly not only into the possession of Americans but into their consciousness. Within two decades, two states (Louisiana and Missouri) formed from eastern sections of the Louisiana territory had been admitted into the Union. Americans also had flowed over into the Floridas, which were acquired from Spain, and by the mid-1820's settlers were moving into Mexican-held Texas. In 1810, New York City had taken the lead from Philadelphia. Registering about 33,000 in the first census of 1790, New York City stood at 200,000 in the census of 1830. Even more striking was the westward movement of the population. In 1829 the fourth largest state was Ohio, which had entered the Union fourteen years after Washington's inauguration. As *Niles' Weekly Register* reminded its readers in 1826, in commenting on the astonishing growth of that state, "within the perfect recollection of middle aged men, Ohio, and all beyond was the home of the savage—hardly ever trodden by the foot of civilized man." Now Cincinnati was larger than Boston had been in 1789. Beyond Ohio two newer states, Indiana (1816) and Illinois (1818), also had been admitted to the Union.

In the South, Eli Whitney's invention of the cotton gin in 1793 spurred a rapid expansion into the agricultural lands of the lower South and altered the whole economy of the region. In 1790, only 3,000 bales of cotton were produced in the United States; by 1820 cotton production was approaching 350,000 bales per year, and cotton, the youngest of all the Southern staple crops, exceeded in value all the others. With the rapid growth of a cotton economy came not only economic expansion but also major alterations in the social order of the region and new barriers to solving the problem of slavery. The shift of population to the lower South brought two new states into the Union: Mississippi (1817) and Alabama (1819). It also marked the beginning of the decline of the nationally oriented leadership of Virginia in the South and the rise of the sectionally oriented leadership of South Carolina.

By the 1820's the face of the country was rapidly being changed by the building of canals. When the Erie Canal was authorized by the New York legislature in 1817, the longest canal in the country was less than twenty-eight miles. When the Erie Canal was completed across the 364 miles between Albany and Buffalo in 1825, it was the longest canal in the world. Its immediate economic success touched off a canal-building frenzy in the United States, the magnitude of which the even more dramatic success of the railroad was to obscure. The steamboat too altered American ways and outlook after Robert Fulton in 1807 sailed the *Clermont* from New York to Albany in thirty-two hours. An Ohio newspaper editor reminded his readers in 1827 "that *forty* years ago, the idea of a vessel being driven by the propulsion of a steam engine was not suggested—and that *fifteen* years ago, there was not one steam boat running on either the Mississippi or any of its vast tributaries. Now, the power of steam, as a mechanical agent, is applied to almost every human purpose both on the land and on the water. . . . And now, there are about one hundred and twenty steam vessels on the Mississippi and its tributaries; and upwards of 300 on the waters of the United States alone." Even more astonishing changes lay just ahead. "By the construction of railroads, and the introduction of the locomotive engine upon them," he concluded, *"distance itself will become annihilated! and the remotest parts of this vast empire will be brought within the limits of a single neighborhood!"*

With the expansion of the country came growth in the size of the national government. The membership of the House of Representatives, which increased from the constitutional apportionment of 65 to 105 after the first census, doubled to 213 following the fourth census in 1820. Accompanying appointments in the congressional establishment altered markedly the appearance of the small assembly whose members had grouped around the fireplaces in the old congressional hall in Philadelphia. One member who had been in Congress since 1791 protested in 1827 that "formerly two men were sufficient for doorkeepers, etc. to the two Houses, but now there is a regiment." Such increases, however, were due more to the growth of the country than to expanding functions of the national government. The federal bureaucracy had not, in fact, increased significantly since the Federalists had left office in 1801. Twenty years after the Republicans had come into office, there were only two more clerks in the Department of State than there had been in 1801. In the Treasury Department, although the number of employees in the Washington office more than doubled between 1801 and 1826, the total Treasury staff throughout the country, as a result of the elimination of the internal revenue service, was actually less at the close than at the opening of the Jeffersonian era. Republican emphasis on simplicity and frugality in government had checked a burgeoning federal bureaucracy, but the growth of population and territory made an increase in the size of government operations inevitable. This was clearly reflected in the principal public service maintained by the national government: the postal service. In 1790 there were seventy-five post offices and 1,875 miles of post roads; by 1829 there were over 8,000 post offices and 115,000 miles of post roads. However much Americans may have longed to keep their government small and simple, the expansion of the country was making it increasingly impossible to do so.

The course of national development was most clearly set during the years from Washington to Jackson in the area of political institutions. Above all, this period was the crucial formative era of American political processes and structures. In the Federalist decade of the 1790's the nation was absorbed in establishing a new government—creating the machinery of government, setting the direction of national policy, and maintaining the independence of the young republic in the midst of wars and revolutions in Europe. The outline of government provided by the Constitution was implemented and the operations of government institutionalized by the creation of executive departments, the formation of the cabinet, and the working out of relationships between the president and the Congress.

The pattern of political party development in the United States was early determined. The framers of the Constitution had not anticipated the rise of national political parties and, in fact, believed, as Madison argued in the *Federalist* papers, that the Constitution was designed to guard against the evil of parties. The view which Washington stressed in his farewell address (Document 5), that parties were dangers to be avoided, was shared by most Americans, even those busily engaged in building political parties. "The situation of the public good, in the hands of two parties nearly poised as to numbers, must be extremely perilous," wrote John Taylor of Caroline County, Virginia, in 1794. "Truth is a thing, not of divisibility into conflicting parts, but of unity." The viewpoint expressed by Taylor led each party to regard itself as the rightful manifestation of the public good and its opponents alone as dangerous to the republic. Washington's administration had begun under nonparty conditions, but as early as 1792 the lines of conflict between Alexander Hamilton and Thomas Jefferson in the cabinet had been clearly drawn and two voting blocs or factions were forming in Congress. In the presidential election of 1792 there was an effort made by the emerging Republican interest to unseat John Adams as vice president. Before the end of Washington's second term, two national political parties had been distinctly formed in the United States, and the election to choose the successor to the first president in 1796 was clearly a party contest between the Federalist supporters of Adams and the Republican followers of Jefferson. A Republican campaign circular sent out from Philadelphia in 1796 proclaimed that the race for the presidency was "between two men of very dissimilar politics, indeed—THOMAS JEFFERSON and JOHN ADAMS. It remains with the Citizens of Pennsylvania to decide, in which they will repose confidence,—the uniform advocate of equal rights among citizens, or the champion of rank, titles and hereditary distinctions;—the steady supporter of our present republican constitution; or the warm panegyrist of the British Monarchical form of Government." An American style of partisan exaggeration was thus evident in this first political campaign for the presidential office.

The election of Adams, by a margin of three electoral votes over Jefferson, set the stage for uninhibited national party development; for as long as Washington, who took the position of being above political parties, remained president, party opposition had been limited. During the Federalist administration of Adams, the Jeffersonian Republicans devoted considerable attention to building party organization, directing political campaigns, and publicizing their policy differences with the Federalists. In the hard-fought party contest of 1800, the Jeffersonians not only defeated Adams in his bid for re-election and elected their party leader to the presidency, but they also won control of both houses of Congress. Though Jefferson exaggerated when he spoke of the "revolution of 1800," the election of 1800 was a decisive Republican victory, and the event was of immense importance in the nation's political development. It brought the first transfer of the vast power of the national goverment from one political party to another, and it did so in a peaceful and orderly fashion.

The Republicans in contesting the re-election of Adams had used every political stratagem and party mechanism that they could devise, but they had also presented to the voters a platform; and Jefferson reiterated this program in his first inaugural address —his best summary of the principles of Jeffersonian democracy (Document 7). Once in office the Jeffersonians proceeded to carry out the policies of simplicity and frugality that they had promised in the campaign: cutting taxes and governmental expenditures, taking steps to pay off the national debt, and reducing the size of the army, the navy, and the diplomatic establishment. These policies of retrenchment were accompanied by a demonstration of concern for the protection of individual rights, which the Jeffersonians had seen threatened by the alien and sedition laws under Adams, and the reinstitution of the five-year residency requirement for naturalization, which had been raised to fourteen years by the Federalists. Thus, with Jefferson's election political parties reached a maturity sufficient to demonstrate that the direction of governmental policy could be effectively altered through the working of the party system.

The adoption of the Constitution had provided the political environment in which the first American party system emerged in the 1790's. Although that early party structure was not to survive, it initiated the two-party tradition in national politics and set many of the patterns of later party development in the United States. So successful were the Jeffersonian Republicans in retaining power that the Federalists never succeeded in making a political comeback in national politics, and after the War of 1812 a one-party period in national politics existed briefly. But by 1824 the Republican congressional nominating caucus, which had nominated the successful presidential candidates since 1800, broke down (Document 24), and national politics entered a new phase of development. The contest for the presidency resulted in the restoration of a two-party system in the age of Jackson.

Throughout the period ran the debate over the interpretation of the Constitution. Jefferson and Hamilton, in the opinions which they wrote on the constitutionality of the national bank in 1791 (Documents 12A, B), early defined the basic distinction between strict construction and loose construction. "I consider the foundation of the Constitution as laid on this ground," wrote Jefferson: "That 'all powers not delegated to the United States, by the Constitution, nor prohibited by it to the States, are reserved to the States or to the People.' To take a single step beyond the boundaries thus specially drawn around the powers of Congress, is to take possession of a boundless field of power, no longer susceptible of any definition." Replied Hamilton: "If the end be clearly comprehended within any of the specified powers, and if the measure have an obvious relation to that end, and is not forbidden by any particular provision of the constitution—it may safely be deemed to come within the compass of the national authority." President Washington agreed with Hamilton and signed the bill chartering the first Bank of the United States. Twenty-eight years later the Supreme Court in the decision in *McCulloch v. Maryland* (Document 15), upholding the constitutionality of the second Bank of the United States, gave judicial sanction to the Hamiltonian interpretation of implied powers. Even the language used by Chief Justice John Marshall was strikingly similar to that used by Washington's Secretary of the Treasury. The political triumph of the Jeffersonians thus did not bring the triumph of Jeffersonian strict construction. Indeed, Jefferson had been in office but two years when the Supreme Court, in a precedent-setting exercise of the power of judicial review in *Marbury v. Madison*, first struck down an act of Congress as unconstitutional. During Marshall's long tenure as Chief Justice (1801–1835), the Supreme Court in a series of momentous decisions went far toward establishing the Hamiltonian ideal of the supremacy of the national government. These were the years in which judicial approval was given to the Hamiltonian interpretation of the implied powers clause, the commerce clause was construed broadly, and the whole constitutional basis for a state-rights interpretation of the Constitution was undermined.

Paradoxically, this was also the period in which a systematic doctrine of state rights was formulated and perpetuated. In 1798 and 1799, the Jeffersonian Republicans—in seeking to combat what they regarded as violations of constitutional guarantees of civil liberties by the alien and sedition acts—appealed for an interposition of state power to restrain the national government, then controlled by the Federalists under Adams. In the Kentucky and Virginia Resolutions (Document 13), Jefferson and Madison articulated a systematic doctrine of state rights. Though they went no further than to protest, they provided the theoretical basis for the compact interpretation of the Constitution, to which later plaintiffs with different causes would resort. Driven from national power by the Jeffersonians in 1800, the Federalists in New England raised the banner of state rights against the Republicans after the purchase of Louisiana; and during the War of 1812 some New England Federalists verged on carrying the doctrine to its ultimate extreme of secession. As the Jacksonian era opened, John C. Calhoun, in the *South Carolina Exposition* (Document 16), was restating the doctrine of state rights in protest against the tariff, and the ground was being prepared for one of the major confrontations of state and national power in the nation's history—the nullification crisis of 1832. Thus, although the direction of constitutional interpretation was firmly set by the Marshall court, the crucial issue of state rights remained unresolved.

Throughout the period that opened with the final protests of the Antifederalists of 1787 and closed with the first outcrys of the South Carolina nullifiers, particularism persisted. Along the way, Americans wrestled with the Kentucky and Virginia Resolutions, the Hartford Convention, and the Missouri Compromise. But despite the tensions between states and sections and the lack of unity that at times threatened the survival of the early republic, the advance of American nationalism moved irresistibly forward. Nowhere can this be better seen than in the area of foreign relations.

In setting the direction of the nation's foreign policy there were frequent conflicts, much floundering, and many reversals, yet by 1823 President James Monroe was able to define an American position (Document 11) which future generations would uphold. Foreign affairs were never far from the minds of American leaders during the first decades of nationhood, for these were years of great convulsion in Europe. The problems of the young American republic cannot be understood without a knowledge of the period of crisis in Europe. Only a few weeks after Washington took the oath of office as president, the Estates General met in France; and before the First Congress could complete its organizational session, the National Assembly was proclaimed at Versailles, the Bastille was stormed, and the Declaration of the Rights of Man and the Citizen was issued. For the next decade the French Revolution and the wars that ensued shaped events on both sides of the Atlantic. Throughout Jefferson's eight years as president, Napoleon ruled France, and with but short pauses his armies were at war with Great Britain and much of Europe. Although Jefferson began his administration under policies of governmental retrenchment on the national level, developments in world affairs produced dramatic alterations in Jeffersonian simplicity and frugality. His first administration was highlighted by the crisis over the Mississippi outlet to the sea, resulting in the vast expansion of the territory of the United States by the Louisiana Purchase in 1803. In his second term, Jefferson was increasingly absorbed in the problems of maritime rights, brought sharply to the forefront by the attack on the *Chesapeake* in June, 1807, and the subsequent enactment of the embargo.

Madison's administration from the outset was dominated by the threat of war with Great Britain, and before the end of his first term Madison had become the nation's first wartime president (Document 8). With the War of 1812, the young nation, militarily weak, ineffectually mobilized, and divided in sentiment (Documents 9A, B), faced the most serious crisis of the period. The lack of unity in support of the war seemed at one time to threaten the survival of the Union. But the wars in Europe ended, peace with Great Britain was obtained, and the nation surged forward in a new phase of quickening national development.

Although this book focuses primary attention on the domestic problems of the new nation, it is important to point out how greatly the policies and actions of the national government were influenced by the world situation. Every president from Washington to John Quincy Adams faced one or more serious crises in foreign affairs. Political success at home not infrequently depended upon the state of foreign relations. The Jay Treaty, the XYZ inci-

dent, the embargo, and the War of 1812 were all intimately en-
twined in domestic politics. The extent to which foreign affairs occupied the attention of Washington's administration can be seen
in his famous farewell address (Document 5). And the continuing
concern with foreign affairs and the formation of the nation's foreign policy can be traced through the messages of Jefferson, Madison, and Monroe (Documents 7, 8, and 11); for the dictum
against permanent or entangling alliances laid down by Washington was reiterated by Jefferson in his first inaugural and reaffirmed
for world attention under President Monroe. From the first years
of Washington's administration to the end of the War of 1812,
Americans were greatly preoccupied with the problems of foreign
affairs. With peace in Europe in 1815, Americans could turn their
attention more fully to domestic affairs. As Henry Adams wrote in
bringing to a close his monumental study of the Jefferson and
Madison administrations: "Every serious difficulty which seemed
alarming to the people of the Union in 1800 had been removed
or had sunk from notice in 1816. With the disappearance of every
immediate peril, foreign or domestic, society could devote all its
energies, intellectual and physical, to its favorite objects. . . . The
continent lay before them, like an uncovered ore-bed."[1]

The forty years from Washington to Jackson produced considerable controversy over national economic policy and left many basic
issues unsettled, as is indicated by the fact that the most critical
controversies of Jackson's presidency centered around two long-
standing issues—the national bank and the tariff. Nevertheless, the
period was a significant one in setting the direction of the national
economy, and the impact of the first Secretary of the Treasury may
well have been greater than that of any subsequent Treasury head.
For five and a half years Alexander Hamilton was the major source
of ideas, information, and recommendations which molded congressional legislation on economic matters; and the most important
domestic legislation during Washington's administration was in
the economic area: the funding of the national debt, the assumption of state debts, the chartering of the national bank, the excise
tax, and the tariff. Congress refused to go as far in planning and

[1] Henry Adams, History of the United States of America during the Administrations of Thomas Jefferson and James Madison (9 vols., New York:
Charles Scribner's Sons, 1889–91), IX, 173.

directing the national economy as Hamilton recommended in his famous Report on Manufactures (Document 17), but for a nation of farmers a large part of the program of the commercially oriented, industrial-minded Secretary of the Treasury was adopted.

The election of the agrarian-minded Jefferson to the presidency brought a redirection of national economic policy but not an uprooting of the Hamiltonian foundations. Jefferson's Secretary of the Treasury, Albert Gallatin, took steps for the orderly retirement of the national debt, both that inherited from the Federalists and the new addition necessitated by the Louisiana Purchase. The Republicans never accepted the Hamiltonian argument that a national debt could be a national blessing by attaching creditors to the support of the government, and they began the process of paying off the debt which was eventually to be completed during Jackson's presidency. Although Jefferson continued to worry about the power of the national bank, Gallatin found it useful. Yet, when the charter of the first Bank of the United States expired in 1812, Republicans could not bring themselves to continue the institution that they had earlier denounced as unconstitutional. The difficulties of financial management during the War of 1812 caused many Republicans to change their minds, and the Hamiltonian triumph on the bank issue appeared complete when President Madison, who had led the opposition in Congress to the first bank, recommended the establishment of a second national bank. Congress responded by chartering the bank in 1816, and the constitutionality of the measure was upheld by the Supreme Court in *McCulloch v. Maryland* in 1819 (Document 15). The bank issue did not subside from politics, however, and was to burst forth anew under Jackson.

Major questions of the role of the national government in relation to protective tariffs and internal improvements were raised during the Republican era. Gallatin in 1808 proposed a major program of internal improvements (Document 18), and after the War of 1812 young Republican leaders such as Henry Clay and John C. Calhoun pushed for extensive programs of internal improvements and for protective tariffs (Document 19). The trend of legislation was in this direction with the Tariff of 1816 and the bonus bill of 1817, which would have applied the bonus and future dividends from the second Bank of the United States to a program of building roads and canals at federal expense. The latter measure, however, was vetoed by President Madison as his last act of office. The extent of participation of the national government in internal improvements remained unsettled throughout the remainder of the Republican era. National tariff policy likewise remained unresolved. The protective features of the Tariff of 1824 aroused major controversy which, following the passage of the Tariff of Abominations of 1828, grew into the nullification crisis which threatened the survival of the Union.

During the postwar years after 1815 the country not only experienced a great burst of economic development but also faced the first great financial crisis in its history—the panic of 1819. Though the nation would recover from this shock, the statistics available on unemployment, declining foreign trade, bank and business failures, and the deep depression in agriculture demonstrate that the nation early learned of the frightening experience of an economic depression. It was not to learn so quickly how to deal with such crises.

The launching of the government under the Constitution opened a new era of American history, and, though of lesser proportions, the inauguration of President Jackson also marked the beginning of a new phase of American development. Thus, the intervening years provide a logical segment of the nation's past for exploration. This was the age of youth, a period of nation building, a time when much thought and effort were directed toward developing a society that could maintain its freedom and independence, and a period when people were not yet, as they soon would be, obsessed by sectional interests. The documents in this book seek to provide a basis for exploring the major problems of a young country in the process of becoming a nation. Most of these problems developed out of the task of establishing the character, policies, and machinery of a new government and determining who was to operate the machinery and exercise the power of the nation. Some of these problems were new; others, like the debt or slavery, were inherited from the past. Still others resulted from conflicting constitutional interpretations. Many of the nation's problems sprang from the pressures of world events, for the early republic was not left alone to solve its internal problems in unhurried isolation. In the course of working out the problems relating to the power and purposes of the national government,

Americans formed political parties, pressure groups, and other organizations; and as groups and individuals they formulated opposing positions on public practices, policies, and issues. Through a process that can never be fully described they succeeded in giving legitimacy and strength to the new government.

In the records of the first four decades under the Constitution are a strikingly large number of what might be called "famous" public documents—documents that had far-reaching influence on the development of the United States. Washington's farewell address together with the Monroe Doctrine provided the theoretical and historical basis for American isolationism for over a century. The decisions of the Supreme Court, presided over by Chief Justice John Marshall from 1801 to 1835, in themselves form a whole collection of fundamental documents defining the nature of the federal union and the powers of the national government. The state papers prepared by Alexander Hamilton and Albert Gallatin provide impressive examples of the economic thought of American policy makers whose influence persisted far beyond their own careers. As a lasting document, expressing with eloquence the basic principles of American democracy, Jefferson's address at his first inauguration—the first in the new capital on the Potomac— still endures as one of the great inaugural addresses in American history.

Some writings which were originally prepared as private papers have subsequently taken on the character of public documents. For example, the opinions of Jefferson and Hamilton on the constitutionality of a national bank were written for President Washington's use, and only in subsequent years did they become publicly known and recognized as classic expositions of the doctrines of strict construction and loose construction. The opportunity to see what contemporaries frequently could not is a great advantage enjoyed by the student of history. This advantage is most apparent in the historian's access to the personal correspondence which passed between men immersed in the affairs of an earlier day. Thus, we can read a private letter in which Alexander Hamilton unburdened himself about politics to his friend, Edward Carrington in 1792 (Document 3A), or study the confidential letter of a party leader, such as Robert Goodloe Harper in 1812 (Document 22), mapping election campaign tactics. And we can share the reflections of two former presidents, John Adams and Thomas Jefferson, when in retirement they renewed their correspondence (Documents 27A, B).

The documents of the age reveal the ability of Americans to debate and to examine critically the problems and issues of their time—in Congress and other public forums, in newspapers and pamphlets, and in private letters. Major crises, such as the War of 1812 or the Missouri controversy of 1820, produced the most extensive debates, but the records abound with evidence of the intensity of concern and interest with which Americans resolved the problems of their day. It was an age when petitions, resolutions, and remonstrances flowed regularly to the seats of authority. The assumption of state debts prompted the General Assembly of Virginia to remonstrate to Congress before the First Congress finished its work (Document 2); the threat of war with France in 1798 moved the students of the College of William and Mary to issue an address to their representatives in Congress urging a policy of peace (Document 6A); the problem of slavery inspired a number of memorials to Congress (Document 10A); acts of Congress led frequently to public protests. Some of these protests, such as Jefferson's indictment of the alien and sedition laws in the Kentucky Resolutions of 1798 (Document 13) or Calhoun's protest against the tariff in the *South Carolina Exposition* of 1828 (Document 16), are among the most significant statements of constitutional theory in American history.

The emphasis in the present collection of documents on the political, constitutional, and economic development of the nation is justified by the preoccupation of the age with those matters. That Americans were more interested in the practical matters of government and economic concerns than in the arts and letters can be seen in the address of architect Benjamin Henry Latrobe to the Society of Artists in 1811 (Document 26). And though the age produced some of the most versatile intellectuals in American history, the foremost of these, Thomas Jefferson, made his greatest contribution in political service. The documents in this book are only a selection, but they reflect fairly, it is believed, the records that hold the keys to understanding the problems of the early republic.

I

Establishing a New Government

The problems of establishing a new government under the Constitution involved not only structuring the political system outlined by the Constitution but also setting policy directions and determining the level of power that the new national government was to wield. During Washington's first term as president, the proposed programs of Secretary of the Treasury Alexander Hamilton provided the major basis for debate and for action in domestic affairs, and the enactment of one of these measures—the excise tax—occasioned, in the Whisky Rebellion crisis, the first real test of the power and determination of the national government to enforce its authority. Hamilton's proposals also raised fundamental questions of constitutional interpretation, and both his policies and actions contributed to the emergence of national political parties. The concern of Washington's administration with problems of foreign affairs was clearly revealed in the president's farewell address. The crises in foreign relations, particularly over the Jay Treaty, had brought issues of foreign affairs into the center of domestic politics. Under President John Adams the entwinement of foreign and domestic policies increased, and the problems of foreign relations together with the repercussions of these crises in domestic affairs dominated politics. The four years under Adams were years of partisan conflict between Republicans and Federalists for control of the national administration, ending with the Jeffersonian victory in the election of 1800.

1. The Election of Washington

On February 4, 1789, presidential electors in ten of the eleven states ratifying the Constitution cast their electoral votes in their respective states in the nation's first presidential election. The New York Assembly, by failing to reach agreement on the method of choosing electors, had prevented that state from participating; two other states, North Carolina and Rhode Island, had not yet ratified the Constitution. The electoral votes could not be counted until Congress assembled. This meeting was scheduled for March 4, but it was April 6 before both houses had a quorum and the electoral votes could be counted. The returns showed that Washington had received the vote of every one of the sixty-nine electors. The second votes of the electors were widely scattered; John Adams, whose thirty-four electoral votes gave him the second largest number, was elected vice president. Charles Thomson, who had been secretary of the former Congress since 1774, was dispatched to carry the notification to Mount Vernon. Thomson's report on this misison is given below. Although Washington reached New York on April 23, the inauguration did not take place until April 30. The text is taken from American State Papers: Documents, Legislative and Executive (38 vols., Washington, D.C., 1832–61), Miscellaneous, I, 5–6.

Return of the Messenger Appointed to Deliver to George Washington the Certificate of His Election to the Office of President of the United States.

COMMUNICATED TO THE SENATE, APRIL 25, 1789

SIR: NEW YORK, April 24, 1789

In pursuance of the orders I received from the Senate, I left New York on Tuesday, the 7th of the present month; and though much impeded by tempestuous weather, bad roads, and the many large rivers I had to cross, yet, by unremitted diligence I reached Mount Vernon, the seat of his excellency General Washington, on Tuesday, the 14th, about 12 o'clock. I found his excellency at home; and after communicating to him the object of my mission and the substance of my instructions, I took an opportunity, on the day of my arrival, to address him as follows:

"Sir, the President of the Senate, chosen for the special occasion, having opened and counted the votes of the electors in the presence of the Senate and the House of Representatives, I was honored with the commands of the Senate to wait upon your excellency with the information of your being elected to the office of President of the United States of America. This commission was intrusted to me on account of my having been long in the confidence of the late Congress, and charged with the duties of one of the principal civil departments of Government.

"I have now, sir, to inform you, that the proofs you have given of your patriotism, and of your readiness to sacrifice domestic ease and private enjoyment to preserve the liberty and promote the happiness of your country, did not permit the two Houses to harbor a doubt of your undertaking this great, this important office, to which you are called not only by the unanimous votes of the electors but by the voice of America; I have it therefore in command to accompany you to New York, where the Senate and the House of Representatives are convened for the despatch of public business. In executing this part of my commission, where personal gratification coincides with duty, I shall wait your time, and be wholly governed by your convenience."

To this his excellency was pleased to make the following reply:

"Sir, I have been long accustomed to entertain so great a respect for the opinion of my fellow-citizens, that the knowledge of their unanimous suffrages having been given in my favor, scarcely leaves me the alternative for an option. Whatever may have been my private feelings and sentiments, I believe I cannot give a greater evidence of my sensibility for the honor they have done me, than by accepting the appointment.

"I am so much affected by this fresh proof of my country's esteem and confidence, that silence can best explain my gratitude—while I realize the arduous nature of the task which is conferred on me, and feel my inability to perform it, I wish there may not be reason for regretting the choice. All I can promise is, only that which can be accomplished by an honest zeal.

"Upon considering how long time some of the gentlemen of both Houses of Congress have been at New York, how anxiously desirous they must be to proceed to business, and how deeply the public mind appears to be impressed with the necessity of doing it immediately, I cannot find myself at liberty to delay my journey. I shall therefore be in readiness to set out the day after to-morrow, and shall be happy in the pleasure of your company; for you will permit me to say that it was a peculiar gratification to have received the communication from you."

His excellency set out accordingly on Thursday, the 16th. His progress was retarded by the tender and affectionate leave which his neighbors and friends took of him; by the congratulatory addresses which he was obliged to receive by the way; and by the testimonies of public esteem and joy, to which it was necessary for him to pay attention, in the several States through which he passed; but that this might occasion as little delay as possible, he commenced his journey every morning at sun-rise, continued it incessantly throughout the day, and supported the fatigues of it, eight days successively, till he reached this place.

His happy and safe arrival here yesterday having terminated my commission, I submit my conduct in the execution of it to the judgment of the Senate, and have the honor to be, with great esteem and respect,

Sir, your most obedient and most humble servant,

CHARLES THOMSON

The PRESIDENT of the Senate

2. The Remonstrance of Virginia against the Assumption of State Debts

In his first Report on the Public Credit submitted to Congress in January, 1790, Secretary of the Treasury Alexander Hamilton recommended the funding of the foreign and domestic debts and the assumption by the national government of the state debts incurred during the Revolution. Although there was virtually no objection to Hamilton's proposals regarding the foreign debt, his plans for funding the domestic debt and assuming state debts aroused considerable opposition. Both the funding and the assumption measures passed Congress in the summer of 1790, but only after a bargain was reached whereby the permanent capital was to be established on the Potomac. Opposition to assumption continued, however, and the Virginia Assembly in December, 1790, sent the following remonstrance to Congress outlining the reasons for Virginia's discontent and calling for repeal of assumption. The document is significant not merely because it indicates the state interests of Virginia but also because it raises broader questions of the interpretation of the Constitution and of the tendency of Hamilton's legislation to promote a large moneyed interest in the United States. The text is taken from American State Papers, Finance, I, 90–91.

IN THE HOUSE OF DELEGATES,
Thursday, the 16th of December, 1790

The General Assembly of the Commonwealth of Virginia to the United States in Congress assembled, represent:

That it is with great concern they find themselves compelled, from a sense of duty, to call the attention of Congress to an act of their last session, entitled "An act making provision for the debt of the United States," which the General Assembly conceives neither policy, justice, nor the constitution, warrants. Republican policy, in the opinion of your memorialists, could scarcely have suggested those clauses in the aforesaid act, which limit the right of the

United States, in their redemption of the public debt. On the contrary, they discern a striking resemblance between this system and that which was introduced into England at the Revolution—a system which has perpetuated upon that nation an enormous debt, and has, moreover, insinuated into the hands of the Executive an unbounded influence, which, pervading every branch of the Government, bears down all opposition, and daily threatens the destruction of every thing that appertains to English liberty. The same causes produce the same effects.

In an agricultural country like this, therefore, to erect and concentrate and perpetuate a large moneyed interest, is a measure which your memorialists apprehend must, in the course of human events, produce one or other of two evils; the prostration of agriculture at the feet of commerce, or a change in the present form of Federal Government, fatal to the existence of American liberty.

The General Assembly pass by various other parts of the said act, which they apprehend will have a dangerous and impolitic tendency, and proceed to shew the injustice of it, as it applies to this Commonwealth. It pledges the faith of the United States for the payment of certain debts due by the several States in the Union, contracted by them during the late war.

A large proportion of the debt thus contracted by this State has been already redeemed by the collection of heavy taxes levied on its citizens, and measures have been taken for the gradual payment of the balance, so as to afford the most certain prospect of extinguishing the whole at a period not very distant. But, by the operation of the aforesaid act, a heavy debt, and consequently heavy taxes, will be entailed on the citizens of this Commonwealth, from which they never can be relieved by all the efforts of the General Assembly, whilst any part of the debts contracted by any State in the American Union, and so assumed, shall remain unpaid: for it is with great anxiety your memorialists perceive, that the said act, without the smallest necessity, is calculated to extort from the General Assembly the power of taxing their own constituents for the payment of their own debts, in such a manner as would be best suited to their own ease and convenience.

Your memorialists cannot suppress their uneasiness at the discriminating preference which is given to the holders of the principal of the Continental debt, over the holders of the principal of the State debts, in those instances where States have made ample provision for the annual payment of the interest, and where, of course, there can be no interest to compound with the principal; which happens to be the situation of this Commonwealth.

The continental creditors have preferences in other respects, which the General Assembly forbear to mention, satisfied that Congress must allow, that policy, justice, and the principles of public credit, abhor discriminations between fair creditors.

Your memorialists turn away from the impolicy and injustice of the said act, and view it in another light, in which, to them, it appears still more odious and deformed.

During the whole discussion of the federal constitution, by the convention of Virginia, your memorialists were taught to believe, "that every power not granted, was retained;" under this impression, and upon this positive condition, declared in the instrument of ratification, the said Government was adopted by the people of this Commonwealth; but your memorialists can find no clause in the constitution, authorizing Congress to assume debts of the States! As the guardians, then, of the rights and interests of their constituents; as sentinels placed by them over the ministers of the Federal Government, to shield it from their encroachments, or at least to sound the alarm when it is threatened with invasion; they can never reconcile it to their consciences silently to acquiesce in a measure which violates that hallowed maxim—a maxim, on the truth and sacredness of which, the Federal Government depended for its adoption in this Commonwealth. But this injudicious act not only deserves the censure of the General Assembly, because it is not warranted by the constitution of the United States, but, because it is repugnant to an express provision of that constitution. This provision is, "that all debts contracted, and engagements entered into, before the adoption of this constitution, shall be as valid against the United States, under this constitution, as under the Confederation;" which amounts to a constitutional ratification of the contracts respecting the State debts in the situation in which they existed under the Confederation; and, resorting to that standard, there can be no doubt that, in the present question, the rights of States, as contracting parties with the United States, must be considered as sacred.

The General Assembly of the Commonwealth of Virginia confide so fully in the justice and wisdom of Congress, upon the present occasion, as to hope that they will revise and amend the aforesaid act generally, and repeal, in particular, so much of it as relates to the assumption of the State debts.

1790, December 23.
> Agreed to by the Senate

3. The Emergence of Political Parties

The development of national political parties in the United States was a complicated, evolutionary process in which the formation of voting blocs in Congress was of greater significance for institutionalizing parties than the divisions within Washington's cabinet. Nevertheless, the differences between Alexander Hamilton and Thomas Jefferson were catalytic ingredients in the growth of parties, providing as they did articulated positions on public issues. Although neither man singlehandedly created a party in his own image, both men provided active leadership in the process of party formation. The statements of these two leaders at the time when political parties in the national government were emerging in 1792 provide an opportunity to view party origins from the perspectives of two leading antagonists. Hamilton, in writing to his close friend Edward Carrington of Virginia, poured out his feelings of resentment over the opposition of Madison and Jefferson, examining their motives and answering the charges against Federalist policies. He indicated that he regarded the emerging Republican interest as "actuated by views . . . subversive of the principles of good government and dangerous to the Union, peace, and happiness of the country." Jefferson's view on the rising party conflict can be found in his letter to President Washington, September 9, 1792, in which he was replying to the admonition that the president, in private letters to both Hamilton and Jefferson, had made against partisan conflict. Hamilton's formal reply to the president lacked the revealing frankness of his letter to Carrington, but Jefferson's reply to Washington provides the best statement, written contemporaneously with the events, of his view of his differences with Hamilton and the emerging party conflict. Hamilton's letter is reprinted from Henry Cabot Lodge (ed.), The Works of Alexander Hamilton (12 vols., New York [1904]), IX, 513–535. Jefferson's letter is from Paul L. Ford (ed.), The Writings of Thomas Jefferson (10 vols., New York, 1892–99), VI, 101–109.

A. *Alexander Hamilton to Edward Carrington, May 26, 1792*

Believing that I possess a share of your personal friendship and confidence, and yielding to that which I feel towards you; persuaded also, that our political creed is the same on two essential points—first, the necessity of Union to the respectability and happiness of this country, and second, the necessity of an efficient general government to maintain the Union, I have concluded to unbosom myself to you, on the present state of political parties and views. . . .When I accepted the office I now hold, it was under full persuasion, that from similarity of thinking, conspiring with personal good-will, I should have the firm support of Mr. Madison, in the general course of my administration. Aware of the intrinsic difficulties of the situation, and of the powers of Mr. Madison, I do not believe I should have accepted under a different supposition. I have mentioned the similarity of thinking between that gentleman and myself. This was relative, not merely to the general principles of national policy and government, but to the leading points, which were likely to constitute questions in the administration of the finances. I mean, first, the expediency of funding the debt; second, the inexpediency of discrimination between original and present holders; third, the expediency of assuming the State debts. . . .

Under these circumstances you will naturally imagine that it must have been matter of surprise to me when I was apprised that it was Mr. Madison's intention to oppose my plan on both the last-mentioned points. Before the debate commenced, I had a conversation with him on my report; in the course of which I alluded to the calculation I had made of his sentiments, and the grounds of that calculation. He did not deny them; but alleged in his justification that the very considerable alienation of the debt, subsequent to the periods at which he had opposed a discrimination, had essentially changed the state of the question; and that as to the assumption, he had contemplated it to take place as matters stood at the peace. While the change of opinion avowed on the point of discrimination diminished my respect for the force of Mr. Madison's mind and the soundness of his judgment; and while the idea of reserving and setting afloat a vast mass of already extinguished debt, as the condition of a measure, the leading objects of which were an accession of strength to the national government, and an assurance of order and vigor in the national finances, by doing away with the necessity of thirteen complicated and conflicting systems of finance, appeared to me somewhat extraordinary, yet my previous impressions of the fairness of Mr. Madison's character, and my reliance on his good-will towards me, disposed me to believe that his suggestions were sincere, and even on the point of an assumption of the debts of the States as they stood at the peace, to lean towards a co-operation in his views, till on feeling the ground I found the thing impracticable, and on further reflection I thought it liable to immense difficulties. It was tried and failed with little countenance.

At this time and afterwards repeated intimations were given to me that Mr. Madison, from a spirit of rivalship, or some other cause, had become personally unfriendly to me; and one gentleman in particular, whose honor I have no reason to doubt, assured me that Mr. Madison, in a conversation with him, had made a pretty direct attempt to insinuate unfavorable impressions of me. Still I suspended my opinion on the subject. I knew the malevolent officiousness of mankind too well to yield a very ready acquiescence to the suggestions which were made, and resolved to wait till time and more experience should afford a solution. It was not till the last session that I became unequivocally convinced of the following truth: "that Mr. Madison, cooperating with Mr. Jefferson, is at the head of a faction decidedly hostile to me and my administration; and actuated by views, in my judgment, subversive of the principles of good government and dangerous to the Union, peace, and happiness of the country."

These are strong expressions, they may pain your friendship for one or both of the gentlemen whom I have named. I have not lightly resolved to hazard them. They are the result of a serious alarm in my mind for the public welfare, and of a full conviction that what I have alleged is a truth, and a truth which ought to be told, and well attended to by all the friends of the Union and efficient national government. The suggestion will, I hope, at least awaken attention free from the bias of former prepossessions.

This conviction, in my mind, is the result of a long train of circumstances, many of them minute. To attempt to detail them all would fill a volume. I shall therefore confine myself to the mention of a few.

First.—As to the point of opposition to me and my administration.

Mr. Jefferson, with very little reserve, manifests his dislike of the funding system generally, calling in question the expediency of funding a debt at all. Some expressions, which he has dropped in my presence (sometimes without sufficient attention to delicacy), will not permit me to doubt on this point representations which I have had from various respectable quarters. I do not mean that he advocates directly the undoing of what has been done, but he censures the whole, on principles which, if they should become general, could not but end in the subversion of the system. In various conversations, with foreigners as well as citizens, he has thrown censure on my principles of government and on my measures of administration. He has predicted that the people would not long tolerate my proceedings, and that I should not long maintain my ground. Some of those whom he immediately and notoriously moves have even whispered suspicions of the rectitude of my motives and conduct. In the question concerning the bank he not only delivered an opinion in writing against its constitutionality and expediency, but he did it in a style and manner which I felt as partaking of asperity and ill humor toward me. As one of the trustees of the sinking fund, I have experienced in almost every leading question opposition from him. When any turn of things in the community has threatened either odium or embarrassment to me, he has not been able to suppress the satisfaction which it gave him. A part of this is, of course, information, and might be misrepresentation, but it comes through so many channels, and so well accords with what falls under my own observation, that I can entertain no doubt.

I find a strong confirmation in the following circumstances: Freneau, the present printer of the *National Gazette*, who was a journeyman with Childs & Swain, at New York, was a known Anti-federalist. It is reduced to a certainty that he was brought to Philadelphia by Mr. Jefferson to be the conductor of a newspaper. It is notorious that contemporarily with the commencement of his paper he was a clerk in the Department of State, for foreign languages. Hence a clear inference that his paper has been set on foot and is conducted under the patronage and not against the views of Mr. Jefferson. What then is the complexion of this paper? Let any impartial man peruse all the numbers down to the present day, and I never was more mistaken if he does not pronounce that it is a paper devoted to the subversion of me and the measures in which I have had an agency; and I am little less mistaken if he does not pronounce that it is a paper of a tendency generally unfriendly to the government of the United States. . . .

With regard to Mr. Madison, the matter stands thus: I have

not heard, but in the one instance to which I have alluded, of his having held language unfriendly to me in private conversation, but in his public conduct there has been a more uniform and persevering opposition than I have been able to resolve into a sincere difference of opinion. I cannot persuade myself that Mr. Madison and I, whose politics had formerly so much the same point of departure, should now diverge so widely in our opinions of the measures which are proper to be pursued. The opinion I once entertained of the candor and simplicity and fairness of Mr. Madison's character, has, I acknowledge, given way to a decided opinion that it is one of a peculiarly artificial and complicated kind. For a considerable part of the last session Mr. Madison lay in a great measure perdu. But it was evident from his votes and a variety of little movements and appearances, that he was the prompter of Mr. Giles and others who were the open instruments of the opposition. Two facts occurred in the course of the session which I view as unequivocal demonstrations of his disposition towards me. In one, a direct and decisive blow was aimed. When the Department of the Treasury was established, Mr. Madison was an unequivocal advocate of the principles which prevailed in it, and of the powers and duties which were assigned by it to the head of the department. This appeared, both from his private and public discourse, and I will add, that I have personal evidence that Mr. Madison is as well convinced as any man in the United States of the necessity of the arrangement which characterizes that establishment, to the orderly conducting of the business of the finances. Mr. Madison nevertheless opposed a reference to me to report ways and means for the Western expedition, and combated, on principle, the propriety of such references.

He well knew that if he had prevailed a certain consequence was my resignation; that I would not be fool enough to make pecuniary sacrifices and endure a life of extreme drudgery without opportunity either to do material good or to acquire reputation, and frequently with a responsibility in reputation for measures in which I had no hand, and in respect to which the part I had acted, if any, could not be known. To accomplish this point an effectual train, as was supposed, was laid. Besides those who ordinarily acted under Mr. Madison's banners, several who had generally acted with me, from various motives—vanity, self-importance, etc., etc.,—were enlisted.

My overthrow was anticipated as certain, and Mr. Madison, laying aside his wonted caution, boldly led his troops, as he imagined, to a certain victory. He was disappointed. Though late, I became apprised of the danger. Measures of counteraction were adopted, and when the question was called Mr. Madison was confounded to find characters voting against him whom he counted upon as certain. Towards the close of the session another, though a more covert, attack was made. It was in the shape of a proposition to insert in the supplementary act respecting the public debt something by way of instruction to the trustees "to make their purchases of the debt at the lowest market price." In the course of the discussion of this point Mr. Madison dealt much in insidious insinuations calculated to give an impression that the public money, under my particular direction, had been unfaithfully applied to put undue advantages in the pockets of speculators, and to support the debt at an artificial price for their benefit. The whole manner of this transaction left no doubt in any one's mind that Mr. Madison was actuated by personal and political animosity. As to this last instance, it is but candid to acknowledge that Mr. Madison had a better right to act the enemy than on any former occasion. I had, some short time before, subsequent to his conduct respecting the reference, declared openly my opinion of the views by which he was actuated towards me, and my determination to consider and treat him as a political enemy. . . .

Secondly, as to the tendency of the views of the two gentlemen who have been named. Mr. Jefferson is an avowed enemy to a funded debt. Mr. Madison disavows, in public, any intention to undo what has been done, but, in private conversation with Mr. Charles Carroll, Senator, . . . he favored the sentiment in Mr. Mercer's speech, that a Legislature had no right to fund the debt by mortgaging permanently the public revenues, because they had no right to bind posterity. The inference is that what has been unlawfully done may be undone.

The discourse of partisans in the Legislature, and the publication in the party newspapers, direct their main battery against the principle of a funded debt, and represent it in the most odious light as a perfect Pandora's box. . . .

In almost all the questions, great and small, which have arisen since the first session of Congress, Mr. Jefferson and Mr. Madison have been found among those who are disposed to narrow the federal authority. The question of a national bank is one example. The question of bounties to the fisheries is another. Mr. Madison resisted it on the ground of constitutionality, till it was evident, by the intermediate questions taken, that the bill would pass; and he then, under the wretched subterfuge of a change of a single word, "bounty" for "allowance," went over to the majority, and voted for the bill. On the militia bill, and in a variety of minor cases, he has leaned to abridging the exercise of federal authority, and leaving as much as possible to the States; and he lost no opportunity of sounding the alarm, with great affected solemnity, at encroachments, meditated on the rights of the States, and of holding up the bugbear of a faction in the government having designs unfriendly to liberty.

This kind of conduct has appeared to me the more extraordinary on the part of Mr. Madison, as I know for a certainty, it was a primary article in his creed, that the real danger in our system was the subversion of the national authority by the preponderancy of the State governments. All his measures have proceeded on an opposite supposition. I recur again to the instance of Freneau's paper. In matters of this kind one cannot have direct proof of men's latent views; they must be inferred from circumstances. As coadjutor of Mr. Jefferson in the establishment of this paper, I include Mr. Madison in the consequences imputable to it. In respect to foreign politics, the views of these gentlemen are, in my judgment, equally unsound and dangerous. They have a womanish attachment to France and a womanish resentment against Great Britain. They would draw us into the closest embrace of the former, and involve us in all the consequences of her politics; and they would risk the peace of the country in their endeavors to keep us at the greatest possible distance from the latter. This disposition goes to a length, particularly in Mr. Jefferson, of which, till lately, I had no adequate idea. Various circumstances prove to me that if these gentlemen were left to pursue their own course, there would be, in less than six months, an open war between the United States and Great Britain. I trust I have a due sense of the conduct of France towards this country in the late revolution; and that I shall always be among the foremost in making her every suitable return; but there is a wide difference between this and implicating ourselves in all her politics; between bearing good-will to her and hating and wrangling with all those whom she hates. The neutral and the pacific policy appears to me to mark the true path to the United States.

Having delineated to you what I conceive to be the true complexion of the politics of these gentlemen, I will not attempt a solution of these strange appearances. Mr. Jefferson, it is known, did not in the first instance cordially acquiesce in the new Constitution for the United States; he had many doubts and reserves. He left this country before we had experienced the imbecilities of the former.

In France, he saw government only on the side of its abuses. He drank freely of the French philosophy, in religion, in science, in politics. He came from France in the moment of a fermentation, which he had a share in exciting, and in the passions and feelings of which he shared both from temperament and situation. He came here probably with a too partial idea of his own powers; and with the expectation of a greater share in the direction of our councils than he has in reality enjoyed. I am not sure that he had not peculiarly marked out for himself the department of the finances.

He came, electrified with attachment to France, and with the project of knitting together the two countries in the closest political bands.

Mr. Madison had always entertained an exalted opinion of the talents, knowledge, and virtues of Mr. Jefferson. The sentiment was probably reciprocal. A close correspondence subsisted between them during the time of Mr. Jefferson's absence from the country. A close intimacy arose upon his return.

Whether any peculiar opinions of Mr. Jefferson's concerning the public debt wrought a change in the sentiments of Mr. Madison (for it is certain that the former is more radically wrong than the latter), or whether Mr. Madison, seduced by the expectation of popularity, and possibly by the calculation of advantage to the State of Virginia, was led to change his own opinion, certain it is that a very material change took place, and that the two gentlemen were united in the new ideas. Mr. Jefferson was indiscreetly open in his approbation of Mr. Madison's principles, upon his first coming to the seat of government. I say indiscreetly, because a gentleman in the administration, in one department, ought not to have taken sides against another, in another department. The course of this business and a variety of circumstances which took place left Mr. Madison a very discontented and chagrined man, and begot some degree of ill-humor in Mr. Jefferson. Attempts were made by these gentlemen, in different ways, to produce a commercial warfare with Great Britain. In this, too, they were disappointed. And, as they had the liveliest wishes on the subject, their dissatisfaction has been proportionably great; and, as I had not favored the project, I was comprehended in their displeasure.

These causes, and perhaps some others, created, much sooner than I was aware of it, a systematic opposition to me, on the part of these gentlemen. My subversion, I am now satisfied, has been long an object with them.

Subsequent events have increased the spirit of opposition and the feelings of personal mortification on the part of these gentlemen.

A mighty stand was made on the affair of the bank. There was much commitment in that case. I prevailed. On the mint business I was opposed from the same quarters and with still less success. In the affair of ways and means for the Western expedition, on the supplementary arrangements concerning the debt, except as to the additional assumption, my views have been equally prevalent in opposition to theirs. This current of success on the one side and of defeat on the other has rendered the opposition furious, and has produced a disposition to subvert their competitors, even at the expense of the government.

Another circumstance has contributed to widening the breach. 'T is evident, beyond a question, from every movement, that Mr. Jefferson aims with ardent desire at the Presidential chair. This, too, is an important object of the party-politics. It is supposed, from the nature of my former personal and political connections, that I may favor some other candidate more than Mr. Jefferson, when the question shall occur by the retreat of the present gentleman. My influence, therefore, with the community becomes a thing, on ambitious and personal grounds, to be resisted and destroyed. You know how much it was a point to establish the Secretary of State, as the officer who was to administer the government in defect of the President and Vice-President. Here, I acknowledge, though I took far less part than was supposed, I ran counter to Mr. Jefferson's wishes; but if I had had no other reason for it, I had already experienced opposition from him, which rendered it a measure of self-defence. It is possible, too, (for men easily heat their imaginations when their passions are heated), that they have by degrees persuaded themselves of what they may have at first only sported to influence others, namely, that there is some dreadful combination against State government and republicanism; which, according to them, are convertible terms. But there is so much absurdity in this supposition, that the admission of it tends to apologize for their hearts at the expense of their heads. Under the influence of all these circumstances the attachment to the government of the United States, originally weak in Mr. Jefferson's mind, has given way to something very like dislike in Mr. Madison's. It is so counteracted by personal feelings as to be more an affair of the head than of the heart; more the result of a conviction of the necessity of Union than of cordiality to the thing itself. I hope it does not stand worse than this with him. In such a state of mind both these gentlemen are prepared to hazard a great deal to effect a change. Most of the important measures of every government are connected with the treasury. To subvert the present head of it, they deem it expedient to risk rendering the government itself odious; perhaps foolishly thinking that they can easily recover the lost affections and confidence of the people, and not appreciating, as they ought to do, the natural resistance to government, which in every community results from the human passions, the degree to which this is strengthened by the organized rivalry of State governments, and the infinite danger that the national government, once rendered odious, will be kept so by these powerful and indefatigable enemies. . . .

A word on another point. I am told serious apprehensions are disseminated in your State as to the existence of a monarchical party meditating the destruction of State and republican government. If it is possible that so absurd an idea can gain ground, it is necessary that it should be combated. I assure you, on my private faith and honor as a man, that there is not, in my judgment, a shadow of foundation for it. A very small number of men indeed may entertain theories less republican than Mr. Jefferson and Mr. Madison, but I am persuaded there is not a man among them who would not regard as both criminal and visionary any attempt to subvert the republican system of the country. Most of these men rather fear that it may not justify itself by its fruits, than feel a predilection for a different form; and their fears are not diminished by the factious and fanatical politics which they find prevailing among a certain set of gentlemen and threatening to disturb the tranquillity and order of the government.

As to the destruction of State governments, the great and real anxiety is to be able to preserve the national from the too potent and counteracting influence of those governments. As to my own political creed, I give it to you with the utmost sincerity. I am affectionately attached to the republican theory. I desire above all things to see the equality of political rights, exclusive of all hereditary distinction, firmly established by a practical demonstration of its being consistent with the order and happiness of society. As to State governments, the prevailing bias of my judgment is that if they can be circumscribed within bounds, consistent with the preservation of the national government, they will prove useful and salutary. If the States were all of the size of Connecticut, Maryland, or New Jersey, I should decidedly regard the local governments as both safe and useful. As the thing now is, however, I acknowledge the most serious apprehensions, that the government of the United States will not be able to maintain itself against their influence. I see that influence already penetrating into the national councils and preventing their direction. Hence, a disposition on my part towards a liberal construction of the powers of the national government, and to erect every fence, to guard it from depredations which is, in my opinion, consistent with constitutional propriety. As to any combination to prostrate the State governments, I disavow and deny it. From an apprehension lest the judiciary should not work efficiently or harmoniously, I have been desirous of seeing some national scheme of connection adopted as an amendment to the Constitution, otherwise I am for maintaining things as they are; though I doubt much the possibility of it, from a tendency in the nature of things towards the preponderancy of the State governments.

I said that I was affectionately attached to the republican theory. This is the real language of my heart, which I open to you in the sincerity of friendship; and I add that I have strong hopes of the success of that theory; but, in candor, I ought also to add that I am far from being without doubts. I consider its success as yet a problem. It is yet to be determined by experience whether it be consistent with that stability and order in government which are essential to public strength and private security and happiness.

On the whole, the only enemy which Republicanism has to fear in this country is in the spirit of faction and anarchy. If this will not permit the ends of government to be attained under it, if it engenders disorders in the community, all regular and orderly minds will wish for a change, and the demagogues who have produced the disorder will make it for their own aggrandizement. This is the old story. If I were disposed to promote monarchy and overthrow State governments, I would mount the hobby-horse of popularity; I would cry out "usurpation," "danger to liberty," etc., etc.; I would endeavor to prostrate the national government, raise a ferment, and then "ride in the whirlwind, and direct the storm." That there are men acting with Jefferson and Madison who have this in view, I verily believe; I could lay my finger on some of them. That Madison does not mean it, I also verily believe; and I rather believe the same of Jefferson, but I read him upon the whole thus: "A man of profound ambition and violent passions."

You must be by this time tired of my epistle. Perhaps I have treated certain characters with too much severity. I have, however, not meant to do them injustice, and, from the bottom of my soul, believe I have drawn them truly; and it is of the utmost consequence to the public weal they should be viewed in their true colors. I yield to this impression. I will only add that I make no clandestine attacks on the gentlemen concerned. They are both apprised indirectly from myself of the opinion I entertain of their views.

B.   Thomas Jefferson to President Washington, September 9, 1792

. . . I now take the liberty of proceeding to that part of your letter wherein you notice the internal dissentions which have taken place within our government, and their disagreeable effect on it's movements. That such dissentions have taken place is certain, and even among those who are nearest to you in the administration. To no one have they given deeper concern than myself; to no one equal mortification at being myself a part of them. Tho' I take to myself no more than my share of the general observations of your letter, yet I am so desirous ever that you should know the whole truth, and believe no more than the truth, that

I am glad to seize every occasion of developing to you whatever I do or think relative to the government; and shall therefore ask permission to be more lengthy now than the occasion particularly calls for, or could otherwise perhaps justify.

When I embarked in the government, it was with a determination to intermeddle not at all with the legislature, and as little as possible with my co-departments. The first and only instance of variance from the former part of my resolution, I was duped into by the Secretary of the Treasury and made a tool for forwarding his schemes, not then sufficiently understood by me; and of all the errors of my political life, this has occasioned me the deepest regret. It has ever been my purpose to explain this to you, when, from being actors on the scene, we shall have become uninterested spectators only. The second part of my resolution has been religiously observed with the war department; and as to that of the Treasury, has never been farther swerved from than by the mere enunciation of my sentiments in conversation, and chiefly among those who, expressing the same sentiments, drew mine from me. If it has been supposed that I have ever intrigued among the members of the legislatures to defeat the plans of the Secretary of the Treasury, it is contrary to all truth. As I never had the desire to influence the members, so neither had I any other means than my friendship, which I valued too highly to risk by usurpations on their freedom of judgment, and the conscientious pursuit of their own sense of duty. That I have utterly, in my private conversations, disapproved of the system of the Secretary of the treasury, I acknowledge and avow: and this was not merely a speculative difference. His system flowed from principles adverse to liberty, and was calculated to undermine and demolish the republic, by creating an influence of his department over the members of the legislature. I saw this influence actually produced, and it's first fruits to be the establishment of the great outlines of his project by the votes of the very persons who, having swallowed his bait were laying themselves out to profit by his plans: and that had these persons withdrawn, as those interested in a question ever should, the vote of the disinterested majority was clearly the reverse of what they made it. These were no longer the votes then of the representatives of the people, but of deserters from the rights and interests of the people: and it was impossible to consider their decisions, which had nothing in view but to enrich themselves, as the measures of the fair majority, which ought always to be respected. If what was actually doing begat uneasiness in those who wished for virtuous government, what was further proposed was not less threatening to the friends of the Constitution. For, in a Report on the subject of manufactures (still to be acted on) it was expressly assumed that the general government has a right to exercise all powers which may be for the *general welfare*, that is to say, all the legitimate powers of government: since no government has a legitimate right to do what is not for the welfare of the governed. There was indeed a sham-limitation of the universality of this power *to cases where money is to be employed*. But about what is it that money cannot be employed? Thus the object of these plans taken together is to draw all the powers of government into the hands of the general legislature, to establish means for corrupting a sufficient corps in that legislature to divide the honest votes and preponderate, by their own, the scale which suited, and to have that corps under the command of the Secretary of the Treasury for the purpose of subverting step by step the principles of the constitution, which he has so often declared to be a thing of nothing which must be changed. Such views might have justified something more than mere expressions of dissent, beyond which, nevertheless, I never went. Has abstinence from the department committed to me been equally observed by him? To say nothing of other interferences equally known, in the case of the two nations with which we have the most intimate connections, France and England, my system was to give some satisfactory distinctions to the former, of little cost to us, in return for the solid advantages yielded us by them; and to have met the English with some restrictions which might induce them to abate their severities against our commerce. I have always supposed this coincided with your sentiments. Yet the Secretary of the treasury, by his cabals with members of the legislature, and by high-toned declamation on other occasions, has forced down his own system, which was exactly the reverse. He undertook, of his own authority, the conferences with the ministers of those two nations, and was, on every consultation, provided with some report of a conversation with the one or the other of them, adapted to his views. These views, thus made to prevail, their execution fell of course to me; and I can safely appeal to you, who have seen all my letters and proceedings, whether I have not carried them into execution as sincerely as if they had been my own, tho' I ever considered them as inconsistent with the honor and interest of our country. That they have been inconsistent with our interest is but too fatally proved by the stab to our navigation given by the French. So that if the question be By whose fault is it that Colonel Hamilton and myself have not drawn together? the answer will depend on that to two other questions; whose principles of administration best justify, by their purity, conscientious adherence? and which of us has, notwithstanding, stepped farthest into the controul of the department of the other?

To this justification of opinions, expressed in the way of conversation, against the views of Colonel Hamilton, I beg leave to add some notice of his late charges against me in Fenno's gazette; for neither the stile, matter, nor venom of the pieces alluded to can leave a doubt of their author. Spelling my name and character at full length to the public, while he conceals his own under the signature of "an American" he charges me 1. With having written letters from Europe to my friends to oppose the present constitution while depending. 2. With a desire of not paying the public debt. 3. With setting up a paper to decry and slander the government. 1. The first charge is most false. No man in the U.S. I suppose, approved of every title in the constitution: no one, I believe approved more of it than I did: and more of it was certainly disproved by my accuser than by me, and of it's parts most vitally republican. Of this the few letters I wrote on the subject (not half a dozen I believe) will be a proof: and for my own satisfaction and justification, I must tax you with the reading of them when I return to where they are. You will there see that my objection to the constitution was that it wanted a bill of rights securing freedom of religion, freedom of the press, freedom from standing armies, trial by jury, and a constant Habeas corpus act. Colonel Hamilton's was that it wanted a king and house of lords. The sense of America has approved my objection and added the bill of rights, not the king and lords. I also thought a longer term of service, insusceptible of renewal, would have made a President more independant. My country has thought otherwise, and I have acquiesced implicitly. He wishes the general government should have power to make laws binding the states in all cases whatsoever. Our country has thought otherwise: has he acquiesced? . . . 2. The second charge is equally untrue. My whole correspondence while in France, and every word, letter, and act on the subject since my return, prove that no man is more ardently intent to see the public debt soon and sacredly paid off than I am. This exactly marks the difference between Colonel Hamilton's views and mine, that I would wish the debt paid tomorrow; he wishes it never to be paid, but always to be a thing where with to corrupt and manage the legislature. 3. I have never enquired what number of sons, relations and friends of Senators, representatives, printers or other useful partisans Colonel Hamilton has provided for among the hundred clerks of his department, the thousand excisemen, customhouse officers, loan officers etc. etc. etc. appointed by him, or at his nod, and spread over the Union; nor could ever have imagined that the man who has the shuffling of millions backwards and forwards from paper into money and money into paper, from Europe to America, and America to Europe, the dealing out of Treasury-secrets among his friends in what time and measure he pleases, and who never slips an occasion of making friends with his means, that such an one I say would have brought forward a charge against me for having appointed the poet Freneau translating clerk to my office, with a salary of 250 dollars a year. That fact stands thus. While the government was at New York I was applied to on behalf of Freneau to know if there was any place within my department to which he could be appointed. I answered there were but four clerkships, all of which I found full, and continued without any change. When we removed to Philadelphia, Mr. Pintard the translating clerk, did not chuse to remove with us. His office then became vacant. I was again applied to there for Freneau, and had no hesitation to promise the clerkship for him. I cannot recollect whether it was at the same time, or afterwards, that I was told he had a thought of setting up a newspaper there. But whether then, or afterwards, I considered it as a circumstance of some value, as it might enable me to do, what I had long wished to have done, that is, to have the material parts of the Leyden gazette brought under your eye and that of the public, in order to possess yourself and them of a juster view of the affairs of Europe than could be obtained from any other public source. This I had ineffectually attempted through the press of Mr. Fenno while in New York, selecting and translating passages myself at first then having it done by Mr. Pintard the translating clerk, but they found their way too slowly into Mr. Fenno's papers. Mr. Bache essayed it for me in

Philadelphia, but his being a daily paper, did not circulate sufficiently in the other states. He even tried, at my request, the plan of a weekly paper of recapitulation from his daily paper, in hopes that that might go into the other states, but in this too we failed. Freneau, as translating clerk, and the printer of a periodical paper likely to circulate thro' the states (uniting in one person the parts of Pintard and Fenno) revived my hopes that the thing could at length be effected. On the establishment of his paper therefore, I furnished him with the Leyden gazettes, with an expression of my wish that he could always translate and publish the material intelligence they contained; and have continued to furnish them from time to time, as regularly as I received them. But as to any other direction or indication of my wish how his press should be conducted, what sort of intelligence he should give, what essays encourage, I can protest in the presence of heaven, that I never did by myself or any other, directly or indirectly, say a syllable, nor attempt any kind of influence. I can further protest, in the same awful presence, that I never did by myself or any other, directly or indirectly, write, dictate or procure any one sentence or sentiment to be inserted in his, or any other gazette, to which my name was not affixed or that of my office. I surely need not except here a thing so foreign to the present subject as a little paragraph about our Algerine captives, which I put once into Fenno's paper. Freneau's proposition to publish a paper, having been about the time that the writings of Publicola, and the discourses on Davila had a good deal excited the public attention, I took for granted from Freneau's character, which had been marked as that of a good whig, that he would give free place to pieces written against the aristocratical and monarchical principles these papers had inculcated. This having been in my mind, it is likely enough I may have expressed it in conversation with others; tho' I do not recollect that I did. To Freneau I think I could not, because I had still seen him but once, and that was at a public table, at breakfast, at Mrs. Elsworth's, as I passed thro' New York the last year. And I can safely declare that my expectations looked only to the chastisement of the aristocratical and monarchical writers, and not to any criticisms on the proceedings of government: Colonel Hamilton can see no motive for any appointment but that of making a convenient partizan. But you Sir, who have received from me recommendations of a Rittenhouse, Barlow, Paine, will believe that

talents and science are sufficient motives with me in appointments
to which they are fitted: and that Freneau, as a man of genius,
might find a preference in my eye to be a translating clerk, and
make good title to the little aids I could give him as the editor of a
gazette, by procuring subscriptions to his paper, as I did some,
before it appeared, and as I have with pleasure done for the
labours of other men of genius. . . . As to the merits or demerits of
his paper, they certainly concern me not. He and Fenno are rivals
for the public favor. The one courts them by flattery, the other
by censure, and I believe it will be admitted that the one has been
as servile, as the other severe. But is not the dignity, and even
decency of government committed, when one of it's principal ministers enlists himself as an anonymous writer or paragraphist for
either the one or the other of them? No government ought to be
without censors: and where the press is free, no one ever will. If
virtuous, it need not fear the fair operation of attack and defence.
Nature has given to man no other means of sifting out the truth
either in religion, law, or politics. I think it as honorable to the
government neither to know, nor notice, it's sycophants or censors,
as it would be undignified and criminal to pamper the former and
persecute the latter. . . .

. . . I confide that yourself are satisfied that, as to dissensions
in the newspapers, not a syllable of them has ever proceeded from
me; and that no cabals or intrigues of mine have produced those
in the legislature, and I hope I may promise, both to you and
myself, that none will receive aliment from me during the short
space I have to remain in office. . . .

4. Opposition to the Excise Tax in Pennsylvania

By 1794 the opposition to the excise tax on distilled whisky enacted
in 1791 had assumed, it appeared to many, a level of defiance in western
Pennsylvania that required action on the part of the national government to uphold federal law. On August 7, 1794, President Washington,
acting under the Militia Act of 1792 and having been informed by a
federal judge as required by the act that the laws of the United States
were being opposed by "combinations too powerful to be suppressed
by the ordinary course of judicial proceedings, or by the powers vested
in the marshal," called for militia forces to take the field. The president
reviewed his actions in the following message to Congress, November

20, 1794. In the face of the show of military force, all opposition evapo-
rated, leading Jefferson to comment that "an insurrection was announced and proclaimed and armed against, but could never be found."
Hamilton, on the other hand, who had been Washington's closest ad-
viser during the crisis, argued that the government had gained "reputation and strength" by showing that it was capable of enforcing obedience to federal laws. In any case, as the first occasion for the use of the
militia to support the enforcement of federal legislation, the Whisky
Rebellion has significance beyond the immediate circumstances of the
event. The text of Washington's message is taken from American State
Papers, Miscellaneous, I, 83–85.

Fellow-citizens of the Senate and of the House of Representatives:

When we call to mind the gracious indulgence of Heaven, by
which the American people became a nation; when we survey the
general prosperity of our country, and look forward to the riches,
power, and happiness, to which it seems destined; with the deepest
regret do I announce to you that, during your recess, some of the
citizens of the United States have been found capable of an insurrection. It is due, however, to the character of our Government,
and to its stability, which cannot be shaken by the enemies of
order, freely to unfold the course of this event.

During the session of the year one thousand seven hundred and
ninety, it was expedient to exercise the legislative power, granted
by the constitution of the United States "to lay and collect excises." In a majority of the States, scarcely an objection was heard
to this mode of taxation. In some, indeed, alarms were at first
conceived, until they were banished by reason and patriotism. In
the four western counties of Pennsylvania, a prejudice, fostered and
imbittered by the artifice of men, who labored for an ascendency
over the will of others, by the guidance of their passions, produced
symptoms of riot and violence. It is well known that Congress did
not hesitate to examine the complaints which were presented; and
to relieve them, as far as justice dictated, or general convenience
would permit. But the impression which this moderation made on
the discontented did not correspond with what it deserved. The
arts of delusion were no longer confined to the efforts of designing
individuals. The very forbearance to press prosecutions was misinterpreted into a fear of urging the execution of the laws, and associations of men began to denounce threats against the officers
employed. From a belief that, by a more formal concert, their

operation might be defeated, certain self-created societies assumed the tone of condemnation. Hence, while the greater part of Pennsylvania itself were conforming themselves to the acts of excise, a few counties were resolved to frustrate them. It was now perceived, that every expectation from the tenderness which had been hitherto pursued was unavailing, and that further delay could only create an opinion of impotency or irresolution in the Government. Legal process was therefore delivered to the marshal against the rioters and delinquent distillers.

No sooner was he understood to be engaged in this duty, than the vengeance of armed men was aimed at his person, and the person and property of the inspector of the revenue. They fired upon the marshal, arrested him, and detained him, for some time, as a prisoner. He was obliged, by the jeopardy of his life, to renounce the service of other process, on the west side of the Allegany mountain; and a deputation was afterwards sent to him to demand a surrender of that which he had served. A numerous body repeatedly attacked the house of the inspector, seized his papers of office, and finally destroyed by fire his buildings and whatsoever they contained. Both of these officers, from a just regard to their safety, fled to the seat of Government—it being avowed, that the motives to such outrages were to compel the resignation of the inspectors; to withstand by force of arms the authority of the United States; and thereby to extort a repeal of the laws of excise, and an alteration in the conduct of Government.

Upon the testimony of these facts, an associate justice of the Supreme Court of the United States notified to me that, "in the counties of Washington and Allegany, in Pennsylvania, laws of the United States were opposed, and the execution thereof obstructed, by combinations too powerful to be suppressed by the ordinary course of judicial proceedings, or by the powers vested in the marshal of that district." On this call, momentous in the extreme, I sought and weighed what might best subdue the crisis. On the one hand, the judiciary was pronounced to be stripped of its capacity to enforce the laws; crimes, which reached the very existence of social order, were perpetrated without control; the friends of Government were insulted, abused, and overawed into silence, or an apparent acquiescence; and, to yield to the treasonable fury of so small a portion of the United States, would be to violate the fundamental principle of our constitution, which enjoins that the will of the majority shall prevail. On the other, to array citizen against citizen, to publish the dishonor of such excesses, to encounter the expense, and other embarrassments, of so distant an expedition, were steps too delicate, too closely interwoven with many affecting considerations, to be lightly adopted. I postponed, therefore, the summoning of the militia immediately into the field; but I required them to be held in readiness, that, if my anxious endeavors to reclaim the deluded, and to convince the malignant of their danger, should be fruitless, military force might be prepared to act before the season should be too far advanced.

My proclamation of the 7th of August last was accordingly issued, and accompanied by the appointment of commissioners, who were charged to repair to the scene of insurrection. They were authorized to confer with any bodies of men or individuals. They were instructed to be candid and explicit in stating the sensations which had been excited in the Executive, and his earnest wish to avoid a resort to coercion; to represent, however, that, without submission, coercion *must* be the resort; but to invite them, at the same time, to return to the demeanor of faithful citizens, by such accommodations as lay within the sphere of Executive power. Pardon, too, was tendered to them by the Government of the United States, and that of Pennsylvania, upon no other condition than a satisfactory assurance of obedience to the laws.

Although the report of the commissioners marks their firmness and abilities, and must unite all virtuous men, by showing that the means of conciliation have been exhausted, all of those who had committed or abetted the tumults did not subscribe the mild form which was proposed as the atonement; and the indications of a peaceable temper were neither sufficiently general nor conclusive to recommend or warrant the further suspension of the march of the militia.

Thus, the painful alternative could not be discarded. I ordered the militia to march, after once more admonishing the insurgents, in my proclamation of the 25th of September last.

It was a task too difficult to ascertain, with precision, the lowest degree of force competent to the quelling of the insurrection. From a respect, indeed, to economy, and the ease of my fellow-citizens belonging to the militia, it would have gratified me to accomplish such an estimate. My very reluctance to ascribe too much importance to the opposition, had its extent been accurately seen, would have been a decided inducement to the smallest efficient numbers. In this uncertainty, therefore, I put in motion fifteen thousand men, as being an army which, according to all human calculation, would be prompt and adequate in every view, and might, perhaps, by rendering resistance desperate, prevent the effusion of blood. Quotas had been assigned to the States of New Jersey, Pennsylvania, Maryland, and Virginia; the Governor of Pennsylvania having declared, on this occasion, an opinion which justified a requisition to the other States.

As commander-in-chief of the militia, when called into the actual service of the United States, I have visited the places of general rendezvous, to obtain more exact information, and to direct a plan for ulterior movements. Had there been room for persuasion that the laws were secure from obstruction; that the civil magistrate was able to bring to justice such of the most culpable as have not embraced the proffered terms of amnesty, and may be deemed fit objects of example; that the friends to peace and good government were not in need of that aid and countenance which they ought always to receive, and, I trust, ever will receive, against the vicious and turbulent; I should have caught with avidity the opportunity of restoring the militia to their families and home. But, succeeding intelligence has tended to manifest the necessity of what has been done; it being now confessed by those who were not inclined to exaggerate the ill conduct of the insurgents, that their malevolence was not pointed merely to a particular law, but that a spirit, inimical to all order, has actuated many of the offenders. If the state of things had afforded reason for the continuance of my presence with the army, it would not have been withholden. But every appearance assuring such an issue as will redound to the reputation and strength of the United States, I have judged it most proper to resume my duties at the seat of Government, leaving the chief command with the Governor of Virginia.

Still, however, as it is probable that, in a commotion like the present, whatsoever may be the pretence, the purposes of mischiefs and revenge may not be laid aside, the stationing of a small force, for a certain period, in the four western counties of Pennsylvania, will be indispensable, whether we contemplate the situation of those who are connected with the execution of the laws, or of others, who may have exposed themselves by an honorable attachment to them. Thirty days from the commencement of this session being the legal limitation of the employment of the militia, Congress cannot be too early occupied with this subject.

Among the discussions which may arise from this aspect of our affairs, and from the documents which will be submitted to Congress, it will not escape their observation, that not only the inspector of the revenue, but other officers of the United States, in Pennsylvania, have, from their fidelity in the discharge of their functions, sustained material injuries to their property. The obligation and policy of indemnifying them are strong and obvious. It may also merit attention, whether policy will not enlarge this provision to the retribution of other citizens, who, though not under the ties of office, may have suffered damage by their generous exertions for upholding the constitution and the laws. The amount, even if all the injured were included, would not be great; and, on future emergencies, the Government would be amply repaid by the influence of an example, that he, who incurs a loss in its defence, shall find a recompense in its liberality.

While there is cause to lament that occurrences of this nature should have disgraced the name or interrupted the tranquility of any part of our community, or should have diverted, to a new application, any portion of the public resources, there are not wanting real and substantial consolations for the misfortune. It has demonstrated that our prosperity rests on solid foundations, by furnishing an additional proof that my fellow-citizens understand the true principles of Government and liberty; that they feel their inseparable union; that, notwithstanding all the devices which have been used to sway them from their interest and duty, they are now as ready to maintain the authority of the laws against licentious invasions, as they were to defend their rights against usurpation. It has been a spectacle, displaying to the highest advantage the value of republican Government, to behold the most and the least wealthy of our citizens standing in the same ranks as private soldiers, preeminently distinguished by being the army of the constitution; undeterred by a march of three hundred miles over rugged mountains, by the approach of an inclement season, or by any other discouragement. Nor ought I to omit to acknowledge the efficacious and patriotic co-operation which I have experienced from the Chief Magistrates of the States to which my requisitions have been addressed.

To every description, indeed, of citizens let praise be given. But let them persevere in their affectionate vigilance over that precious depository of American happiness, the constitution of the United States. Let them cherish it, too, for the sake of those who, from every clime, are daily seeking a dwelling in our land. And when, in the calm moments of reflection, they shall have retraced the origin and progress of the insurrection, let them determine whether it has not been fomented by combinations of men, who, careless of consequences, and disregarding the unerring truth, that those who rouse cannot always appease a civil convulsion, have disseminated, from an ignorance or perversion of facts, suspicions, jealousies, and accusations, of the whole Government.

5. Washington's Farewell Address, September 19, 1796

One of the most famous documents in American history, Washington's farewell address of September 19, 1796, was issued to announce his retirement at the end of his second term. The address reflected the problems that had occupied much of the attention of his administration, especially the concern with foreign affairs and the rise of political parties. The recapitulation of the American position of nonentanglement, which had formed the basis of United States policy during Washington's administration, provided a statement of principle that would not only be reaffirmed by Jefferson and Monroe and other presidents in the nineteenth century but would also be revived in the twentieth century in support of American isolationism. Although the hand of Hamilton, who assisted the president in drafting the address, may be suspected in the denunciation of parties, Washington personally considered himself to be above parties, and in denouncing their evils he expressed a concern that was widely shared by his contemporaries. The text is taken from John C. Fitzpatrick (ed.), The Writings of George Washington (39 vols., Washington, D.C., 1931–44), XXXV, 214–238.

Friends, and Fellow-Citizens: The period for a new election of a Citizen, to Administer the Executive government of the United States, being not far distant, and the time actually arrived, when your thoughts must be employed in designating the person, who is to be cloathed with that important trust, it appears to me proper, especially as it may conduce to a more distinct expression of the public voice, that I should now apprise you of the resolution

I have formed, to decline being considered among the number of those, out of whom a choice is to be made.

I beg you, at the same time, to do me the justice to be assured, that this resolution has not been taken, without a strict regard to all the considerations appertaining to the relation, which binds a dutiful citizen to his country, and that, in with drawing the tender of service which silence in my situation might imply, I am influenced by no diminution of zeal for your future interest, no deficiency of grateful respect for your past kindness; but am supported by a full conviction that the step is compatible with both.

The acceptance of, and continuance hitherto in, the office to which your Suffrages have twice called me, have been a uniform sacrifice of inclination to the opinion of duty, and to a deference for what appeared to be your desire. I constantly hoped, that it would have been much earlier in my power, consistently with motives, which I was not at liberty to disregard, to return to that retirement, from which I had been reluctantly drawn. The strength of my inclination to do this, previous to the last Election, had even led to the preparation of an address to declare it to you; but mature reflection on the then perplexed and critical posture of our Affairs with foreign Nations, and the unanimous advice of persons entitled to my confidence, impelled me to abandon the idea.

I rejoice, that the state of your concerns, external as well as internal, no longer renders the pursuit of inclination incompatible with the sentiment of duty, or propriety; and am persuaded whatever partiality may be retained for my services, that in the present circumstances of our country, you will not disapprove my determination to retire. . . .

In looking forward to the moment, which is intended to terminate the career of my public life, my feelings do not permit me to suspend the deep acknowledgment of that debt of gratitude which I owe to my beloved country, for the many honors it has conferred upon me; still more for the stedfast confidence with which it has supported me; and for the opportunities I have thence enjoyed of manifesting my inviolable attachment, by services faithful and persevering, though in usefulness unequal to my zeal. If benefits have resulted to our country from these services, let it always be remembered to your praise, and as an instructive example in our annals, that, under circumstances in which the Passions agitated in every direction were liable to mislead, amidst appearances sometimes dubious, viscissitudes of fortune often discouraging, in situations in which not unfrequently want of Success has countenanced the spirit of criticism, the constancy of your support was the essential prop of the efforts, and a guarantee of the plans by which they were effected. Profoundly penetrated with this idea, I shall carry it with me to my grave, as a strong incitement to unceasing vows that Heaven may continue to you the choicest tokens of its beneficence; that your Union and brotherly affection may be perpetual; that the free constitution, which is the work of your hands, may be sacredly maintained; that its Administration in every department may be stamped with wisdom and Virtue; that, in fine, the happiness of the people of these States, under the auspices of liberty, may be made complete, by so careful a preservation and so prudent a use of this blessing as will acquire to them the glory of recommending it to the applause, the affection, and adoption of every nation which is yet a stranger to it.

Here, perhaps, I ought to stop. But a solicitude for your welfare, which cannot end but with my life, and the apprehension of danger, natural to that solicitude, urge me on an occasion like the present, to offer to your solemn contemplation, and to recommend to your frequent review, some sentiments; which are the result of much reflection, of no inconsiderable observation, and which appear to me all important to the permanency of your felicity as a People. These will be offered to you with the more freedom, as you can only see in them the disinterested warnings of a parting friend, who can possibly have no personal motive to biass his counsel. Nor can I forget, as an encouragement to it, your endulgent reception of my sentiments on a former and not dissimilar occasion.

Interwoven as is the love of liberty with every ligament of your hearts, no recommendation of mine is necessary to fortify or confirm the attachment.

The Unity of Government which constitutes you one people is also now dear to you. It is justly so; for it is a main Pillar in the Edifice of your real independence, the support of your tranquility at home; your peace abroad; of your safety; of your prosperity; of that very Liberty which you so highly prize. But as it is easy to foresee, that from different causes and from different quarters, much pains will be taken, many artifices employed, to weaken in your minds the conviction of this truth; as this is the point in your political fortress against which the batteries of internal and external enemies will be most constantly and actively (though often covertly and insidiously) directed, it is of infinite moment, that you should properly estimate the immense value of your national Union to your collective and individual happiness; that you should cherish a cordial, habitual and immoveable attachment to it; accustoming yourselves to think and speak of it as of the Palladium of your political safety and prosperity; watching for its preservation with jealous anxiety; discountenancing whatever may suggest even a suspicion that it can in any event be abandoned, and indignantly frowning upon the first dawning of every attempt to alienate any portion of our Country from the rest, or to enfeeble the sacred ties which now link together the various parts.

For this you have every inducement of sympathy and interest. Citizens by birth or choice, of a common country, that country has a right to concentrate your affections. The name of AMERICAN, which belongs to you, in your national capacity, must always exalt the just pride of Patriotism, more than any appellation derived from local discriminations. With slight shades of difference, you have the same Religeon, Manners, Habits and political Principles. You have in a common cause fought and triumphed together. The independence and liberty you possess are the work of joint councils, and joint efforts; of common dangers, sufferings and successes.

But these considerations, however powerfully they address themselves to your sensibility are greatly outweighed by those which apply more immediately to your Interest. Here every portion of our country finds the most commanding motives for carefully guarding and preserving the Union of the whole.

The North, in an unrestrained intercourse with the South, protected by the equal Laws of a common government, finds in the productions of the latter, great additional resources of Maratime and commercial enterprise and precious materials of manufacturing industry. The South in the same Intercourse, benefitting by the Agency of the North, sees its agriculture grow and its commerce expand. Turning partly into its own channels the seamen of the North, it finds its particular navigation envigorated; and while it contributes, in different ways, to nourish and increase the general mass of the National navigation, it looks forward to the protection of a Maratime strength, to which itself is unequally adapted. The

East, in a like intercourse with the *West*, already finds, and in the progressive improvement of interior communications, by land and water, will more and more find a valuable vent for the commodities which it brings from abroad, or manufactures at home. The *West* derives from the *East* supplies requisite to its growth and comfort, and what is perhaps of still greater consequence, it must of necessity owe the *secure* enjoyment of indispensable *outlets* for its own productions to the weight, influence, and the future Maritime strength of the Atlantic side of the Union, directed by an indissoluble community of Interest as *one Nation*. Any other tenure by which the *West* can hold this essential advantage, whether derived from its own separate strength, or from an apostate and unnatural connection with any foreign Power, must be intrinsically precarious.

While then every part of our country thus feels an immediate and particular Interest in Union, all the parts combined cannot fail to find in the united mass of means and efforts greater strength, greater resource, proportionately greater security from external danger, a less frequent interruption of their Peace by foreign Nations; and, what is of inestimable value! they must derive from Union an exemption from those broils and Wars between themselves, which so frequently afflict neighboring countries, not tied together by the same government; which their own rivalships alone would be sufficient to produce, but which opposite foreign alliances, attachments and intriegues would stimulate and imbitter. Hence likewise they will avoid the necessity of those overgrown Military establishments, which under any form of Government are inauspicious to liberty, and which are to be regarded as particularly hostile to Republican Liberty: In this sense it is, that your Union ought to be considered as a main prop of your liberty, and that the love of the one ought to endear to you the preservation of the other.

These considerations speak a persuasive language to every reflecting and virtuous mind, and exhibit the continuance of the UNION as a primary object of Patriotic desire. Is there a doubt, whether a common government can embrace so large a sphere? Let experience solve it. To listen to mere speculation in such a case were criminal. We are authorized to hope that a proper organization of the whole, with the auxiliary agency of governments for the respective Sub divisions, will afford a happy issue to the experi-

ment. 'Tis well worth a fair and full experiment. With such powerful and obvious motives to Union, affecting all parts of our country,
while experience shall not have demonstrated its impracticability,
there will always be reason, to distrust the patriotism of those, who
in any quarter may endeavor to weaken its bands.

In contemplating the causes which may disturb our Union, it
occurs as matter of serious concern, that any ground should have
been furnished for characterizing parties by *Geographical* discriminations: *Northern* and *Southern; Atlantic* and *Western;* whence
designing men may endeavour to excite a belief that there is a
real difference of local interests and views. One of the expedients
of Party to acquire influence, within particular districts, is to mis-
represent the opinions and aims of other Districts. You cannot
shield yourselves too much against the jealousies and heart burn-
ings which spring from these misrepresentations. They tend to
render Alien to each other those who ought to be bound together
by fraternal affection. The Inhabitants of our Western country
have lately had a useful lesson on this head. They have seen, in the
Negociation by the Executive, and in the unanimous ratification
by the Senate, of the Treaty with Spain, and in the universal satisfaction at that event, throughout the United States, a decisive
proof how unfounded were the suspicions propagated among
them of a policy in the General Government and in the Atlantic
States unfriendly to their Interests in regard to the MISSISSIPPI.
They have been witnesses to the formation of two Treaties, that
with G: Britain and that with Spain, which secure to them every
thing they could desire, in respect to our Foreign relations, towards confirming their prosperity. Will it not be their wisdom
to rely for the preservation of these advantages on the UNION by
which they were procured? Will they not henceforth be deaf to
those advisers, if such there are, who would sever them from their
Brethren and connect them with Aliens?

To the efficacy and permanency of Your Union, a Government
for the whole is indispensable. No Alliances however strict between
the parts can be an adequate substitute. They must inevitably experience the infractions and interruptions which all Alliances in all
times have experienced. Sensible of this momentous truth, you have
improved upon your first essay, by the adoption of a Constitution
of Government, better calculated than your former for an intimate
Union, and for the efficacious management of your common con-

cerns. This government, the offspring of our own choice uninfluenced and unawed, adopted upon full investigation and mature deliberation, completely free in its principles, in the distribution of its powers, uniting security with energy, and containing within itself a provision for its own amendment, has a just claim to your confidence and your support. Respect for its authority, compliance with its Laws, acquiescence in its measures, are duties enjoined by the fundamental maxims of true Liberty. The basis of our political systems is the right of the people to make and to alter their Constitutions of Government. But the Constitution which at any time exists, 'till changed by an explicit and authentic act of the whole People, is sacredly obligatory upon all. The very idea of the power and the right of the People to establish Government presupposes the duty of every Individual to obey the established Government.

All obstructions to the execution of the Laws, all combinations and Associations, under whatever plausible character, with the real design to direct, controul counteract, or awe the regular deliberation and action of the Constituted authorities are distructive of this fundamental principle and of fatal tendency. They serve to organize faction, to give it an artificial and extraordinary force; to put in the place of the delegated will of the Nation, the will of a party; often a small but artful and enterprizing minority of the Community; and, according to the alternate triumphs of different parties, to make the public administration the Mirror of the ill concerted and incongruous projects of faction, rather than the organ of consistent and wholesome plans digested by common councils and modefied by mutual interests. However combinations or Associations of the above description may now and then answer popular ends, they are likely, in the course of time and things, to become potent engines, by which cunning, ambitious and unprincipled men will be enabled to subvert the Power of the People, and to usurp for themselves the reins of Government; destroying afterwards the very engines which have lifted them to unjust dominion.

Towards the preservation of your Government and the permanency of your present happy state, it is requisite, not only that you steadily discountenance irregular oppositions to its acknowledged authority, but also that you resist with care the spirit of innovation upon its principles however specious the pretexts. One method of assault may be to effect, in the forms of the Constitution, alterations which will impair the energy of the system, and thus to undermine what cannot be directly overthrown. In all the changes to which you may be invited, remember that time and habit are at least as necessary to fix the true character of Governments, as of other human institutions; that experience is the surest standard, by which to test the real tendency of the existing Constitution of a country; that facility in changes upon the credit of mere hypotheses and opinion exposes to perpetual change, from the endless variety of hypotheses and opinion: and remember, especially, that for the efficient management of your common interests, in a country so extensive as ours, a Government of as much vigour as is consistent with the perfect security of Liberty is indispensable. Liberty itself will find in such a Government, with powers properly distributed and adjusted, its surest Guardian. It is indeed little else than a name, where the Government is too feeble to withstand the enterprises of faction, to confine each member of the Society within the limits prescribed by the laws and to maintain all in the secure and tranquil enjoyment of the rights of person and property.

I have already intimated to you the danger of Parties in the State, with particular reference to the founding of them on Geographical discriminations. Let me now take a more comprehensive view, and warn you in the most solemn manner against the baneful effects of the Spirit of Party, generally.

This spirit, unfortunately, is inseperable from our nature, having its root in the strongest passions of the human Mind. It exists under different shapes in all Governments, more or less stifled, controuled, or repressed; but, in those of the popular form it is seen in its greatest rankness and is truly their worst enemy.

The alternate domination of one faction over another, sharpened by the spirit of revenge natural to party dissention, which in different ages and countries has perpetuated the most horrid enormities, is itself a frightful despotism. But this leads at length to a more formal and permanent despotism. The disorders and miseries, which result, gradually incline the minds of men to seek security and respose in the absolute power of an Individual: and sooner or later the chief of some prevailing faction more able or more fortunate than his competitors, turns this disposition to the purposes of his own elevation, on the ruins of Public Liberty.

Without looking forward to an extremity of this kind (which nevertheless ought not to be entirely out of sight) the common and continual mischiefs of the spirit of Party are sufficient to make it the interest and the duty of a wise People to discourage and restrain it.

It serves always to distract the Public Councils and enfeeble the Public administration. It agitates the Community with ill founded jealousies and false alarms, kindles the animosity of one part against another, foments occasionally riot and insurrection. It opens the door to foreign influence and corruption, which find a facilitated access to the government itself through the channels of party passions. Thus the policy and the will of one country, are subjected to the policy and will of another.

There is an opinion that parties in free countries are useful checks upon the Administration of the Government and serve to keep alive the spirit of Liberty. This within certain limits is probably true, and in Governments of a Monarchical cast Patriotism may look with endulgence, if not with favour, upon the spirit of party. But in those of the popular character, in Governments purely elective, it is a spirit not to be encouraged. From their natural tendency, it is certain there will always be enough of that spirit for every salutary purpose. And there being constant danger of excess, the effort ought to be, by force of public opinion, to mitigate and assuage it. A fire not to be quenched; it demands a uniform vigilance to prevent its bursting into a flame, lest, instead of warming it should consume. . . .

Of all the dispositions and habits which lead to political prosperity, Religion and morality are indispensable supports. In vain would that man claim the tribute of Patriotism, who should labour to subvert these great Pillars of human happiness, these firmest props of the duties of Men and citizens. The mere Politician, equally with the pious man ought to respect and to cherish them. A volume could not trace all their connections with private and public felicity. Let it simply be asked where is the security for property, for reputation, for life, if the sense of religious obligation desert the oaths, which are the instruments of investigation in Courts of Justice? And let us with caution indulge the supposition, that morality can be maintained without religion. Whatever may be conceded to the influence of refined education on minds of peculiar structure, reason and experience both forbid us to expect that National morality can prevail in exclusion of religious principle.

'Tis substantially true, that virtue or morality is a necessary spring of popular government. The rule indeed extends with more or less force to every species of free Government. Who that is a sincere friend to it, can look with indifference upon attempts to shake the foundation of the fabric.

Promote then as an object of primary importance, Institutions for the general diffusion of knowledge. In proportion as the structure of a government gives force to public opinion, it is essential that public opinion should be enlightened.

As a very important source of strength and security, cherish public credit. One method of preserving it is to use it as sparingly as possible: avoiding occasions of expence by cultivating peace, but remembering also that timely disbursements to prepare for danger frequently prevent much greater disbursements to repel it; avoiding likewise the accumulation of debt, not only by shunning occasions of expence, but by vigorous exertions in time of Peace to discharge the Debts which unavoidable wars may have occasioned, not ungenerously throwing upon posterity the burthen which we ourselves ought to bear. The execution of these maxims belongs to your Representatives, but it is necessary that public opinion should cooperate. To facilitate to them the performance of their duty, it is essential that you should practically bear in mind, that towards the payment of debts there must be Revenue; that to have Revenue there must be taxes; that no taxes can be devised which are not more or less inconvenient and unpleasant; that the intrinsic embarrassment inseparable from the selection of the proper objects (which is always a choice of difficulties) ought to be a decisive motive for a candid construction of the Conduct of the Government in making it, and for a spirit of acquiescence in the measures for obtaining Revenue which the public exigencies may at any time dictate.

Observe good faith and justice towards all Nations. Cultivate peace and harmony with all. Religion and morality enjoin this conduct; and can it be that good policy does not equally enjoin it? It will be worthy of a free, enlightened, and, at no distant period, a great Nation, to give to mankind the magnanimous and too novel example of a People always guided by an exalted justice and benevolence. Who can doubt that in the course of time and things the fruits of such a plan would richly repay any temporary advantages which might be lost by a steady adherence to it? Can it be, that Providence has not connected the permanent felicity of a Nation with its virtue? The experiment, at least, is recommended by every sentiment which ennobles human Nature. Alas! is it rendered impossible by its vices?

In the execution of such a plan nothing is more essential than that permanent, inveterate antipathies against particular Nations and passionate attachments for others should be excluded; and that in place of them just and amicable feelings towards all should be cultivated. The Nation, which indulges towards another an habitual hatred, or an habitual fondness, is in some degree a slave. It is a slave to its animosity or to its affection, either of which is sufficient to lead it astray from its duty and its interest. Antipathy in one Nation against another, disposes each more readily to offer insult and injury, to lay hold of slight causes of umbrage, and to be haughty and intractable, when accidental or trifling occasions of dispute occur. Hence frequent collisions, obstinate envenomed and bloody contests. The Nation, prompted by illwill and resentment sometimes impels to War the Government, contrary to the best calculations of policy. The Government sometimes participates in the national propensity, and adopts through passion what reason would reject; at other times, it makes the animosity of the Nation subservient to projects of hostility instigated by pride, ambition and other sinister and pernicious motives. The peace often, sometimes perhaps the Liberty, of Nations has been the victim.

So likewise, a passionate attachment of one Nation for another produces a variety of evils. Sympathy for the favourite nation, facilitating the illusion of an imaginary common interest, in cases where no real common interest exists, and infusing into one the enmities of the other, betrays the former into a participation in the quarrels and Wars of the latter, without adequate inducement or justification: It leads also to concessions to the favourite Nation of priviledges denied to others, which is apt doubly to injure the Nation making the concessions; by unnecessarily parting with what ought to have been retained; and by exciting jealousy, ill will, and a disposition to retaliate, in the parties from whom equal priviledges are withheld: And it gives to ambitious, corrupted, or deluded citizens (who devote themselves to the favourite Nation) facility to betray, or sacrifice the interests of their own country, without odium, sometimes even with popularity; gilding with the appearances of a virtuous sense of obligation a commendable deference for public opinion, or a laudable zeal for public good, the base or foolish compliances of ambition corruption or infatuation.

As avenues to foreign influence in innumerable ways, such attachments are particularly alarming to the truly enlightened and independent Patriot. How many opportunities do they afford to tamper with domestic factions, to practice the arts of seduction, to mislead public opinion, to influence or awe the public Councils! Such an attachment of a small or weak, towards a great and powerful Nation, dooms the former to be the satellite of the latter.

Against the insidious wiles of foreign influence, (I conjure you to believe me fellow citizens) the jealousy of a free people ought to be *constantly* awake; since history and experience prove that foreign influence is one of the most baneful foes of Republican Government. But that jealousy to be useful must be impartial; else it becomes the instrument of the very influence to be avoided, instead of a defence against it. Excessive partiality for one foreign nation and excessive dislike of another, cause those whom they actuate to see danger only on one side, and serve to veil and even second the arts of influence on the other. Real Patriots, who may resist the intriegues of the favourite, are liable to become suspected and odious; while its tools and dupes usurp the applause and confidence of the people, to surrender their interests.

The Great rule of conduct for us, in regard to foreign Nations is in extending our commercial relations to have with them as little *political* connection as possible. So far as we have already formed engagements let them be fulfilled, with perfect good faith. Here let us stop.

Europe has a set of primary interests, which to us have none, or a very remote relation. Hence she must be engaged in frequent controversies, the causes of which are essentially foreign to our concerns. Hence therefore it must be unwise in us to implicate ourselves, by artificial ties, in the ordinary vicissitudes of her politics, or the ordinary combinations and collisions of her friendships, or enmities:

Our detached and distant situation invites and enables us to pursue a different course. If we remain one People, under an efficient government, the period is not far off, when we may defy material injury from external annoyance; when we may take such an attitude as will cause the neutrality we may at any time resolve upon to be scrupulously respected; when belligerent nations, under the impossibility of making acquisitions upon us, will not lightly hazard the giving us provocation; when we may choose peace or war, as our interest guided by our justice shall Counsel.

Why forego the advantages of so peculiar a situation? Why quit our own to stand upon foreign ground? Why, by interweaving our destiny with that of any part of Europe, entangle our peace and prosperity in the toils of European Ambition, Rivalship, Interest, Humour or Caprice?

'Tis our true policy to steer clear of permanent Alliances, with any portion of the foreign world. So far, I mean, as we are now at liberty to do it, for let me not be understood as capable of patronising infidility to existing engagements (I hold the maxim no less applicable to public than to private affairs, that honesty is always the best policy). I repeat it therefore, let those engagements be observed in their genuine sense. But in my opinion, it is unnecessary and would be unwise to extend them.

Taking care always to keep ourselves, by suitable establishments, on a respectably defensive posture, we may safely trust to temporary alliances for extraordinary emergencies.

Harmony, liberal intercourse with all Nations, are recommended by policy, humanity and interest. But even our Commercial policy should hold an equal and impartial hand: neither seeking nor granting exclusive favours or preferences; consulting the natural course of things; diffusing and deversifying by gentle means the streams of Commerce, but forcing nothing; establishing with Powers so disposed; in order to give to trade a stable course, to define the rights of our Merchants, and to enable the Government to support them; conventional rules of intercourse, the best that present circumstances and mutual opinion will permit, but temporary, and liable to be from time to time abandoned or varied, as experience and circumstances shall dictate; constantly keeping in view, that 'tis folly in one Nation to look for disinterested favors from another; that it must pay with a portion of its Independence for whatever it may accept under that character; that by such acceptance, it may place itself in the condition of having given equivalents for nominal favours and yet of being reproached with ingratitude for not giving more. There can be no greater error than to expect, or calculate upon real favours from Nation to

Nation. 'Tis an illusion which experience must cure, which a just pride ought to discard.

In offering to you, my Countrymen these counsels of an old and affectionate friend, I dare not hope they will make the strong and lasting impression, I could wish; that they will controul the usual current of the passions, or prevent our Nation from running the course which has hitherto marked the Destiny of Nations: But if I may even flatter myself, that they may be productive of some partial benefit, some occasional good; that they may now and then recur to moderate the fury of party spirit, to warn against the mischiefs of foreign Intriegue, to guard against the Impostures of pretended patriotism; this hope will be a full recompense for the solicitude for your welfare, by which they have been dictated. . . .

6. Problems of John Adams's Administration

The major problems of Adams's presidency grew out of the crisis with France following the XYZ incident and the responses of the administration and a Federalist-controlled Congress to the war threat. In reaction to the French challenge, Congress expanded the army, created a navy, passed the alien and sedition laws, raised the residence requirements for naturalization, and increased taxes. The possibility of war with France alarmed many Americans, among them the students of the College of William and Mary who prepared an address to the Virginia delegation in Congress arguing the case for peace. This address is reprinted below from the Philadelphia Aurora, June 18, 1798. The crisis, however, worked to the political advantage of the Federalists, who increased their majority in Congress in the congressional elections of 1798–99. Although a full-scale war was avoided and President Adams himself pushed through the second peace mission to France, which reached an understanding with Napoleon in 1800, Republicans were aroused by the increased military establishment, the restrictions on freedom of speech and the press, and other Federalist measures. A strong statement of the Republican position examining the principal measures of Federalist policy was the series of resolutions adopted in Dinwiddie County, Virginia, in November, 1798. These resolutions display what the Republicans regarded as the main issues of the Adams administration, which became in fact the key issues of the presidential election of 1800. The Dinwiddie County resolutions are reprinted from the Richmond Examiner, December 6, 1798.

A. *An Address from Students of the College of William and Mary, June 8, 1798*

At a meeting of the Students of William and Mary College, Virginia, on Friday 8th of June, JOHN BOSWELL JOHNSON being appointed to the chair, and JOHN TAYLOE LOMAX, Secretary, the following address, to the Virginia delegation in Congress, was agreed to, (there being only one dissenting voice) and ordered to be published:

GENTLEMEN,

The students of William and Mary College regard the brooding hostilities, between the United States of America and the Republic of France, as forming a crisis in our political affairs which involves the future destiny of our country. Although we do not yet, by the laws of this state, possess the full powers of constituents, yet, on a subject so interesting to ourselves, we conceive it but reasonable and just that our opinions should be heard and respected by the representatives of the people. War between the two republics seems daily denounced to us in the measures of our government. Those measures appear to us not the inevitable offsprings of necessity; we are, therefore, left at full liberty to offer you some of our objections to being plunged into a state of hostility.

Our wishes for a temper of pacification, on the part of our government are grounded, not on any juvenile predilections, or preference of the interest of one foreign nation to that of any other; but on a conviction of the injuries which would result to our own from a contrary conduct. One of the principal of these is, the unavoidable and acknowledged accumulation of our national debt. Though we do not pretend to an intimate acquaintance with the existing revenues of the nation, or the resources by which those revenues may be augmented; yet, we think, we cannot be deceived, when we say, that that debt must be increased to an enormous and insupportable amount. Hence too will arise a proportionate increase in the taxes of our citizens. We submit it, however, to your consideration, whether it would be advantageous to the people, or prudent for their representatives to encrease them, whilst their present weight is already the subject of murmurs and complaints.

Nor will the effects of a war on commerce and agriculture have a less pernicious tendency. Though our merchants have been considerably injured by the depredations on our commerce, yet, from a declaration of war, and the consequent stoppage of all commercial intercourse, their sufferings, instead of redress, would be increased and aggravated in the highest degree. They would, in that case, lose the whole profits of their stock; whereas, in the present, many of their losses are compensated by the advanced prices of their goods. These advanced prices are now paid by the agricultural interest, which, therefore, experiences a real injury from the present situation of our country: but, in case of a war, and the interruption of commerce, the home market will, of course, be the only one remaining for the purchasing and consumption of the produce of the farmers. Now, it is evident that the number of farmers, remaining in our country during the continuance of the war, notwithstanding the numbers drafted off for the supply of the army and navy, would bear a much greater proportion to the then existing demand, than the number of farmers before the war would bear to the demand which at that time existed. The demand will not be sufficient to give employment to the farmers who will remain; or in other words there will be a greater competition amongst the sellers than among the buyers, in which case we may ever look for the lowest possible price of any commodity.—This low price of produce will inevitably tend to discourage the further improvement of land, and consequently retard the growing improvement of our country: We conceive that its effects would proceed still farther; that they will not only stop the present rapidly progressing state of our country towards wealth, population and improvement, but will tend to throw it back from the state, to which it has already attained: For this low price of produce, together with the numbers who will be called off from their farms, will occasion a neglect of a considerable portion of those lands which are now under cultivation. The increase of the taxes, also, must fall chiefly on farmers; the diminution in the price of whose produce must create a proportionable inability to pay this increase. From this agricultural interest arises another powerful dissuasive from a rupture with France; or any other country. In the populous nations of Europe the prosecution of hostilities is generally attended with consequences disadvantageous to agriculture and improvement. How injurious then must it be to this country, where we experience a deficiency of population, where our inhabitants are chiefly husbandmen, where agriculture is, and ought to be, our primary object, and where every deviation from, and obstacle to, the pursuit of that object, is a deviation from, and perversion of, the real interest of the community? Of all countries, then, this should entertain the greatest aversion to entering into a war, and more particularly with the republic of France, than with any other country whatever. By a war with any power we sacrifice some of the greatest interests of our country—by a war with France we add to the sacrifice that, perhaps, of Republican Liberty.

We believe an increase of power and influence in the executive branch of our government to be an inevitable effect of war. The history of all governments, and particularly of the representative governments of modern Europe, warn us to look with certainty for the event. The present powers of the executive are sufficient to answer the ends of efficient government. To increase them, will be to weaken the co-ordinate branches, Legislative and Judiciary, to turn the balance of powers between the three departments and to take away the only support of liberty. Power, moreover, we believe, to be of a rooted and increasing, rather than of an unstable and decreasing nature. The executive, acquiring an additional energy in time of war, is too apt, upon the return of peace, to preserve, exert and augment that energy; although the necessity of its existence has passed away. By our constitution the president possesses the command of the army and navy, the appointment of officers in both, and the management of the monies necessary for their equipment and maintenance. That love which the soldier bears to his commander will ever operate in making him a powerful friend to the executive. The splendour of office, and rewards for services, also, are too gratifying to man, not to create in him, who receives them, the strongest and most permanent attachment to his benefactor. The army of Ceasar, was, at first, the army of Rome; but they were soon taught to kiss the hand that cherished them. We would wish to believe that the President feels too much the dignity of being the chief magistrate of a FREE PEOPLE, ever to make use of an army, committed to his care for the welfare of his country, as an engine for the destruction of our liberties so dearly purchased, and of exchanging the honourable appellation, at present enjoyed, for the degraded one of a tyrant, did not the nature of man, did not the history of all men entrusted with power, did not the general conduct of our own administration itself forbid us to entertain the flattering idea. We consider, moreover, an implicit confidence in any government whatever, however well administered, as the certain harbinger of oppression, as being incompatible with that political suspicion, the only true safeguard of Liberty.

An alliance with Great Britain seems too evidently to be the inevitable offspring of a war with France, for us to resist the belief that it will be—nay it is daily proclaimed to us by those who seem to be secret advocates of the war, that an alliance with that government must be formed. Of all the evils resulting from a war, none appears to us to be more serious, more alarming than this. It will be well recollected, that our constitution is formed on the plan of, what is commonly termed, the constitution of Great Britain.—The abuses and corruptions which have crept into the British government, should therefore, stand as useful monitors to warn us, how we pursue that course which has already proved fatal to that nation. If a stronger assimilation of the American government to that of the British would tend to introduce the same abuses here; it would be madness to disobey that voice which so loudly calls upon us to change our course—it would be a voluntary devotion of ourselves, as victims, at that altar on which G. Britain bleeds. We need not, we trust, attempt to prove that an alliance between the two nations will soon beget a strong attachment bewixt the people of the one nation and those of the other, and equally as strong a one between the two governments. But friendships between nations, like those between individuals, will ever generate a similarity of views and dispositions. This similarity would soon dissipate those horrors, which we have hitherto felt at monarchical governments, and might quickly involve the people of this country in a common fate, with those of Great Britain.

Moreover, by establishing a connection with a nation, of so much importance on the political theatre of Europe, we would be led into those troubles, discords and contentions, by which Europe is continually torn, distracted and divided; which must increase our burdens, disorganize our government and disturb the general tranquility of the nation. Hitherto we have considered the effects of this war as confined solely to America; but they will not stop here; they will have a more general and extensive range. —It may well be recollected with what anxiety the advocates for Republics looked forward to the day when they should become the prevailing governments, and with what pleasure they anticipated in them an end to those wars and contentions, by which the world had been so long harrassed, and the peace and harmony which, from them, would ensue to all mankind. Let us not then, *without obvious necessity*, blast these hopes, so rationally and so virtuously formed.—With what triumph will the despot point to these two infant Republics, and with what ridicule will he exclaim "this is the boasted harmony which republics are to create." And how will he exult in the contemplation of an alliance, established betwixt one of those boasted republics and a monarchy, for the very purpose of war?

Permit us, gentlemen, after having thus laid freely before you the inconveniences & dangers of a war, with equal freedom to express our warmest disapprobation of certain measures of government, which have led us into our present gloomy situation and which seem to be daily drawing us still nearer the precipice. These measures appears to us to be justified neither by reason nor necessity; but can only meet with support in that weak temerity, which would stifle all kinds of negociation, and hurry us into a war. That our situation requires measures of internal defence and security, we cannot but acknowledge. Hence we highly approve of fortifying our coast, and a proper regulation of the militia. But, under this head, give us leave to say, that we cannot perceive the necessity of resorting to the dangerous and expensive expedient of establishing a standing army, when the more usual, and less offensive, method of calling out the militia, taken from the great body of the people, could, we apprehend, have answered every laudable end.

But that our situation will justify us in measures of an offensive nature, is a question which still remains to be proved to our mind. And hence we cannot but strongly disapprove of those late acts by which our merchantmen are empowered to arm, and our national vessels to make lawful prizes of French vessels, wherever they may be found. For as yet all hopes of negociation were not lost. By the latest accounts from France our envoys were received; and it is highly probable that a negociation was going on between them and the Directory. In this negociation, the friends of peace, with pleasure foresaw a reconciliation of our differences, & that friendship, which had been so unfortunately suspended, would again be established betwixt the two Republics. These acts will now irritate the mind of France, as amounting to a declaration of war, put a stop to the negociation and produce the unavoidable consequence of WAR.

The force of these acts in rousing the French to resentment, will be doubly augmented by the late publication of the dispatches from our envoys—dispatches which contained mere conversations betwixt our envoys and private individuals, no way concerned in the government, wholly unauthorized to act for it—dispatches which could throw no light on the wishes and intentions of France, or which could give no important information whatever—But which, by libelling its government and inflaming the nation, may make them more inimical to peace; and by rousing the citizens of this country make them less averse to war. The virulence used by the Executive of this country in its expressions, concerning France, in its daily communications will compleat this mournful procession of acts, and will give the finishing stroke to this melancholy painting.

After expressing these sentiments on the existing prospect of war, between the two Republics we think proper to observe that it is one of the noblest marks of a free government for the minority to advance and to endeavor to support by reason and argument their opinions against any proposed measure, which they may suppose will be prejudicial to the general welfare and happiness of the community; but always to acquiesce in that measure, when determined on by the fair & legal decision of a majority. This is all we attempt at present. Should the Representatives of the people exercising their constitutional authorities, either declare, or by their acts bring on a commencement of hostilities, we shall no longer conceive ourselves justified in using the sceptre of remonstrance to our government; but throwing aside our opposition to measures which we conceive to have been so highly improper, we will imitate the glorious example of our predecessors at William and Mary, in being ready to defend our rights and liberties against foreign invasion.

B. *Resolutions of the Freeholders of the County of Dinwiddie, Virginia, November 19, 1798*

At a meeting of a number of the Freeholders of the county of Dinwiddie, on the 3d Monday in November, 1798, assembled in pursuance of a previous notice, for the purpose of expressing their opinions on the administration of the affairs of the United States

1. *Resolved as the opinion of this meeting,* That a militia composed of the body of the people, is the proper, natural and safe defence of a free state, and that regular armies, except in case of an invasion, or the certain prospect of an invasion, are not only highly detrimental to the public welfare, but dangerous to liberty:

Detrimental to the public welfare, because industrious men are heavily taxed to support those who do nothing; because indolence among the poor is publicly encouraged: the army being an asylum for all who do not choose to labour: because the young men who form the mass of an army, instead of being a drawback on the productive labor of the community, might be more beneficially employed in supporting by their industry themselves and their families, and paying their proportions of the public debt: because the same object, immediate defence against a sudden invasion, might be attained infinitely cheaper, by putting arms into the hands of every man capable of bearing them: and because, the spirit which leads to war, the curse and the disgrace of humanity, is greatly augmented by standing armies, to whose leaders it opens a prospect of greater wealth, and higher military honors: and

Dangerous to liberty, because when numerous, they have tyrannized, as the experience of all ages has proved, both over the people and the government, and when limited, have always been subservient to the views of the executive department, from which they derive their honors and emoluments: because these honors and emoluments furnish an ample fund, by means of which the executive is enabled to reward its partizans and increase the number of its adherents: because a people accustomed to look for protection from external violence, to a standing army, become abject, debased and gradually enslaved; but knowing themselves to be the only defenders of their country, soon acquire that discipline and courage, which insure safety not only from foreign enemies, but domestic tyrants; and because, military establishments are in their nature progressive, the vast expense attending them, producing discontent and disturbances, and these furnishing a pretext for providing a force still more formidable; thus finally occasioning the oppression, the ruin, the SLAVERY of the people.

2. *Resolved as the opinion of this meeting,* That the plan for establishing a great naval armament is impolitic and pernicious;

because it enlarges still more the fund for increasing executive influence: because the expense is incalculable, and in fact cannot be supported by legitimate taxation: because this country cannot hope to protect its commerce by a fleet, as no other country has ever done so, or to guard from invasion a coast fifteen hundred miles in extent: because it will teach the people to look for protection, not in themselves, their patriotism, their union, and their courage; but in a system in which they will not find it; because if the people of the United States, following the councils of their late president, avoid all political connexions with European powers, they may reasonably expect to be seldom involved in the calamities of war, and having, fortunately, no islands in the West Indies, or Mediterranean, to defend, or conquests in the east to maintain, their ships must perish in the intervals of peace, to be preserved at an expense no less monstrous than unnecessary: and because experience has proved that even in a country whose existence is admitted now to depend on a fleet, seamen cannot be obtained, but by impressments, incompatible with law, liberty and humanity.

When therefore the navy of the United States is competent to the protection, not of our extensive coast, nor of our commerce throughout the world, but of our sea ports and coasting trade, from privateering and piratical depredations, it has attained the point, beyond which it ought not to go: beyond which benefit is partial, trifling, and precarious, and expense insupportable.

3. *Resolved also, as the opinion of this meeting,* that the government of the United States ought not to form an alliance with any nation on earth; that the people of America are competent to their own defence; that they are decidedly opposed to the plan of being drawn into the "foul abominations" of European politics, by any alliance with any government whatever, conscious that they must pay full value for what they receive, besides being entangled in ruinous connexions.

They reprobate therefore the practice of maintaining ministers resident in foreign countries, in the extent to which it is carried by the executive of the United States; because it adds still more to the already enormous mass of presidential patronage; because every important political view might be accomplished by a single minister advantageously stationed, and every valuable commercial purpose might be effected under the ordinary consular establishments; and because at a time like this, when money is borrowed to supply the deficiency of the taxes, every expense not absolutely necessary ought to be avoided.

Under these impressions they condemn the mission of William Smith to Lisbon, and of John Quincy Adams to Berlin: because there is but little commerce with Portugal and none with Prussia. In both cases therefore, and especially the latter, unless some political connection between the two countries is contemplated, an event surely not to be apprehended, the office is a sinecure and the salary thrown away.

4. *Resolved also, as the opinion of this meeting*, that the only proper way to raise money for national purposes, is by taxes, duties, excises and imposts, and that the power of borrowing money, ought not to be exercised except in cases of absolute necessity; that if money be really wanted, the people ought to be taxed to pay it; if not wanted, it ought not to be raised; if the public exigencies are supplied in the way first mentioned, economy must be observed: the people feeling immediately the effect of every public measure, would see that no unnecessary expense was incurred, and the money raised was duly expended; that the latter plan increases executive influence, augments the public debt, without the direct knowledge of the people; creates a paper monied interest, always adverse to the general welfare, and thrown on posterity, a burthen, which must either ruin them by its weight, or be shaken off in the struggles of a revolution.

5. *Resolved also, as the opinion of this meeting*, that the alien bill passed at the last session of Congress, is unnecessary, repugnant to humanity, and contrary to the constitution: the first, because its warmest advocates though called on, could mention neither persons nor facts to justify it: the second because it subjects the natives of foreign countries, who have sought here an asylum from persecution, to the despotism of a single individual: and the last, because the punishment of exile is inflicted without a public accusation of the party in the presence of the witnesses, and a trial by jury, which the constitution of the United States solemnly guarantees to every member of the community.

6. *Resolved also, as the opinion of this meeting*, that the freedom of the press is the great bulwark of liberty and can never be restrained but by a despotic government.

The people here present solemnly impressed with this momentous truth, regard with astonishment, regret and indignation, the act of congress passed at the last session, commonly called the Sedition Bill. They denounce it to their fellow citizens, as a daring and unconstitutional violation of a sacred and essential right, without which, liberty, political science, and national prosperity are at an end.

At a crisis like this, it becomes the real friends of order, of liberty, and of equal government, to come forward with an unequivocal declaration of their sentiments and wishes. The people of Dinwiddie therefore now assembled, solemnly aver that their minds impressed with affection and good will towards their fellow citizens from Georgia to New-Hampshire, and that they have no doubt either as to the importance or necessity of union between the states.

They declare that they are exclusively attached to their own country; that they abhor the idea of foreign influence, and that they will be at all times ready to support their government, and to unite with their fellow-citizens in repelling it, whether sought to be established by force or by intrigue.

They reprobate the practice, of which the example has been given by the executive department, of using intemperate and abusive expressions towards the French republic. The language of reproach, will not afford relief to America, nor compel France from terror, to adopt a system of moderation, justice, and good faith. It can only tend to irritate a nation always proud of its strength and its resources, and now still more proud of its victories and success.

But as those who have exercised here the privilege of freemen, in condemning the measures of their own government have been stigmatised, as the enemies of the United States, and the partizans of France, the freeholders of Dinwiddie, though they reprobate the fatal steps which led to the present crisis, are unanimous in saying, that they will be among the first to resist the invaders of their country, and that they consider the refusal of the French Directory to receive our late envoys, as a violation of the law of nations, & the rights of humanity.

They confidently aver that they despise and hate sedition, riot, and insurrection, and condemn calumnies against individuals or the government, as much as those who passed the law to punish the offences; deriving their subsistence from their lands and their happiness from their families, they knew full well the importance of order, and the blessings of tranquility: but valuing life, only as it is connected with law and liberty, they think it a duty which they owe to themselves to protect their rights from violation, and to transmit them unimpaired to their children: and this duty, nothing but despair, shall deter them from performing.

They condemn therefore, after the most mature deliberation, so much of the law last mentioned as relates to libels.

1st. Because congress possesses no power, but what is expressly given, or is necessary to carry a given power into effect, & the power of punishing libels is not expressly given, nor necessary to carry a given power into effect.

2dly. Because the constitution of the United States expressly declares that congress shall make no law abridging the freedom of speech or of the press.

And 3dly. Because it is a direct and palpable violation of every principle of republicanism, policy, and common sense; that the Representatives, the Senators, and President, who, whatever they may think to the contrary, are the trustees and servants of the people, and responsible to them for their misconduct, should pass a law to protect themselves from censure and their conduct from enquiry.

The freeholders of Dinwiddie, viewing this measure of the government as a blow which strikes at the vitals of the constitution and the liberty of the people, cannot remain calm spectators of the event. They solemnly, in the sacred names of liberty, and domestic peace, adjure the congress of the United States, to repeal this law: they most seriously declare, that the public tranquility has been greatly disturbed, and the public happiness greatly impaired, by the invasion of a right, which the state convention of 1776, the convention of 1788, and the congress of 1789, have concurred in assuring them, ought to be held in the highest estimation: and they do not hesitate to say, that unless a change takes place, the peace and welfare of the union are endangered, merely to preserve a law, which forty of the representatives of the people have opposed as unconstitutional, and which the warmest friends of the administration, concede to be not only unnecessary but pernicious.

If this appeal to the integrity and patriotism of congress, though heard, shall be disregarded, the people of Dinwiddie, look up at this awful moment with no less confidence than pleasure, to the general assembly of Virginia, the members of which have always proved themselves the faithful servants of their constituents, and the decided friends of liberty and the constitution. They are now solemnly required to protect, as they are bound to do, the rights of their fellow-citizens, and the people here present, with one voice pledge themselves to support such measures as their greater experience and better judgment shall direct.

The freedom of the press, it would be cowardice, it would be sacrilege to surrender.

7. *Resolved also, as the opinion of this meeting,* that there is one, and only one way to prevent unconstitutional laws, and the perpetuation of the present system of debts, taxes, standing armies, naval armaments, foreign intercourse, and executive influence, and that is, by an annual election of representatives and senators.

The foregoing resolutions were unanimously agreed to, this 19th day of November, 1798.

BULLER CLAIBORNE, Chm.
GEORGE PEGRAM, Sec'ry.

II

Maintaining the New Republic

The Jeffersonians who assumed control of the national government in 1801 established a Republican domination of its administration that kept the Federalists from returning to power and enabled the Republicans to govern the nation until the break up of the first party structure in 1824. The note sounded by Jefferson in his first inaugural address suggesting a return to a simpler government, while implemented in such specific policies as the reduction of military forces and government employees, was not to set the tone for the Republican era. To look back from the mid-1820's over the first quarter of the century was to see most clearly that the size of the country had been nearly doubled by the Louisiana Purchase and that the republic had maintained itself through a long period of foreign threats and a major war with Great Britain. From a war that had divided the country so deeply and humiliated it so severely, the nation emerged into a period of growing nationalism, which reached a high point of expression in Monroe's message to Congress in 1823 announcing that the American continents were closed to further colonization and intervention by European powers. Although the United States lacked the strength to enforce its dictum, the assertion of the American position demonstrated the self-confidence of the postwar nation. The so-called "era of good feelings" was clearly not a period without strains and conflicts within the nation, and the controversy over the admission of Missouri revealed how deep and serious a national problem was posed by the institution of slavery. But America entered the Jacksonian era with a confidence and optimism nurtured by having maintained the Constitution and the republic through the testing years of young nationhood.

7. Jefferson's First Inaugural Address, March 4, 1801

Speaking softly before nearly a thousand persons crowded into the Senate chamber for the first inaugural ceremony in the new capital on March 4, 1801, Jefferson delivered an eloquent affirmation of his basic political principles. His address, in which he repeated many of the *beliefs he had expressed in letters during the preceding presidential campaign, provides the finest summary of the principles of Jeffersonian democracy. Although Jefferson was soon to abandon his efforts to reconcile the Federalists, his appeal for the reconciliation of parties reflected a genuine desire for political harmony and suggested that he shared the common belief that two parties did not serve the national interest. The text is transcribed from Jefferson's final manuscript copy, Thomas Jefferson Papers, Library of Congress.*

Friends and fellow citizens

Called upon to undertake the duties of the first Executive office of our country, I avail myself of the presence of that portion of my fellow citizens which is here assembled to express my grateful thanks for the favor with which they have been pleased to look towards me, to declare a sincere consciousness that the task is above my talents, and that I approach it with those anxious and awful presentiments which the greatness of the charge, and the weakness of my powers so justly inspire. A rising nation, spread over a wide and fruitful land, traversing all the seas with the rich productions of their industry, engaged in commerce with nations who feel power and forget right, advancing rapidly to destinies beyond the reach of mortal eye, when I contemplate these transcendent objects, and see the honour, the happiness, and the hopes of this beloved country committed to the issue and the auspices of this day, I shrink from the contemplation, and humble myself before the magnitude of the undertaking. Utterly indeed should I despair, did not the presence of many, whom I here see, remind me, that, in the other high authorities provided by our constitution, I shall find resources of wisdom, of virtue, and of zeal, on which to rely under all difficulties. To you, then, gentlemen, who are charged with the sovereign functions of legislation, and to those associated with you, I look with encouragement for that guidance and support which may enable us to steer with safety the vessel in which we are all embarked, amidst the conflicting elements of a troubled world.

During the contest of opinion through which we have past, the animation of discussions and of exertions has sometimes worn an aspect which might impose on strangers unused to think freely, and to speak and to write what they think. But this being now decided by the voice of the nation, enounced according to the rules of the constitution, all will of course arrange themselves under the will of the law, and unite in common efforts for the common good. All too will bear in mind this sacred principle that though the will of the majority is in all cases to prevail, that will, to be rightful, must be reasonable; that the minority possess their equal rights, which equal laws must protect, and to violate would be oppression. Let us then fellow citizens unite with one heart and one mind, let us restore to social intercourse that harmony and affection without which liberty, and even life itself, are but dreary things. And let us reflect that having banished from our land that religious intolerance under which mankind so long bled and suffered, we have yet gained little, if we countenance a political intolerance, as despotic, as wicked, and capable of as bitter and bloody persecutions. During the throes and convulsions of the ancient world, during the agonizing spasms of infuriated man, seeking through blood and slaughter his long lost liberty, it was not wonderful that the agitation of the billows should reach even this distant and peaceful shore; that this should be more felt and feared by some, and less by others; and should divide opinions as to measures of safety. But every difference of opinion is not a difference of principle. We have called by different names brethren of the same principle. We are all republicans: we are all federalists. If there be any among us who would wish to dissolve this Union or to change it's republican form, let them stand undisturbed as monuments of the safety with which error of opinion may be tolerated, where reason is left free to combat it. I know indeed that some honest men fear that a republican government cannot be strong, that this government is not strong enough. But would the honest patriot in the full tide of successful experiment abandon a government which has so far kept us free and firm, on the theoretic and visionary fear, that this government, the world's best hope, may, by possibility, want energy to preserve itself? I trust not. I believe this, on the contrary, the strongest government on earth. I believe it the only one, where every man, at the call of the law, would fly to the standard of the law, and would meet invasions of the public order as his own personal concern. Sometimes it is said that man cannot be trusted with the government of himself. Can he then be trusted with the government of others? Or have we found angels in the form of kings, to govern him? Let history answer this question.

Let us then, with courage and confidence, pursue our own federal and republican principles; our attachment to union and representative government. Kindly separated by nature and a wide ocean from the exterminating havoc of one quarter of the globe; too high-minded to endure the degradations of the others, possessing a chosen country, with room enough for our descendants to the thousandth and thousandth generation, entertaining a due sense of our equal right to the use of our own faculties, to the acquisitions of our own industry, to honour and confidence from our fellow citizens, resulting not from birth, but from our actions and their sense of them, enlightened by a benign religion, professed indeed and practised in various forms, yet all of them inculcating Honesty, truth, temperance, gratitude and the love of man, acknoleging and adoring an overruling providence, which by all it's dispensations proves that it delights in the happiness of man here, and his greater happiness hereafter; with all these blessings, what more is necessary to make us a happy and prosperous people? Still one thing more fellow citizens, a wise and frugal government, which shall restrain men from injuring one another, shall leave them otherwise free to regulate their own pursuits of industry and improvement, and shall not take from the mouth of labor the bread it has earned. This is the sum of good government; and this is necessary to close the circle of our felicities.

About to enter, fellow citizens, on the exercise of duties which comprehend every thing dear and valuable to you, it is proper you should understand what I deem the essential principles of our government, and consequently those which ought to shape it's administration. I will compress them within the narrowest compass they will bear, stating the general principle, but not all it's limitations.—Equal and exact justice to all men, of whatever state or persuasion, religious or political:—Peace, commerce, and honest friendship with all nations, entangling alliances with none:—the support of the state governments in all their rights as the most competent administrations for our domestic concerns, and the surest bulwarks against anti-republican tendencies:—the preservation of the general government in it's whole constitutional vigour as the sheet anchor of our peace at home, and safety abroad:—a jealous care of the right of election by the people, a mild and safe corrective of abuses which are lopped by the sword of revolution where peaceable remedies are unprovided:—absolute acquiescence in the decisions of the majority, the vital principle of republics, from which is no appeal but to force, the vital principle and immediate parent of despotism:—a well disciplined militia, our best reliance in peace, and for the first moments of war, till regulars may relieve them:—the supremacy of the civil over the military authority:—economy in the Public expense, that labor may be lightly burthened:—the honest payment of our debts and sacred preservation of the public faith:—encouragement of agriculture; and of commerce as it's handmaid:—the diffusion of information, and arraignment of all abuses at the bar of the public reason:— freedom of religion; freedom of the press; and freedom of person, under the protection of the Habeas corpus:—and trial by juries impartially selected. These principles form the bright constellation, which has gone before us and guided our steps through an age of revolution and reformation. The wisdom of our sages and blood of our heroes have been devoted to their attainment: they should be the creed of our political faith, the text of civic instruction, the touchstone by which to try the services of those we trust. And should we wander from them in moments of error or of alarm, let us hasten to retrace our steps, and to regain the road which alone leads to Peace, liberty and safety.

I repair then, fellow citizens, to the post you have assigned me. With experience enough in subordinate offices to have seen the difficulties of this the greatest of all, I have learnt to expect that it will rarely fall to the lot of imperfect man to retire from this station with the reputation, and the favor, which bring him into it. Without pretensions to that high confidence you reposed in our first and greatest revolutionary character, whose preeminent services had entitled him to the first place in his country's love, and destined for him the fairest page in the volume of faithful history, I ask so much confidence only as may give firmness and effect to the legal administration of your affairs. I shall often go wrong through defect of judgment. When right, I shall often be thought wrong by those whose positions will not command a view of the whole ground. I ask your indulgence for my own errors, which will never be intentional; and your support against the errors of others, who may condemn what they would not, if seen in all it's parts. The approbation implied by your suffrage is a great consolation to me for the past, and my future solicitude will be to retain the good opinion of those who have bestowed it in advance, to conciliate that of others by doing them all the good in my power, and to be instrumental to the happiness and freedom of all.

Relying then on the patronage of your good will, I advance with obedience to the work, ready to retire from it whenever you become sensible how much better choices it is in your power to make. And may that infinite power which rules the destinies of the universe lead our councils to what is best, and give them a favourable issue for your peace and prosperity.

8. Upholding National Rights:
Madison's War Message, June 1, 1812

President Madison's message to Congress recommending a declaration of war against Great Britain was the culmination of conflicts that had been mounting since the renewal of the Napoleonic wars in Europe in 1803. Under President Jefferson the nation had faced a war crisis following the British attack on the Chesapeake in 1807 and had unsuccessfully attempted to bring Britain to terms through a general embargo on American shipping. Madison assumed the presidency in 1809 with the difficulties still unsettled. As various measures of commercial restriction failed, the administration moved toward a policy of war. Whether Congress or the president was more responsible for leading the nation in this direction, historians have not agreed. Nor have they agreed that the reasons given by Madison in his war message fully explained the American declaration of war. In emphasizing the British practice of impressment and violations of American neutral rights as the principal grievances, while referring also to British responsibility for Indian warfare on the frontiers, Madison stated the case for war as necessary to uphold national rights. The text of Madison's message is taken from Gaillard Hunt (ed.), The Writings of James Madison (9 vols., New York, 1900–1910), VIII, 192–200.

WASHINGTON, JUNE 1, 1812

I communicate to Congress certain documents, being a continuation of those heretofore laid before them on the subject of our affairs with Great Britain.

Without going back beyond the renewal in 1803 of the war in which Great Britain is engaged, and omitting unrepaired wrongs of inferior magnitude, the conduct of her Government presents a series of acts hostile to the United States as an independent and neutral nation.

British cruisers have been in the continued practice of violating the American flag on the great highway of nations, and of seizing and carrying off persons sailing under it, not in the exercise of a belligerent right founded on the law of nations against an enemy, but of a municipal prerogative over British subjects. British jurisdiction is thus extended to neutral vessels in a situation where no laws can operate but the law of nations and the laws of the country to which the vessels belong, and a self-redress is assumed which, if British subjects were wrongfully detained and alone concerned, is that substitution of force for a resort to the responsible sovereign which falls within the definition of war. Could the seizure of British subjects in such cases be regarded as within the exercise of a belligerent right, the acknowledged laws of war, which forbid an article of captured property to be adjudged without a regular investigation before a competent tribunal, would imperiously demand the fairest trial where the sacred rights of persons were at issue. In place of such a trial these rights are subjected to the will of every petty commander.

The practice, hence, is so far from affecting British subjects alone that, under the pretext of searching for these, thousands of American citizens, under the safeguard of public law and of their national flag, have been torn from their country and from everything dear to them; have been dragged on board ships of war of a foreign nation and exposed, under the severities of their discipline, to be exiled to the most distant and deadly climes, to risk their lives in the battles of their oppressors, and to be the melancholy instruments of taking away those of their own brethren.

Against this crying enormity, which Great Britain would be so prompt to avenge if committed against herself, the United States have in vain exhausted remonstrances and expostulations, and that no proof might be wanting of their conciliatory dispositions, and no pretext left for a continuance of the practice, the British Government was formally assured of the readiness of the United States to enter into arrangements such as could not be rejected if the recovery of British subjects were the real and the sole object. The communication passed without effect.

British cruisers have been in the practice also of violating the rights and the peace of our coasts. They hover over and harass our entering and departing commerce. To the most insulting pretensions they have added the most lawless proceedings in our very harbors, and have wantonly spilt American blood within the sanctuary of our territorial jurisdiction. The principles and rules enforced by that nation, when a neutral nation, against armed vessels of belligerents hovering near her coasts and disturbing her commerce are well known. When called on, nevertheless, by the United States to punish the greater offenses committed by her own vessels, her Government has bestowed on their commanders additional marks of honor and confidence.

Under pretended blockades, without the presence of an adequate force and sometimes without the practicability of applying one, our commerce has been plundered in every sea, the great staples of our country have been cut off from their legitimate markets, and a destructive blow aimed at our agricultural and maritime interests. In aggravation of these predatory measures they have been considered as in force from the dates of their notification, a retrospective effect being thus added, as has been done in other important cases, to the unlawfulness of the course pursued. And to render the outrage the more signal these mock blockades have been reiterated and enforced in the face of official communications from the British Government declaring as the true definition of a legal blockade "that particular ports must be actually invested and previous warning given to vessels bound to them not to enter."

Not content with these occasional expedients for laying waste our neutral trade, the cabinet of Britain resorted at length to the sweeping system of blockades, under the name of orders in council, which has been molded and managed as might best suit its political views, its commercial jealousies, or the avidity of British cruisers.

To our remonstrances against the complicated and transcendent injustice of this innovation the first reply was that the orders were reluctantly adopted by Great Britain as a necessary retaliation on decrees of her enemy proclaiming a general blockade of the British Isles at a time when the naval force of that enemy dared not issue from his own ports. She was reminded without effect that her own prior blockades, unsupported by an adequate naval force actually applied and continued, were a bar to this plea; that executed edicts against millions of our property could not be retaliation on edicts confessedly impossible to be executed; that retaliation, to be just, should fall on the party setting the guilty example, not on an innocent party which was not even chargeable with an acquiescence in it.

When deprived of this flimsy veil for a prohibition of our trade with her enemy by the repeal of his prohibition of our trade with Great Britain, her cabinet, instead of a corrresponding repeal or a practical discontinuance of its orders, formally avowed a determination to persist in them against the United States until the markets of her enemy should be laid open to British products, thus asserting an obligation on a neutral power to require one belligerent to encourage by its internal regulations the trade of another belligerent, contradicting her own practice toward all nations, in peace as well as in war, and betraying the insincerity of those professions which inculcated a belief that, having resorted to her orders with regret, she was anxious to find an occasion for putting an end to them.

Abandoning still more all respect for the neutral rights of the United States and for its own consistency, the British Government now demands as prerequisites to a repeal of its orders as they relate to the United States that a formality should be observed in the repeal of the French decrees nowise necessary to their termination nor exemplified by British usage, and that the French repeal, besides including that portion of the decrees which operates within a territorial jurisdiction, as well as that which operates on the high seas, against the commerce of the United States should not be a single and special repeal in relation to the United States, but should be extended to whatever other neutral nations unconnected with them may be affected by those decrees. And as an additional insult, they are called on for a formal disavowal of conditions and pretensions advanced by the French Government for which the United States are so far from having made themselves responsible that, in official explanations which have been published to the world, and in a correspondence of the American minister at London with the British minister for foreign affairs such a responsibility was explicitly and emphatically disclaimed.

It has become, indeed, sufficiently certain that the commerce of the United States is to be sacrificed, not as interfering with the belligerent rights of Great Britain; not as supplying the wants of her enemies, which she herself supplies; but as interfering with the monopoly which she covets for her own commerce and navigation. She carries on a war against the lawful commerce of a friend that she may the better carry on a commerce with an enemy—a commerce polluted by the forgeries and perjuries which are for the most part the only passports by which it can succeed.

Anxious to make every experiment short of the last resort of injured nations, the United States have withheld from Great Britain, under successive modifications, the benefits of a free intercourse with their market, the loss of which could not but outweigh the profits accruing from her restrictions of our commerce with other nations. And to entitle these experiments to the more favorable consideration they were so framed as to enable her to place her adversary under the exclusive operation of them. To these appeals her Government has been equally inflexible, as if willing to make sacrifices of every sort rather than yield to the claims of justice or renounce the errors of a false pride. Nay, so far were the attempts carried to overcome the attachment of the British cabinet to its unjust edicts that it received every encouragement within the competency of the executive branch of our Government to expect that a repeal of them would be followed by a war between the United States and France, unless the French edicts should also be repealed. Even this communication, although silencing forever the plea of a disposition in the United States to acquiesce in those edicts originally the sole plea for them, received no attention.

If no other proof existed of a predetermination of the British Government against a repeal of its orders, it might be found in the correspondence of the minister plenipotentiary of the United States at London and the British secretary for foreign affairs in 1810, on the question whether the blockade of May, 1806, was considered as in force or as not in force. It had been ascertained that the French Government, which urged this blockade as the ground of its Berlin decree, was willing in the event of its removal, to repeal that decree, which, being followed by alternate repeals of the other offensive edicts, might abolish the whole system on both sides. This inviting opportunity for accomplishing an object so important to the United States, and professed so often to be the desire of both the belligerents, was made known to the British Government. As that Government admits that an actual application of an adequate force is necessary to the existence of a legal blockade, and it was notorious that if such a force had ever been applied its long discontinuance had annulled the blockade in question, there could be no sufficient objection on the part of Great Britain to a formal revocation of it, and no imaginable objection to a declaration of the fact that the blockade did not exist. The declaration would have been consistent with her avowed principles of blockade, and would have enabled the United States to demand from France the pledged repeal of her decrees, either with success, in which case the way would have been opened for a general repeal of the belligerent edicts, or without success, in which case the United States would have been justified in turning their measures exclusively against France. The British Government would, however, neither rescind the blockade nor declare its nonexistence, nor permit its nonexistence to be inferred and affirmed by the American plenipotentiary. On the contrary, by representing the blockade to be comprehended in the orders in council, the United States were compelled so to regard it in their subsequent proceedings.

There was a period when a favorable change in the policy of the British cabinet was justly considered as established. The minister plenipotentiary of His Britannic Majesty here proposed an adjustment of the differences more immediately endangering the harmony of the two countries. The proposition was accepted with the promptitude and cordiality corresponding with the invariable professions of this Government. A foundation appeared to be laid for a sincere and lasting reconciliation. The prospect, however, quickly vanished. The whole proceeding was disavowed by the British Government without any explanations which could at that time repress the belief that the disavowal proceeded from a spirit of hostility to the commercial rights and prosperity of the United States; and it has since come into proof that at the very moment when the public minister was holding the language of friendship and inspiring confidence in the sincerity of the negotiation with which he was charged a secret agent of his Government was employed in intrigues having for their object a subversion of our Government and a dismemberment of our happy union.

In reviewing the conduct of Great Britain toward the United States our attention is necessarily drawn to the warfare just renewed by the savages on one of our extensive frontiers—a warfare which is known to spare neither age nor sex and to be distinguished by features peculiarly shocking to humanity. It is difficult to account for the activity and combinations which have for some time been developing themselves among tribes in constant intercourse with British traders and garrisons without connecting their hostility with that influence and without recollecting the authenticated examples of such interpositions heretofore furnished by the officers and agents of that Government.

Such is the spectacle of injuries and indignities which have been heaped on our country, and such the crisis which its unexampled forbearance and conciliatory efforts have not been able to avert. It might at least have been expected that an enlightened nation, if less urged by moral obligations or invited by friendly dispositions on the part of the United States, would have found its true interest alone a sufficient motive to respect their rights and their tranquility on the high seas; that an enlarged policy would have favored that free and general circulation of commerce in which the British nation is at all times interested, and which in times of war is the best alleviation of its calamities to herself as well as to other belligerents; and more especially that the British cabinet would not, for the sake of a precarious and surreptitious intercourse with hostile markets, have persevered in a course of measures which necessarily put at hazard the invaluable market of a great and growing country, disposed to cultivate the mutual advantages of an active commerce.

Other counsels have prevailed. Our moderation and conciliation have had no other effect than to encourage perseverance and to enlarge pretensions. We behold our seafaring citizens still the daily victims of lawless violence, committed on the great common and highway of nations, even within sight of the country which owes them protection. We behold our vessels, freighted with the products of our soil and industry, or returning with the honest proceeds of them, wrested from their lawful destinations, confiscated by prize courts no longer the organs of public law but the instruments of arbitrary edicts, and their unfortunate crews dispersed and lost, or forced or inveigled in British ports into British fleets, whilst arguments are employed in support of these aggressions which have no foundation but in a principle equally supporting a claim to regulate our external commerce in all cases whatsoever.

We behold, in fine, on the side of Great Britain, a state of war against the United States, and on the side of the United States a state of peace toward Great Britain.

Whether the United States shall continue passive under these progressive usurpations and these accumulating wrongs, or, opposing force to force in defense of their national rights, shall commit a just cause into the hands of the Almighty Disposer of Events, avoiding all connections which might entangle it in the contest or views of other powers, and preserving a constant readiness to concur in an honorable re-establishment of peace and friendship, is a solemn question which the Constitution wisely confides to the legislative department of the Government. In recommending it to their early deliberations I am happy in the assurance that the decision will be worthy the enlightened and patriotic councils of a virtuous, a free, and a powerful nation. . . .

9. The Debate over the War of 1812

American disunity over the war against Great Britain was demonstrated in the vote in Congress on the declaration of war, which passed the House of Representatives by 79 to 49 votes, on June 4, 1812, and was approved by the Senate, 19 to 13, on June 17. The debate on the policy of war which preceded the declaration continued after that decision was made, and the nation remained seriously divided throughout the course of the conflict. The two excerpts below present the opposing arguments. Samuel Taggart, a Massachusetts Federalist who served in the House of Representatives from 1803 to 1817, voted against the declaration of war, as did twenty out of thirty New England representatives voting. Taggart gave his reasons in a lengthy speech prepared for delivery in Congress but not given when the debate on the declaration of war was held behind closed doors. The address was published in the Alexandria Gazette, June 24, 1812. The text below is taken from Annals of Congress, 12 Congress, 1 Session, 1638–67. One of the best defenses in support of the War of 1812 was delivered in Congress by Henry Clay, on January 9, 1813, during a debate on a bill to enlist an additional twenty regiments of infantry. Clay, a Republican representative from Kentucky and Speaker since entering the house in 1811, had been a leading proponent of a belligerent policy toward Britain and remained a vigorous champion of the decision for war. The text of Clay's speech is reprinted from James F. Hopkins and Mary W. M. Hargreaves (eds.), The Papers of Henry Clay (Lexington, Ky., 1959–   ), I, 763–773.

A. *Opposing the War: Speech of Samuel Taggart*
Published June 24, 1812

I consider the question now before the House as the most important of any on which I have been called upon to decide since I have been honored with a seat in this House, whether it can be considered in relation to its principles or consequences. It is no less than whether I will give my vote to change the peaceful habits of the people of the United States for the attitude of war and the din of arms, and familiarize our citizens with blood and slaughter. I am happy to find that, so far as my own conduct is concerned, the clearest conviction of duty harmonizes with my own inclination. Having been long conversant in the quiet walks of civil life, and in the exercise of a profession, one important part of the duties of which is to inculcate peace and good will both towards and among men, I cannot contemplate my country as on the verge of a war, especially of a war which to me appears both unnecessary and impolitic in the outset, and which will probably prove disastrous in the issue; a war which, in my view, goes to put not only the lives and property of our most valuable citizens, but also our liberty and independence itself, at hazard, without experiencing the most painful sensations. Believing, as I most conscientiously do, that a war, at this time, would jeopardize the best, the most vital interests, of the country which gave me birth, and in which is contained all that I hold near and dear in life, I have, so far as depended upon my vote, uniformly opposed every measure which I believed had a direct tendency to lead to war. . . .

In the remarks which follow, I shall confine my observations to two principal topics of difference; which are relied upon as the principal causes of the present war, which is now about to be waged on our part, viz: the Orders in Council, and the impressment of seamen; the affair of the Chesapeake, which has been for several years a fruitful source of crimination, being at length removed out of the way. I wish it to be kept in view, that I have no intention, neither do I entertain a wish to vindicate the Orders in Council. Every neutral, and especially every American, must view the principles contained in these orders as injurious to his rights. Nor shall I consider the plea of retaliation mutually set up as sufficient to justify either the decrees or orders. . . . I shall barely consider the Orders in Council on the footing in which we have placed the subject in dispute by the law of the first of May, 1810, in which the Congress of the United States declares, that in case either Great Britain or France shall, before the first day of March next, so revoke or modify her edicts that they shall cease to violate the neutral commerce of the United States, and the other does not, in three months thereafter, revoke and modify in like manner, certain enumerated sections of the former non-intercourse law of 1809 shall be revived. After the multifarious evidence of the Berlin and Milan decrees, which has been laid before the public, the mere expression of a doubt on the subject of the reality of the repeal, at least so far as the neutral commerce of the United States is concerned, has been scouted. The Duke of Cadore has asserted that they were repealed, and that after a certain date, (November 1st, 1810) they would cease to have effect, accompanied however with a proviso as ambiguous as the responses of the Delphic oracle. The President of the United States has made proclamation of the fact, and the law of Congress of March, 1811, has been passed to carry into more complete effect the conditions of the law of May 1st, 1810, and a number of Governors of different States have reechoed the same in their communications to their several Legislatures; and the fact of the repeal has been asserted both in this House and out, in such strong terms as to say that no man of common sense in the nation could doubt of it for a single moment, and that the person who did not believe the repeal on the evidences now before the nation, would not believe it on any evidence whatsoever. Whether I have or have not, in the estimation of these gentlemen, a right to lay claims to the possession of common sense, is a matter of very small consequence in the present inquiry. I can easily state, however, what kind of evidence of this fact would have satisfied me of its reality, as well as give the reasons why I have always doubted whether a repeal in the proper and literal sense of the term, or whether anything like a substantial or even a virtual repeal has taken place.

Sir, if there had been ever anything like a formal explicit act of the French Government, officially communicated, declaring these decrees repealed; if this supposed repeal had been communicated to the ordinary tribunals of justice in France, and they had received directions to act accordingly; if these ordinary tribunals had declined to take cognizance of cases of capture and condemnation under these decrees, for the express reason that they no longer existed; if similar orders had been given to the commanders of French cruisers on the high seas; but more especially if the effects of these decrees had ceased, and American commerce was now no longer subject to vexation, or to capture and condemnation under their operation, this would have afforded such evidence of their repeal as would have been satisfactory to my mind, and it is such evidence as the nature of the case required and was reasonably to be expected. We would then have to complain of no other infringement of our rights on the ocean only what arose from the Orders in Council, and we might with propriety insist upon their repeal, on the grounds which we have set up. . . .

I do not urge these observations with a view either to justify or palliate the Orders in Council, but merely to show that, on the foundation on which we have chosen to place the controversy by our law of May 1st, 1810, they are no cause either of war or of non-importation. France has never in good faith complied with the proposal held out by the United States in that law. The noose which has been placed round our necks by any supposed pledge to France in that law, is no farther binding than we choose to make it by our own voluntary act. There is no need of a sword to cut the gordian knot which we cannot untie. Or supposing there was a slender thread twined around us, which I do not admit, it must have been long since consumed in the flame of our burning ships. Indeed, had it been equally strong with the new ropes, or the green withs wherewith Samson was bound, it must have, before this time, given way before their fires. If we have a right to demand a repeal of the Orders in Council, agreeable to the principles of public law, a point which I am by no means disposed to controvert, we have neither a right to demand, nor is Great Britain under any obligation to grant that repeal, on the grounds on which we have seen fit to place the point in dispute, i. e. on the plea of her plighted faith, to repeal them on a prior repeal of the Berlin and Milan decrees. If she withdraws her Orders in Council, it must be on other and very different considerations, and of these, the number is probably sufficient, and not that she is pledged to do it by any prior act of France. By placing the controversy on this footing, the United States lay themselves under much greater disadvantages in discussion, than they would by considering the Orders in Council on their own merits without having reference to any act of France. I shall not at present attempt to take a comparative view of the degree of injury and vexation which we receive in our lawful commerce, from the decrees and orders. I will admit that the orders have been more vexatious, and more rigorously carried into effect, during the last twelve or eighteen months, and that captures under them have been both more numerous and more valuable than for the same space of time previous to that period. One cause of this may be found in the attitude which we have assumed. So long as we placed both the belligerents upon an equal footing, the Orders in Council were not very rigorously carried into effect. By our non-importation law we have departed from our neutral ground, and have no longer considered the different belligerents as on an equal footing. The consequence has been that the Orders in Council have been more rigorously carried into effect, on the part of Great Britain. And since the additional hostile attitude assumed during the present session of Congress, has been known in Great Britain, I understand, from the public prints, that orders have been given for their still more rigid execution. Unless she saw fit to rescind them, this was naturally to be expected. In proportion as we assume a more hostile attitude towards her, and show a disposition to embrace her enemy in the arms of friendship and affection, it was to be expected that she would either relax and accede to our demands, or adhere more rigorously to her own system. She has chosen the latter.

As it respects the impressment of seamen, this is a delicate and a difficult subject, and if it is ever adjusted to mutual satisfaction it must be by war, and whenever there is mutually a disposition to accommodate, it will be found necessary to concede something on both sides. With respect to the practice of impressments generally, as it respects the citizens or subjects of the country adopting that method of manning her ships, it may be, and doubtless is, in many instances, attended with circumstances of real hardship. The practice may be oppressive, but it is founded upon a principle which is adopted and more or less practised upon by every nation, i. e. that the nation has a right, either in one shape or another, to compel the services of its citizens or subjects in time of war. The practice of draughting militiamen into actual service, which is authorized by our laws, the conscription of France, for the purpose of recruiting her armies, and the impressment of seamen to man a navy, are all greater or less extensions of the same principle. It is vain to contend against the principle itself, since we have sanctioned it by our laws, and daily practise upon it, however hardly we may think of some of the particular modes in which it is applied. I feel satisfaction, however, in the reflection, that it has never had the sanction of my vote. The principle then being admitted, the only ground of complaint is the irregular application of it to Americans. Great Britain does not claim, she never has claimed the right of impressing American citizens. She claims the right of reclaiming her own subjects, even although they should be found on board of American vessels. And in the assertion of that claim, many irregularities have without doubt been committed by her officers, on account of the similarity of language, manners, and habits. American citizens have been frequently mistaken for British subjects; but I do not know of any instance in which a real American has been reclaimed, where sufficient testimony of his being an American has been adduced, in which his liberation has been refused. No person would, I presume, wish to involve this country in a war, for the sake of protecting deserters, either from British vessels or the British service, who may choose to shelter themselves on board of our ships, allured by the prospects of gain. No, sir, we do not want their services. They are a real injury to the American seamen, both by taking their bread from them and exposing them to additional perils of impressment on the high seas. But it is a fact which can easily be substantiated, and will not be disputed by any one having a competent knowledge of the subject, that thousands of men of that description have been and still are employed on board our ships, and have been by some means furnished with all the usual documents of American seamen. Could an efficient plan be devised to prevent men of this description from assuming the garb, personating the character, and claiming the privileges of Americans, I presume the difficulties which occur in settling the question about impressments, might be easily surmounted. But so long as such a large number of foreign seamen are employed on board our vessels, and so long as American protections for these foreigners can be obtained with such facility, and are mere matters of bargain and sale, and English, Scotch, and Irish sailors are furnished with them, I pretend not to say by what means, indiscriminately with American citizens, it will be difficult to adjust that subject by treaty, it will be impossible to settle it by war. Only let us adopt a plan whereby a discrimination can be made, and the controversy may be amicably settled. But to say that the flag of every merchant ship shall protect every foreigner who may choose to take refuge on board of it, is the same as to say, that we will have no accommodation on the subject, because it is a point which, it is well known, never can be conceded. There is another description of citizens about which there may be some difficulty, I mean naturalized foreigners. These, however, are few in number, it being rarely found that seamen take the benefit of our naturalization laws. There are still some. It is I believe a truth, that neither Great Britain nor any other European nation admits of expatriation, and that the United States both admit the expatriation of their own citizens, and, on terms sufficiently liberal, naturalizes foreigners. But we cannot expect, with any color of reason, that our naturalization laws will make any alteration in the policy of foreign nations, any more than the European doctrine of perpetual allegiance will influence us. Both are municipal regulations, which can be executed only in the respective territories of the parties, and make no part of the law of nations, which is alone binding on the high seas. And every nation claims a right to the services of all its citizens or subjects in time of war. If the United States protect these naturalized foreigners in all the rights and privileges of American citizens, so long as they choose to continue among us, it is a protection sufficiently ample, and as much as they can reasonably claim from the Government. As long as they continue in the quiet pursuits of civil life on shore, they are in no danger of being remanded back into the service of the country they have abandoned. But when they chose to abandon the land for the ocean, and place themselves in a situation in which it is entirely optional with them whether they return or not, or whether they continue or renounce their allegiance, to attempt to afford protection to them in this situation, at the risk of a war, is to extend to them the privileges of citizenship much farther than they have a right either to expect or claim. If our protections were thus limited to the proper subjects, it would be easy to render them sufficient. This would narrow down the difficulty in adjusting the affairs of impressments, and would greatly diminish the numbers of supposed impressed Americans, which are said to be contained in these floating hells, as they have been called. They would be found to be comparatively few, probably not so many hundreds as they have been estimated at thousands, the obstacles in the way of their release would be removed, and impressments probably prevented in future. None of these objects will be obtained by war, but rather by grasping at too much, we will fail of obtaining what we have a right to demand. I do not make these observations with a view to excuse the practice of impressments as generally conducted. But when we are insisting on this as one cause of war, it is proper to view the subject as it is, and not through a magnifying mirror, which represents every object as being tenfold larger than the life.

I shall say no more of the causes of war, as they respect the aggressions of foreign nations. I must now beg the attention of the House for a few minutes, to an inquiry, what there is in the present situation of the United States, which so imperiously calls for this war. It is said to be necessary to go to war, for the purpose of securing our commercial rights, of opening a way for obtaining the best market for our produce, and in order to avenge the insults which have been offered to our flag. But what is there in the present situation of the United States, which we could reasonably expect would be ameliorated by war? In a situation of the world which is perhaps without a parallel in the annals of history, it would be strange indeed, if the United States did not suffer some inconveniences, especially in their mercantile connexions and speculations. In a war which has been unequalled for the changes which it has effected in ancient existing establishments, and for innovations in the ancient laws and usages of nations, it would be equally wonderful, if, in every particular, the rights of neutrals were scrupulously respected. But, upon the whole, we have reaped greater advantages, and suffered fewer inconveniences from the existing state of things, than it was natural to expect. During a considerable part of the time, in which so large and fair a portion of Europe has been desolated by the calamities of war, our commerce has flourished to a degree surpassing the most sanguine calculations. Our merchants have been enriched beyond any former example. Our agriculture has been greatly extended, the wilderness has blossomed like a rose, and cities and villages have sprung up, almost, as it were by the force of magic. It is true, that this tide of prosperity has received a check. The aggressions and encroachments of foreign nations have set bounds to our mercantile speculations; heavy losses have been sustained by the merchant, and the cotton planter of the South and West can no longer reap those enormous profits, those immense golden harvests, from that species of agriculture which he did a few years ago. But, if the shackles which we have placed upon commerce by our own restrictive system were completely done away, and the enterprize of the merchant was left free to explore new channels, it is probable that it would at this moment be more extensive and more gainful than in times of profound peace in Europe. During the operation of the war a much greater proportion of the commerce of the world was thrown into the hands of the Americans, than in times less turbulent would have fallen to their share. . . .

. . . I shall now crave the attention of the House while I take another view of the subject, by adverting to the object to be obtained by war, and the mode proposed for the accomplishment of that object. What is the particular achievement to be accomplished by this armament, which is to be kept up at such an enormous expense, and which is to bring the war to a successful termination? Why, the conquest of Canada, and sometimes, although more rarely, remotely, and indirectly, a glance is taken at Nova Scotia. At all events, Canada must be ours; and this is to be the sovereign balm, the universal panacea, which is to heal all the wounds we have received either in our honor, interest, or reputation. This is to be the boon which is to indemnify us, for all past losses on the ocean, secure the liberty of the seas hereafter, protect our seamen from impressments, and remunerate us for all the blood and treasure which is to be expended in the present war. Our rights on the ocean have been assailed, and, however inconsistent it may seem to go as far as possible from the ocean to seek redress, yet this would appear to be the policy. We are to seek it, it seems, by fighting the Indians on the Wabash or at Tippecanoe, or the Canadians at Fort Malden, at Little York, at Kingston, at Montreal, and at Quebec. It may be deemed equally inconsistent in a man who has spent his life in a manner which wholly abstracted him from all concerns with military affairs, to attempt to say anything about the conquest of Canada, as it was in the philosopher in ancient story, who attempted an harangue upon the military art in the presence of Hannibal. But as the members of this House are not all Hannibals, as some of them are men of military experience, and others of little more than myself, I shall hazard a few observations on the subject of the conquest of Canada, which appear to me to be founded upon the plain dictates of common sense. I hope military men will pardon me should I betray a want of knowledge of my subject. Should that even be the case, it will perhaps be an event not entirely new in this House. I shall say nothing of either the morality or the humanity, or of the reverse of both, which will be displayed in attacking an inoffensive neighbor, and endeavor to overwhelm a country which has done us no wrong with a superior military force alone. The conquest of Canada has been represented to be so easy as to be little more than a party of pleasure. We have, it has been said, nothing to do but to march an army into the country and display the standard of the United States, and the Canadians will immediately flock to it and place themselves under our protection. They have been represented as ripe for revolt, panting for emancipation from a tyrannical Government, and longing to enjoy the sweets of liberty under the fostering hand of the United States. On taking a different view of their situation, it has been suggested that, if they should not be disposed to hail us on our arrival as brothers, come to emancipate and not to subdue them, that they are a debased race of poltroons, incapable of making anything like a stand in their own defence, that the mere sight of an army of the United States would immediately put an end to all thoughts of resistance; that we had little else to do only to march, and that in the course of a few weeks one of our valiant commanders, when writing a despatch to the President of the United States, might adopt the phraseology of Julius Cæsar: Veni, Vidi, Vici. This subject deserves a moment's consideration. To presume on the disaffection or treasonable practices of the inhabitants for facilitating the conquest, will probably be to reckon without our host. The Canadians have no cause of disaffection with the British Government. They have ever been treated with indulgence. They enjoy all that security and happiness, in their connexion with Great Britain, that they could reasonably expect in any situation. Lands can be acquired by the industrious settlers at an easy rate, I believe for little more than the office fees for issuing patents, which may amount to three or four cents per acre. They have few or no taxes to pay. I believe none only a trifle for the repairs of highways. They have a good market for their surplus produce, unhampered with embargoes or commercial restrictions of any kind, and are equally secure both in person and property, both in their civil and religious rights, with the citizens of the United States. What have they, therefore, to gain by a connexion with the United States? Would it be any advantage to them to have the price of vacant lands raised from a sum barely sufficient to pay office fees, say three or four dollars one hundred acres, to two dollars per acre? Have we any other boon to hold out to them which can ameliorate their condition? It cannot be pretended. Why, then, should they desire a revolution? They want nothing of us, only not to molest them, and to buy and sell on terms of mutual reciprocity. We, therefore, ought to calculate on every man in Canada as an enemy, or if he is not hostile at the moment of the commencement of the expedition, an invasion of the country will soon make him so, and when an enemy is in the heart of a country, ready to attack our homes and houses it will inspire even a poltroon with courage. . . .

But, let us admit, for the sake of argument, that Canada is at length conquered, and everything settled in that quarter—*Cui bono?* For whose benefit is the capture of Canada? What advantages are we likely to reap from the conquest? Will it secure the liberty of the seas, or compel Great Britain to rescind her Orders in Council? Did we ever know an instance in which Great Britain gave up a favorite measure for the sake of saving a foreign possession, perhaps of very little value to her? Will the advantages to be derived from the conquest of Canada be an equivalent for the loss and damage we may sustain in other quarters? What is Great Britain to be about all the time that we are wresting Canada out of her possession? Is it consistent with the vigor with which she usually acts, to stand by and tamely look on? Either she will attempt a vigorous defence of Canada, or she will not. If she does, some of the difficulties of the enterprise have been stated. If she does not, it will be that she may be the better able to inflict a severe blow in some other quarter. Admitting war to be sincerely intended, no course could be devised more inconsistent with the maxims of sound policy than that which appears to be pursuing by the United States. . . .

B. *Supporting the War: Speech of Henry Clay in Congress, January 9, 1813*

. . . The war was declared because Great Britain arrogated to herself the pretension of regulating our foreign trade under the delusive name of retaliatory orders in council—a pretension by which she undertook to proclaim to American enterprize—"Thus far shalt thou go, and no farther"—Orders which she refused to revoke after the alledged cause of their enactment had ceased; because she persisted in the practice of impressing American seamen; because she had instigated the Indians to commit hostilities against us; and because she refused indemnity for her past injuries upon our commerce. I throw out of the question other wrongs. The war in fact was announced, on our part, to meet the war which she was waging on her part. So undeniable were the causes of the war—so powerfully did they address themselves to the feelings of the whole American people, that when the bill was pending before this House, gentlemen in the opposition—although provoked to debate, would not, or could not, utter one syllable against it. It is true they wrapped themselves up in sullen silence, pretending that they did not choose to debate such a question in secret session. Whilst speaking of the proceedings on that occasion, I beg to be permitted to advert to another fact that transpired, an important fact, material for the nation to know, and which I have often regretted had not been spread upon our journals. My honorable colleague (Mr. M'Kee) moved, in committee of the whole, to comprehend France in the war; and when the question was taken upon the proposition, there appeared but ten votes in support of it, of whom seven belonged to this side of the House, and three only to the other!

It is said that we were inveigled into the war by the perfidy of France; and that had she furnished the document in time, which was first published in England, in May last, it would have been prevented. I will concede to gentlemen every thing they ask about the injustice of France towards this country. I wish to God that our ability was equal to our disposition to make her feel the sense we entertain of that injustice. The manner of the publication of the paper in question, was undoubtedly extremely exceptionable. But I maintain that, had it made its appearance earlier, it would

not have had the effect supposed; and the proof lies in the unequivocal declarations of the British government. I will trouble
you, sir, with going no further back than to the letters of the
British minister, addressed to the Secretary of State, just before
the expiration of his diplomatic functions. It will be recollected
by the committee that he exhibited to this government a despatch
from Lord Castlereagh, in which the principle was distinctly
avowed, that to produce the effect of the repeal of the orders in
council, the French decrees must be absolutely and entirely revoked as to all the world, and not as to American alone. A copy of
that despatch was demanded of him, and he very awkwardly evaded
it. But on the 10th of June, after the bill declaring war had actually
passed this House, and was pending before the Senate (and which,
I have no doubt, was known to him), in a leter to Mr. Monroe, he
says: "I have no hesitation, sir, in saying that Great-Britain, as the
case has hitherto stood, never did, nor ever *could* engage, without
the greatest injustice to herself and her allies, as well as to other
neutral nations, to repeal her orders as affecting America alone,
leaving them in force against other states, upon condition that
France would except singly and especially America from the operation of her decrees." On the 14th of the same month, the bill
still pending before the Senate, he repeats: "I will now say, that I
feel entirely authorised to assure you, that if you can at any time
produce a *full and unconditional* repeal of the French decrees, as
you have a right to demand it in your character of a neutral nation,
and that it be disengaged from any question concerning our maritime rights, we shall be ready to meet you with a revocation of the
orders in council. Previously to your producing *such* an instrument,
which I am sorry to see you regard as unnecessary, you cannot
expect of us to give up our orders in council." Thus, sir, you see
that the British government would not be content with a repeal
of the French decrees as to us only. But the French paper in question was such a repeal. It could not, therefore, satisfy the British
government. It could not, therefore, have induced that government, had it been earlier promulgated, to repeal the orders in
council. It could not, therefore, have averted the war. The withholding of it did not occasion the war, and the promulgation of
it would not have prevented the war. But gentlemen have contended that, in point of fact, it did produce a repeal of the orders
in council. This I deny. After it made its appearance in England,

it was declared by one of the British ministry, in Parliament, not to be satisfactory. And all the world knows, that the repeal of the orders in council resulted from the inquiry, reluctantly acceded to by the ministry, into the effect upon their manufacturing establishments, of our non-importation law, or to the warlike attitude assumed by this government, or to both. But it is said, that the orders in council are done away, no matter from what cause; and that having been the sole motive for declaring the war, the relations of peace ought to be restored. This brings me into an examination of the grounds for continuing the war.

I am far from acknowledging that, had the orders in council been repealed, as they have been, before the war was declared, the declaration would have been prevented. In a body so numerous as this is, from which the declaration emanated, it is impossible to say with any degree of certainty what would have been the effect of such a repeal. Each member must answer for himself. I have no hesitation, then in saying, that I have always considered the impressment of American seamen as much the most serious aggression. But, sir, how have those orders at last been repealed? Great-Britain, it is true, has intimated a willingness to suspend their practical operation, but she still arrogates to herself the right to revive them upon certain contingencies, of which she constitutes herself the sole judge. She waives the temporary use of the rod, but she suspends it in terrorem over our heads. Supposing it was conceded to gentlemen that such a repeal of the orders in council, as took place on the 23d of June last, exceptionable as it is, being known before the war, would have prevented the war, does it follow that it ought to induce us to lay down our arms, without the redress of any other injury? Does it follow, in all cases, that that which would have prevented the war in the first instance, should terminate the war? By no means. It requires a great struggle for a nation, prone to peace as this is, to burst through its habits and encounter the difficulties of war. Such a nation ought but seldom to go to war. When it does, it should be for clear and essential rights alone, and it should firmly resolve to extort, at all hazards, their recognition. The war of the revolution is an example of a war began for one object and prosecuted for another. It was waged, in its commencement, against the right asserted by the parent country to tax the colonies. Then no one thought of absolute independence. The idea of independence was repelled.

But the British government would have relinquished the principle of taxation. The founders of our liberties saw, however, that there was no security short of independence, and they achieved our independence. When nations are engaged in war, those rights in controversy, which are not acknowledged by the Treaty of Peace, are abandoned. And who is prepared to say that American seamen shall be surrendered, the victims to the British principle of impressment? And, sir, what is this principle? She contends that she has a right to the services of her own subjects; that, in the exercise of this right, she may lawfully impress them, even altho' she finds them in our vessels, upon the high seas, without her jurisdiction. Now, I deny that she has any right, without her jurisdiction, to come on board our vessels upon the high seas, for any other purpose but in pursuit of enemies, or their goods, or goods contraband of war. But she further contends, that her subjects cannot renounce their allegiance to her and contract a new obligation to other sovereigns. I do not mean to go into the general question of the right [of] expatriation. If, as is contended, all nations deny it, all nations at the same time admit and practise the right of naturalization. G. Britain herself does. Great-Britain, in the very case of foreign seamen, imposes, perhaps, fewer restraints upon naturalization than any other nation. Then, if subjects cannot break their original allegiance, they may, according to universal usage, contract a new allegiance. What is the effect of this double obligation? Undoubtedly, that the sovereign having the possession of the subject would have the right to the services of the subject. If he return within the jurisdiction of his primitive sovereign, he may resume his right to his services, of which the subject by his own act, could not divest himself. But his primitive sovereign can have no right to go in quest of him, out of his own jurisdiction, into the jurisdiction of another sovereign, or upon the high seas, where there exists either no jurisdiction, or it belongs to the nation owning the ship navigating them. But, sir, this discussion is altogether useless. It is not to the British principle, objectionable as it is, that we are alone to look;—it is to her practice—no matter what guise she puts on. It is in vain to assert the inviolability of the obligation of allegiance. It is in vain to set up the plea of necessity, and to allege that she cannot exist without the impression of HER seamen. The naked truth is, she comes, by her press-gangs, on board of our vessels, seizes OUR native seamen, as well as naturalized, and drags them into her service. It is the case, then, of the assertion of an erroneous principle, and a practice not conformable to the principle—a principle which, if it were theoretically right, must be for ever practically wrong. . . .

The honorable gentleman from New York (Mr. Bleecker), in the very sensible speech with which he favored the committee, made one observation that did not comport with his usual liberal and enlarged views. It was that those who are most interested against the practice of impressment did not desire a continuance of the war on account of it, whilst those (the southern and western members) who had no interest in it, were the zealous advocates of the American seamen. It was a provincial sentiment unworthy of that gentleman. It was one which, in a change of condition, he would not express, because I know he could not feel it. Does not that gentleman feel for the unhappy victims of the tomahawk in the Western country, although his quarter of the union may be exempted from similar barbarities? I am sure he does. If there be a description of rights which, more than any other, should unite all parties in all quarters of the Union, it is unquestionably the rights of the person. No matter what his vocation; whether he seeks subsistence amidst the dangers of the deep, or draws it from the bowels of the earth, or from the humblest occupations of mechanic life: whenever the sacred rights of an American freeman are assailed, all hearts ought to unite and every arm should be braced to vindicate his cause.

The gentleman from Delaware sees in Canada no object worthy of conquest. According to him, it is a cold, sterile, and inhospitable region. And yet, such are the allurements which it offers, that the same gentleman apprehends that, if it be annexed to the United States, already too much weakened by an extension of territory, the people of New England will rush over the line and depopulate that section of the Union! That gentleman considers it honest to hold Canada as a kind of hostage, to regard it as a sort of bond, for the good behaviour of the enemy. But he will not enforce the bond. The actual conquest of that country would, according to him, make no impression upon the enemy, and yet the very apprehension only of such a conquest would at all times have a powerful operation upon him! Other gentlemen consider the invasion of that country as wicked and unjustifiable. Its inhabitants are represented as unoffending, connected with those of the bordering states by a thousand tender ties, interchanging acts of kindness, and all the offices of good neighborhood; Canada, said Mr.

C. innocent! Canada unoffending! Is it not in Canada that the tomahawk of the savage has been moulded into its death-like form? From Canadian magazines, Malden and others, that those supplies have been issued which nourish and sustain the Indian hostilities? Supplies which have enabled the savage hordes to butcher the garrison of Chicago, and to commit other horrible murders? Was it not by the joint cooperation of Canadians and Indians that a remote American fort, Michilimackinac, was fallen upon and reduced, [while the garrison was] in ignorance of a state of war? But, sir, how soon have the opposition changed. When administration was striving, by the operation of peaceful measures, to bring Great Britain back to a sense of justice, they were for old-fashioned war. And now that they have got old-fashioned war, their sensibilities are cruelly shocked, and all their sympathies are lavished upon the harmless inhabitants of the adjoining provinces. What does a state of war present? The united energies of one people arrayed against the combined energies of another—a conflict in which each party aims to inflict all the injury it can, by sea and land, upon the territories, property and citizens of the other, subject only to the rules of mitigated war practised by civilized nations. The gentlemen would not touch the continental provinces of the enemy, nor, I presume, for the same reason, her possessions in the W. Indies. The same humane spirit would spare the seamen and soldiers of the enemy. The sacred person of his majesty must not be attacked, for the learned gentlemen, on the other side, are quite familiar with the maxim, that the king can do no wrong. Indeed, sir, I know of no person on whom we may make war, upon the principles of the honorable gentlemen, but Mr. [James] Stephen, the celebrated author of the orders in council, or the board of admiralty, who authorise and regulate the practice of impressment!

The disasters of the war admonish us, we are told, of the necessity of terminating the contest. If our achievements upon the land have been less splendid than those of our intrepid seamen, it is not because the American soldier is less brave. On the one element organization, discipline, and a thorough knowledge of their duties exist, on the part of the officers and their men. On the other, almost every thing is yet to be acquired. We have however the consolation that our country abounds with the richest materials, and that in no instance when engaged in an action have our arms been tarnished. At Brownstown and at Queenstown the valor of veterans was displayed, and acts of the noblest heroism were performed. It is true, that the disgrace of Detroit remains to be wiped off. That is a subject on which I cannot trust my feelings, it is not fitting I should speak. But this much I will say, it was an event which no human foresight could have anticipated, and for which administration cannot be justly censured. It was the parent of all the misfortunes we have experienced on land. But for it the Indian war would have been in a great measure prevented or terminated; the ascendency on lake Erie acquired, and the war pushed perhaps to Montreal. With the exception of that event, the war, even upon the land, has been attended by a series of the most brilliant exploits, which, whatever interest they may inspire on this side of the mountains, have given the greatest pleasure on the other. . . .

It is alleged that the elections in England are in favor of the ministry, and that those in this country are against the war. If in such a cause (saying nothing of the impurity of their elections) the people of that country have rallied around their government, it affords a salutary lesson to the people here, who at all hazards ought to support theirs, struggling as it is to maintain our just rights. But the people here have not been false to themselves; a great majority approve the war, as is evinced by the recent re-election of the chief magistrate. Suppose it were even true, that an entire section of the Union were opposed to the war, that section being a minority, is the will of the majority to be relinquished? In that section the real strength of the opposition had been greatly exaggerated. Vermont has, by two successive expressions of her opinion, approved the declaration of war. In New-Hampshire, parties are so nearly equipoised that out of 30 or 35 thousand votes, those who approved, and are for supporting it, lost the election by only 1,000 or 1,500 votes. In Massachusetts alone have they obtained any considerable accession. If we come to New-York, we shall find that other and local causes have influenced her elections.

What cause, Mr. Chairman, which existed for declaring the war has been removed? We sought indemnity for the past and security for the future. The orders in council are suspended, not revoked; no compensation for spoliations, Indian hostilities, which were before secretly instigated, now openly encouraged; and the practice of impressment unremittingly persevered in and insisted upon. Yet administration has given the strongest demonstrations of its love of peace. On the 29th June, less than ten days after the declaration of war, the Secretary of State writes to Mr. Russell, authorising him to agree to an armistice, upon two conditions only, and what are they? That the orders in council should be repealed, and the practice of impressing American seamen cease, those already impressed being released. The proposition was for nothing more than a *real* truce; that the war should in fact cease on *both* sides. Again on the 27th July, one month later, anticipating a possible objection to these terms, reasonable as they are, Mr. Monroe empowers Mr. Russell to stipulate in general terms for an armistice, having only an informal understanding on these points. In return, the enemy is offered a prohibition of the employment of his seamen in our service, thus removing entirely all pretext for the practice of impressment. The very proposition which the gentleman from Connecticut (Mr. Pitkin) contends ought to be made has been made. How are these pacific advances met by the other party? Rejected as absolutely inadmissible, cavils are indulged about the inadequacy of Mr. Russell's powers, and the want of an act of Congress is intimated. And yet the constant usage of nations I believe is, where the legislation of one party is necessary to carry into effect a given stipulation, to leave it to the contracting party to provide the requisite laws. If he failed to do so, it is a breach of good faith, and a subject of subsequent remonstrance by the injured party. When Mr. Russell renews the overture, in what was intended as a more agreeable form to the British government, Lord Castlereagh is not content with a simple rejection, but clothes it in the language of insult. Afterwards, in conversation with Mr. Russell, the moderation of our government is misinterpreted and made the occasion of a sneer, that we are tired of the war. The proposition of Admiral Warren is submitted in a spirit not more pacific. He is instructed, he tells us, to propose that the government of the United States shall instantly recall their letters of marque and reprisal against British ships, together with all orders and instructions for any acts of hostility whatever against the territories of his Majesty or the persons or property of his subjects. That small affair being settled, he is further authorised to arrange as to the revocation of the laws which interdict the commerce and ships of war of his Majesty from the harbors and waters of the United States. This messenger of peace comes with one qualified concession in his pocket, not made to the justice of our demands, and is fully empowered to receive our homage, the contrite retraction of all our measures adopted against his master! And in default, he does not fail to assure us, the orders in council are to be forthwith revived. Administration, still anxious to terminate the war, suppresses the indignation which such a proposal ought to have created, and in its answer concludes by informing Admiral Warren, "that if there be no objection to an accommodation of the difference relating to impressment, in the mode proposed, other than the suspension of the British claim to impressment during the armistice, there can be none to proceeding, *without the armistice*, to an immediate discussion and arrangement of an article on that subject." Thus it has left the door of negotiation unclosed, and it remains to be seen if the enemy will accept the invitation tendered to him. The honorable gentleman from North Carolina (Mr. Pearson) supposes, that if Congress would pass a law, prohibiting the employment of British seamen in our service, upon condition of a like prohibition on their part, and repeal the act of non-importation, peace would immediately follow. Sir, I have no doubt if such a law were passed, with all the requisite solemnities, and the repeal to take place, Lord Castlereagh would laugh at our simplicity. No, sir, administration has erred in the steps which it has taken to restore peace, but its error has been not in doing too little but in betraying too great a solicitude for that event. An honorable peace is attainable only by an efficient war. My plan would be to call out the ample resources of the country, give them a judicious direction, prosecute the war with the utmost vigor, strike wherever we can reach the enemy, at sea or on land, and negotiate the terms of a peace at Quebec or Halifax. We are told that England is a proud and lofty nation that disdaining to wait for danger, meets it half way. Haughty as she is, we once triumphed over her, and if we do not listen to the councils of timidity and despair we shall again prevail. In such a cause, with the aid of Providence, we must come out crowned with success; but if we fail, let us fail like men, lash ourselves to our gallant tars, and expire together in one common struggle, fighting for "*seamen's rights and free trade.*"

10. Grappling with the Problem of Slavery

The controversy over the admission of Missouri into the Union, precipitated by the proposal passed by the House of Representatives to grant statehood only if provision were made to prohibit slavery in

Missouri, led to the most extensive debate over slavery that the nation had yet experienced. Documents A and B below illustrate its major lines, which centered on the question of the power of Congress to impose restrictions upon a state in admitting it into the Union. That the debate went beyond the constitutional issues is also displayed in the resolutions adopted by the citizens of Hartford, asserting that slavery should be prohibited in Missouri because it was an evil repugnant to republican government. John Holmes, who argued the case for the Missouri compromise in a letter to his constituents, was a representative from Massachusetts (which included the district of Maine) at the time; with the admission of Maine as a state he was elected one of its senators. It was the receipt of a copy of Holmes's letter that elicited from Jefferson his famous observation on the Missouri controversy: "This momentous question, like a fire-bell in the night, awakened and filled me with terror. I considered it at once as the knell of the Union. It is hushed, indeed, for the moment. But this is a reprieve only, not a final sentence." (Letter to Holmes, April 22, 1820.) The Hartford memorial is in the Broadside Collection, New-York Historical Society. Holmes's printed circular letter is in the Thomas Jefferson Papers, Library of Congress.

A. Memorial of the Citizens of Hartford, December 3, 1819

At a meeting of the citizens of Hartford and its vicinity, held at the State House, on Friday the 3d day of Dec. 1819, pursuant to public notice, for the purpose of taking into consideration the subject of permitting Slavery in such states as may hereafter be admitted into the Union.

Resolved, That the existence of SLAVERY in this Republic, is an evil deeply to be lamented, and utterly repugnant to the principles of a republican government.

Resolved, That in the opinion of this meeting, the peculiar phraseology of the preamble to the Declaration of Indepedence, declaring that "all men are created equal, &c." shows conclusively that the illustrious authors of that document, never contemplated the farther extension of Slavery in these United States.

Resolved, That in the opinion of this meeting, Congress possesses the clear and indisputable right to prescribe the terms upon which any territory may be admitted into the union as an independent state; and that a contrary doctrine would not only tend to destroy that order and harmony so indispensable to the happiness and union of these states, but would prostrate the powers confided to the general government by the constitution.

Resolved, That it is a duty the American people owe to their republican character, and the honor and glory of their country, to endeavor by all honorable and lawful means, to prevent the farther extension of slavery, which we consider to be contrary to the spirit of our free and excellent constitution, and injurious to the highest interests of the nation.

Resolved, That while we lament the efforts which the representatives in the last Congress, from the slave holding states, made to extend an evil which all unite in deploring, the thanks of this meeting are eminently due to those members who so ably and zealously opposed the admission of Slavery into the proposed state of Missouri.

Resolved, That the Senators and Representatives in Congress from this state, be requested to use every honorable and constitutional exertion to prevent the admission of Slavery into any new state which may be formed.

Resolved, That the Hon. Thomas S. Williams, Rev. Thomas H. Gallaudet, Hon. Sylvester Wells, and Hon. John T. Peters, be a committee to draft a memorial to Congress upon this subject, which shall comport with the spirit of these resolutions.

Resolved, That the Chairman of this meeting, be, and is hereby requested to forward a copy of these Resolutions, and Memorial, to the Senators and Representatives in Congress from this state.

Resolved, That Michael Bull, Nathaniel Goodwin, Charles Babcock, Oliver E. Williams, Charles L. Porter, Thomas Huntington, Joseph B. Gilbert, Edward Bolles, Samuel Huntington, Elihu Olmsted, Azor Hatch and Roderick Terry, be a committee to solicit signatures to the said memorial; and that the several printers of newspapers in this state be requested to publish the proceedings of this meeting.

JOHN T. PETERS, Chairman

JONATHAN W. EDWARDS, *Secretary*

The Memorial of the undersigned, inhabitants of the City of Hartford, and its vicinity, in the State of Connecticut, to the Senate and House of Representatives of the United States of America in Congress Assembled—

RESPECTFULLY REPRESENTS—

THAT as your present session will probably furnish the occasion of deciding a question which deeply involves the character and prosperity of the vast Republic over whose interests you are called in providence to preside; the welfare of that countless posterity who are to inherit from us all that can render human life a blessing or a curse; and the fate of thousands of our fellow men whose dearest rights have been so long sacrificed to the plea of necessity or of interest; we deem it a sacred duty which we owe to ourselves, to our country, and to our God, to make use of that invaluable privilege which our excellent constitution affords us, of attempting to influence the councils of the nation, by every consideration and motive which justice, honor, and a sound policy, will sanction, ere the final step be taken, which, if a wrong one, will shroud the prospects of our country's happiness and glory in shades of the deepest gloom.

In doing this, we avow that no influence actuates us but the purest patriotism. We would rise superior to that ignoble jealousy which weighs all political questions in the petty scale of mere state interest, and measures every proceeding of the National Legislature by the contracted standard of advantage to the northern or southern, the eastern or western, sections of our common country. We would feel as Americans, and present to your respectable body only such considerations, as are worthy of the regard of those who, in their least important, as well as most momentous, decisions, should fix a single eye upon the general happiness of the millions who are to constitute, under the auspices of prudent and magnanimous councils, a great and happy people.

We are inspired with a lively hope that what we may venture to suggest will be weighed with carefulness and candour, when we call to mind the honorable and energetic measures which Congress has of late adopted to check the future progress of Slavery in the United States;—measures which we trust will yet derive resistless efficacy from the co-operation of the whole christian world; from a vigilant enforcement by those officers whose province it is to carry them into effect; and from the repeated adoption of such future auxiliary provisions as the elusive cunning of the traffickers in human blood may yet render necessary to wipe from the character of man one of its foulest stains. Most unhappy will be the result, if the accession of new states to the union, by granting them the privilege of holding a portion of their fellow men in bondage, should prove to be the discomfiture of those generous efforts which are made, to prevent our vast portion of this western hemisphere from being any longer the disgraceful prison-house of the unfortunate sons of Africa.

That the Constitution invests Congress with ample power to impose a restriction with regard to slavery upon such states as may from time to time be admitted into the union, the territory of which lies out of the original limits of the United States, we think there can be no doubt. The union is indeed a compact of independent and sovereign states; but it is a compact whose base rests on the *principles* which all the states avowed in their combined struggle for freedom; on the principles of relative justice, of mutual sacrifices of interest for the general welfare, and of a surrender of individual rights to promote the strength and prosperity of *one common Republic*.

These principles, which, under providence, gave vigor to the resistance of the colonies against the usurpations of the mother country, and a happy result to that resistance, did not cease to have a binding force upon the states when the conflict for liberty was over; and, when assuming again, for a little while, their original sovereignty, they deliberated, in their individual capacity, upon the adoption of such a form of government as would best secure to them and their posterity the blessings for which they had been contending. They were unshackled, it is true, by the restrictions of any *written instrument*; but they were still bound to each other by the ties of *honor and justice*. When we find them proclaiming to the world as one of the principles, nay as the fundamental principle, under which they had acted in concert, "that all men are created equal; that they are endowed by their Creator with certain unalienable rights; that among these are life, liberty, and the pursuit of happiness,"—can we cast such a reproach upon the worthies who conducted their councils, as to suppose, that they meant entirely to abandon this principle, or not to feel its force. Its application, indeed, was waved with reference to those states whose policy led them to make it a condition of their adoption of the Federal Constitution, that they should retain the privilege of holding slaves, and that these slaves should go to increase the mass of their population who should be entitled to a voice in our national councils. But this was done in the *spirit of compromise*, and the original principle which was avowed in the declaration of independence, *revives, in all its primitive force*, with reference to any *new states* which may be admitted into the union, and which lie out of the limits of those states who made the compromise. So that no argument in favor of the absolute and entire sovereignty of new states, is more fallacious than that drawn from a supposed analogy between *their* relation to the union, and *that* which existed between the states who *originally* formed this union.

There has never been a period in our history since the time of our first resistance to Great Britain, that a greater or less surrender of the rights of state sovereignty has not been made for the general good; and if for the same object, such a surrender is now demanded of any portion of our country that wishes to enjoy the privilege of becoming a state, it has no right to complain of partial treatment; and unfounded indeed is such a complaint, when the surrender required, or the restriction imposed, is sanctioned by one of the fundamental principles of the great charter of our liberties; a departure from which, for reasons that *no new state* can now urge, was once reluctantly made in order to secure the unanimous adoption of the Federal Constitution.

Surely, if the states who were the original parties to the compact, had a right to stipulate with each other with regard to the surrender which each should make of some portion of its sovereignty for the common weal, they have now the right, through Congress as their organ, to make similar stipulations for the *same object* with those who are to become new parties to the compact. The only question then that remains, is, has the Constitution empowered Congress to act as this organ. The 3d section of the 4th article of that instrument says, "New states may be admitted by the Congress into the union; but no new state shall be formed or erected within the jurisdiction of any other state, nor any state be formed by the junction of two or more states, or parts of states, without the consent of the legislatures of the states concerned, as well as of the congress." The fair construction of this language is, that Congress is to judge of the expediency of admitting new states into the union, and also of the terms of their admission; and, lest this power vested in Congress should seem to encroach upon the sovereignty of the states who were actually parties to the compact, their consent is made necessary in case new states are formed out of them or by their junction, which evidently proves that, *in all other cases,* the power of Congress was to be complete and unrestricted. As the constitution no where gives any portion of territory, or any mass of population, the right to force itself into the union; and as it no where describes the precise conditions upon which new states may be admitted; but refers the whole subject in the most *general terms* to Congress, it seems to result from the very necessity of the case, as well as from the fair interpretation of the constitution, that Congress must judge of the expediency, and of the conditions, of all such admissions. This power Congress has more than once exercised; nor have the various restrictions which it has imposed upon several of the new states, as the terms of their admission into the union, been heretofore considered any infringement of the Constitution, or undue encroachment upon state sovereignty. Good faith, therefore, will be strictly kept with those who have become subject to the government of the United States by the treaty of the cession of Louisiana, if, upon their wishing to be made a new state, they are required, as a condition of this, to pledge themselves to interdict slavery within their limits; for although the treaty stipulates that they shall be incorporated into the union of the United States, and admitted as soon as possible to the enjoyment of all the rights, advantages, and immunities, of citizens of the United States, yet all this is to be done, as the same treaty stipulates, "according to the principles of the Federal Constitution." Like every other citizen of the United States—a citizen of the contemplated new state will have the privilege of holding slaves in those states where slavery is *permitted*, and like other citizens be debarred this privilege in states where slavery is *not permitted*; nor does it at all affect the merits of the case, that *his own* happens to be one of these states. Without going into any detail of argument, the same reasoning applies, mutatis mutandis, with conclusive force to the objection which is raised to the proposed restriction against the existence of slavery in any new state, from that article in the Constitution which provides that, "The citizens of each state shall be entitled to all privileges and immunities of citizens in the several states."

So far from injustice being done to the slave-holding states by the proposed restriction, which it is contended by many would be the case, we feel it a duty we owe to ourselves as citizens of a state in which slavery is forbidden, to urge upon the consideration of your respectable body, the constituted guardian of our political rights and liberties, that the permission of slavery in the new states, will be an unwarrantable departure from the *principles* of *that compromise* which it is confessed led to the formation of that part of the constitution which gives to the slave-holding states such an influence in the councils of the nation from a great mass of the population who are not recognized nor treated as freemen. This was in fact a bargain made between distinct and independent contracting parties, and, in good faith, this bargain ought not to be stretched in its application to any *new* parties, without the consent of all those who *originally* made it.

But these considerations are merged in the more important ones of national policy and interest. The evils which are already felt, and the more dreadful ones which are to be feared, from the existence of slavery in our country, will, in the opinion of your memorialists, be greatly enhanced by the extension to new states of the privilege of holding their fellow men in bondage. With all due regard to the best interests of those of our fellow citizens who are at present immediately exposed to these evils, we do sincerely believe that their safety, as well as that of the union, depends upon keeping the slave population of our country within the narrowest possible limits. If coercion be necessary it can be most easily, promptly, and successfully applied. If dangers are to be apprehended, they will most quickly be perceived. If plans of gradual emancipation are to be adopted, they will be most efficaciously carried into effect. Philanthropy has indeed plead in behalf of those who are in bondage, that their condition will be meliorated by scattering them over a greater extent of territory. Admitting that this might in some instances be the case, yet the prospect of a final deliverance from this miserable captivity would be diminished, if not destroyed; and that cupidity which now is cunning enough to elude the watchful eye of civil authority, would have new temptations presented to excite its more insatiable desires; new markets would be opened for its cruel enterprizes; and the places of those who might be carried to spread the contagion of this terrible moral disease into regions which are yet unsullied by its contamination, would soon be supplied by a succession of fresh victims. Besides, we deprecate the diffusion of the *slave-holding spirit*, so incompatible with the noble and ingenuous character of freemen; so unhappy in the associations, which it forms in the minds of the rising generation who are the hope and stay of our country; so inconsistent with the manly attitude which we have taken among the nations of the earth as the asserters of human freedom; so destructive of the physical strength of a state by impressing on the brow of honest labor the mark of servitude and disgrace; so discouraging to the gradual progress, through a vast and growing territory, of a bold and hardy yeomanry, tillers of their own soil and its most able defenders; so hostile to the temper of that religion which is at once the brightest ornament and surest strength of a people; and so ungrateful in its exercise towards that Being to whose justice we appealed for protection, when we ourselves felt the pressure of that *very yoke of bondage* which now bears with a more galling and cruel weight on thousands of our fellow-men. He delivered us from that yoke, and he has crowned that deliverance with a profusion of the choicest blessings. What do we not owe to his goodness!

In making such appeals, we boast of no moral superiority over our southern brethren. We well know that this dreadful curse was entailed upon them, and that too many of our own citizens have contributed to its continuance. We sympathize with them in any evils from this source which they feel, or dangers which they may fear. We rejoice with them, too, in any prospects which a kind providence may be opening for the gradual and complete deliverance of our common country from this stain upon its reputation and canker of its prosperity; we hail, with them, the dawning of a happier day, when the combined efforts of our own and the other nations of the earth shall generously redress the wrongs of injured Africa, and, if possible, repay her sufferings, by raising her from her present state of moral and political degradation, to the enjoyment of all those privileges for the possession of which she is now stretching forth her supplicating hands.

It is to give our own favored nation the best opportunity to take such a part as wisdom and prudence may suggest in this noble work of benevolence; to shield it against the imputation under which it has too long laboured, that it can wield with one arm the weapons of war against its oppressors, while it rivets with the other the chains of bondage upon its unhappy victims; and, in the mean time, to furnish it with the best safeguard against the evils which may result from its misfortune or its crime, that we have united with others of our fellow citizens in the object of this memorial, which we lay before your respectable body with the assurance, that, as it rests upon the immutable basis of truth and justice, its influence will not be lost.

B. Congressman John Holmes's Letter to the People of Maine on the Missouri Compromise, 1820

FELLOW CITIZENS:

. . . . Four of my colleagues, and a majority of the whole delegation from Maine, having differed from myself and Mr. Hill, on the Missouri Question, and the compromise of it as finally adopted, have deemed it expedient to make an extraordinary appeal to their constituents. Differing from the rest of the delegation with one exception; standing against such talents and numbers, who might urge their pretensions with a confidence which a majority inspires and popular excitement encourages; apprehending that a laboured defence of their own course must, of necessity, operate as an attack upon mine; and understanding that their communication has been circulated into my own district to instruct my particular constituents; I am reluctantly compelled to offer to the people, the reasons for my conduct, and its effect upon the interests of the nation and the independence of Maine.

It will be recollected, that in the last Congress, and before the attempt for the separation of Maine had commenced, a proposition to inhibit slavery in Missouri, as a condition of her admission into the Union, was discussed, and the restriction imposed in the House and rejected in the Senate. At that time, upon mature reflection, and without the aid of popular excitement, I was compelled to the conclusion, that the restriction could not be imposed; and this opinion was expressed in the House of Representatives, and went to the public through the medium of the newspapers. Since that time, I have been called by my constituents to important public duties, wherein the rights and liberties of the people were intimately concerned; have acted with the most intelligent citizens of all classes and from all sections of Maine; and to my recollection, not one word of doubt, distrust, or regret, was ever expressed to me for the vote I had given. Until the commencement of this session of Congress, the people of the United States appeared disposed to submit the question to the uninfluenced decision of the only constitutional tribunal; and, until the circulars from New-York had been obtruded upon the citizens of Maine, they had never felt an excitement, nor entertained a thought of, becoming parties to the discussion.

With a solitary exception, limited in its numbers, I had not, during this protracted discussion, from my constituents or the people of Maine, any instruction urging or requiring that my course should be different from what it had been. On the contrary, the tenor of my communications from gentlemen of the first political standing in the State, was in perfect accordance with my own opinion.

It would surely be paying a poor compliment to the people of Maine, to imagine for a moment, that they would wish or expect that a representative should yield to their opinions on a constitutional question at the expense of his conscience, and in violation of his oath. A high-minded, honourable, generous, and free people would pity and despise the man who should sacrifice his duty to popular feeling, or artificial excitement. Believing, as I most sincerely did, that the political right of regulating the condition of master and slave, belonged exclusively to the people of Missouri, I was constrained to refuse to Congress the exercise of a municipal power, in extent unlimited, and in operation dangerous and destructive to the sovereignty of the States.

For seventeen years the right to hold slaves in Missouri, had been recognised and confirmed. The lands there were purchased from a common fund, and the right of the slave-holder to emigrate, settle, and cultivate them, was co-ordinate with that of the rest of the people.

Parts of this same Territory had been incorporated into three different States, in each of which this right had been conceded. The treaty of cession was imperative—the terms were palpable, explicit, and unequivocal. The most ingenious dissertations to the contrary, were but a manifest perversion of a plain common-sense meaning, which, it was impossible to mistake. Thus did the Constitution, the treaty, and our own plighted faith forbid us to impose this restriction upon Missouri.

But, had the power existed, the effect of the experiment was doubtful and dangerous. Since the year 1808, Congress has been laudably engaged in prohibiting the importation of slaves. Laws have been enacted, amended, and improved; punishments have been augmented and enforced; and the navy of the United States has been put in requisition to arrest the violators of the laws. The gentlemen from the slave-holding States, with a zeal, which is a pledge of their sincerity, have ever been foremost to provide for detecting the offender and bringing him to justice. A common sentiment of indignation and abhorrence at the slave-trade, was beginning to prevail; and a correspondent feeling of humanity towards those already here, was inculcated and extended.

Experience had proved that to confine great numbers of slaves to a single owner, unable to afford them his personal protection, would expose them to the cruelty of overseers and other distresses. The constant emigration of free persons, without their slaves, would increase the evil and expose to danger those who remained. To permit the slave-holders to emigrate to Missouri with their slaves, would be to *disperse* but not to *increase* them. Distributed into the hands of more masters, they would be more intimately connected with their families, become the objects of their affection, and of their moral and religious instruction. Shall then the slaves now in the United States, be confined to the slave-holding States, or be permitted to be carried to Missouri? This is the MISSOURI QUESTION, so much spoken of and so little understood. Not whether more slaves shall be admitted into the United States—against this every hand is raised. Not whether slavery is an evil—all agree that it is a most afflicting, a most dangerous evil. Not whether it ought to be abolished—but what are our Constitutional means, to remove this evil without inflicting a greater? These are questions on which men may honestly differ. The best feelings of the human heart are instantly enlisted in favour of any measure, whose professed object is *liberty to the slave*, and without regarding its tendency or effect, humanity extorts an opinion, which pride forbids us to retract.

Born and nurtured in a land of liberty; habitually entertaining an utter abhorrence of slavery, in whatever disguise; witnessing as I verily believe, the happy moralizing influence of universal freedom; experiencing, moreover, the voluntary tribute of affection from freemen, which I am always proud to reciprocate; I seized with ardent partiality the proposed restriction, examined it with confident hope, and to my utter disappointment and regret was compelled to condemn it as unconstitutional, inexpedient, and dangerous.

The Constitution of the United States was a compromise of

conflicting rights and interests. This having recognised the right of any State to its slaves and the treaty of cession and the laws in the territory having established and confirmed it to Missouri, the people there, complained of the interference of Congress in their internal concerns. Strong as were my impressions against slavery, the right of a people to manage their own affairs in their own way, had been too lately exercised by the citizens of Maine to escape my recollection.—The attempt of Massachusetts to prescribe to us, our duties in regard to *Bowdoin College*, was not forgotten. The indignation felt, at this officious interference, and the very great unanimity with which we, by a Constitutional act, withheld all endowment from that institution, until it should renounce the odious provision, were strong and impressive proofs of our principles; and gave an assurance that we were too magnanimous to impose on Missouri a restraint, which we had so recently, emphatically, and indignantly rejected.

The Senate of the United States by a decisive vote, had rejected the restriction, which the House had, by a small majority, imposed. By this disagreement of the two Houses, the admission of Missouri had been delayed from the last session, the public feeling was greatly excited, and a geographical division of parties was forming, which threatened danger, if not dissolution, to the Union. Meanwhile, slaves might be admitted into all our Territories and the evil, real or supposed, could not be restrained. The north and east were to be arrayed against the south and west, mutual animosities were fomented, recriminations reiterated, parties rallying, and leaders presenting themselves to martial, and conduct these parties to the field.

The friends of the republic began to perceive that the Union was in danger; and that another year's delay would impair if not dissolve it. The contest was approaching a crisis, and a *compromise* was the only remaining resort—the last hope for the restoration of tranquillity.

To this there seemed an insuperable objection. A bill for the admission of Maine into the Union, had passed the House early in the session, and in the Senate had been united with that for the admission of Missouri. This union had been resisted in the House as unprecedented and improper. The discussion which these subjects, thus united, necessarily involved, had increased the excitement and widened the breach, between the parties. The liberal course of some gentlemen from the north, and the evidence exhibited that Maine, when admitted, would not be disposed to combine to enforce the proposed restriction, had induced several members of the Senate to relax, and to consent that Maine should be admitted alone. These, with the minority, originally against the union of the two subjects, would have secured a separate admission of Maine. But the doctrines advanced by a Senator in the second debate, and echoed in the House, the avowal that it was a contest for political power, and the consequent excitement and alarm, determined the majority to insist that both or neither should be admitted.

In this state of irritation, committees of conference were appointed; the members on the part of the Senate were Messrs. Thomas, Barbour, and Pinkney, and, of the House, Holmes, Taylor, Lowndes, Parker, M[ass]. and Kinsey. A compromise was proposed—that Maine should be admitted separately, Missouri without restriction, and that slavery should be inhibited in all the territory north of 36 deg. 30 min. N. lat. To the *principles* of this compromise the Senate's committee, and all those of the House, except Mr. Taylor, agreed. The *time and manner* of executing the compromise occasioned considerable discussion. The committee of the Senate, whose numbers were sufficient to effect a separation of Missouri from Maine, by uniting with those who had opposed their union, offered their pledge that, if the compromise were effectuated in the House, Maine should be admitted unconnected. We objected, and insisted that Maine must be first admitted. The Senate's committee would have consented to this, could we have made a similar pledge in regard to Missouri. This we could not do, and were about to separate on a point of *etiquette*, which could be safely yielded by the House, but not by the Senate. The peace of the Union, as well as the admission of Maine, was involved in it; and at last a majority of the committee of the House, (Mr. Taylor dissenting to the *principles*, and Mr. Parker to the *form*) consented that separate and similar reports should be presented in both branches, and each acted on without any stipulation in regard to priority. The compromise was agreed to—the bills have passed— and the subject is at rest. The restricted territory, equal to that of all the original States, being unsold and uninhabited, was not subject to the Constitutional objection. Maine was admitted into the Union—the slave-holding States obtained a southern latitude for themselves and their slaves, and the north, an exclusion of slavery from an immense territory, sufficient for all their purposes of emigration. The probability that, for a long time, the non-slaveholding States will have a majority in the House, and the slaveholding States, in the Senate, affords each party a security that the compromise will be permanent.

To the people of Maine the event is interesting and important. I have in my possession the most positive proof, from gentlemen of unquestioned veracity and honour, with full liberty to publish it, if I please, *that the Senate would never have yielded further than they did, and that, had not the report of the conferees been accepted, Maine must have been excluded.* It is a matter of satisfaction to Mr. Hill and myself that, while our votes secured the admission of Maine, they were in perfect coincidence with our *principles* in regard to Missouri; and the members of the delegation who have addressed you, have the consolation that they have been subject to no constraint, inasmuch as the previous admission of Maine could never have induced them to vote for a compromise which they condemn, as unequal and unjust.

In reflecting upon the conduct of the people of Maine, during this interesting and arduous struggle, it affords me high satisfaction, reminds me of the virtues of the past, and presents a sure pledge for the wisdom of the future. Just emerging from colonial dependence, commencing her career of policy, and establishing her character with her sister States; it became her to avoid sectional contests, to solicit the favour and friendship of all, and to exhibit a policy, at once national, liberal, and just.

When the tempest of war assailed us; when discord, distrust, and disaffection prevailed; when the hopes of the enemies of freedom were exalted, and the face of the patriot wore paleness and dismay, Maine was firm, confident, and unshaken. At this time, with *present prospects,* and an undiminished fidelity to the Union, was it expected that she would combine to produce a geographical division of party? Could she have wished that her representatives should have persisted in a restriction, which they could not enforce, at the expense of the independence of Maine, the harmony of the Nation, and the safety of the Union? A political combination of the discordant materials of the north, to over-balance the slave-holding States, promises but little to the harmony and prosperity of the Nation. From this, what political or moral benefit would result? Would a northern party, marked by geographical lines, in which all others might be absorbed, produce an amalgamation, very congenial with the feelings and wishes of Maine?

And who are the men against whom you are called to unite? Republicans, honourable and patriotic—brethren, sympathizing and affectionate, who have fought by your side, and triumphed with you in your country's cause. Your interests and prospects imperatively require you to discountenance and resist every attempt to excite local jealousies. Young, interprising, and industrious, you will need the aid and friendship of the slave-holding States. Your navigation, commerce, fisheries, and manufactures must be cherished and improved. Protection to these is generally taxation upon their products of agriculture. On these subjects they have hitherto been liberal and magnanimous. But engage in this crusade against them; compel them to unite on the only subject in which their safety is exclusively concerned; combine against them in an affair so critical and delicate as the management of their slaves; and you provoke a hostility at once destructive of your own interests, and the safety of the nation.

But this attempt was most alarming to the slave-holding States. We, who know nothing of slaves, can have no correct conception of the excitement which the agitation of this question must naturally produce. Whatever may be imagined, the masters have a strong attachment to their slaves. So jealous are they of any attempt to infringe their rights to this species of property, that, to agitate the question, produces the keenest sensibility. Any indication of a wish to emancipate them, endangers the master, and subjects the slave to a more rigorous discipline. The slave-holding States would combine and resist every attempt of ours, at emancipation. Should we hereafter persist in provoking a union of these States, the parties would take their stand with all the inveterate obstinacy, which a deep sense of wrong on the one hand, and a zeal for humanity on the other, would inculcate. Instead of a competition in acts of kindness and magnanimity; instead of an honourable emulation in feelings and duties, of forbearance and charity; instead of patriotic struggles for the safety, prosperity, and glory of the nation; we should be engaged in the unprofitable and fatal strife of inflicting and retaliating injuries, provoking jealousies and deadly hate; throwing obstacles and stumbling blocks in the way of each other's prosperity and happiness; and, at last consummate the hopes of tyrants by destroying the Union, and prostrating, in the dust, the temple of liberty.

I have thus given you, my fellow-citizens, a plain, concise, and candid view of my conduct, and my reasons in this interesting and important question. If I have erred, it is from an excessive zeal for the preservation of the Constitution and a superabundant solicitude for the harmony and safety of the Union.

In reviewing, however, my course, since the question has been decided, I find no cause of regret, but much of felicitation. The framers of the Constitution were obliged to yield much for the sake of union; and the great Washington has told us that such concessions are necessary to preserve it. Those who apprehended that slavery would be extended over the *immeasurable west*, will derive consolation that it is from thence excluded, and that settlements will be commenced and continued, by a people who will never after consent to establish it. Those who claim the territory as a common property for a common retreat, will be satisfied with the reflection, that though their portion is small, it is populous and valuable, and that they are excluded from a latitude where slaves could never be profitably employed. Those who saw, in this contest, an approaching storm with devastation and ruin in its wake, may rejoice "with joy unspeakable," that its fury is assuaged, its clouds are scattering, and the sun of harmony is rising "with healing in his wings and majesty in his beams."

JOHN HOLMES

Washington, 10th April, 1820

11. The Maturing of American Nationalism: Monroe's Message to Congress, December 2, 1823

The immediate problems that led President Monroe to proclaim in his message to Congress on December 2, 1823, the principles that became known as the Monroe Doctrine were the threat of Russian expansion from Alaska into the Oregon country and the threat of intervention by European powers in Latin America to restore the newly proclaimed independent states to European control. The basic principles affirmed, however, were not the product of the immediate circumstances but of the maturing of an American foreign policy that had been long in the process of formulation. The Monroe Doctrine was in direct lineage from the principles of nonentanglement proclaimed during Washington's administration; and the concept of two hemispheres was rooted deep in the colonial past. The affirmation of the principles of noncoloniza- tion and nonintervention in 1823 also reflected the new spirit of nationalism that had followed the termination of the War of 1812. Secretary of State John Quincy Adams was a major influence in the formulation of the Monroe Doctrine, but it was President Monroe who conceived the plan of a public affirmation of principles in his message to Congress. The excerpts below come from two widely separated passages in the message, which is printed in James D. Richardson (ed.), A Compilation of the Messages and Papers of the Presidents, 1789– 1897 (10 vols., Washington, D.C., 1900), II, 209, 217–219.

. . . . At the proposal of the Russian Imperial Government, made through the minister of the Emperor residing here, a full power and instructions have been transmitted to the minister of the United States at St. Petersburg to arrange by amicable negotiation the respective rights and interests of the two nations on the north- west coast of this continent. A similar proposal has been made by his Imperial Majesty to the Government of Great Britain, which has likewise been acceded to. The Government of the United States has been desirous by this friendly proceeding of manifesting the great value which they have invariably attached to the friendship of the Emperor and their solicitude to cultivate the best understanding with his Government. In the discussions to which this interest has given rise and in the arrangements by which they may terminate the occasion has been judged proper for asserting, as a principle in which the rights and interests of the United States are involved, that the American continents, by the free and independent condition which they have assumed and maintain, are henceforth not to be considered as subjects for future colonization by any European powers. . . .

It was stated at the commencement of the last session that a great effort was then making in Spain and Portugal to improve the condition of the people of those countries, and that it appeared to be conducted with extraordinary moderation. It need scarcely be remarked that the result has been so far very different from what was then anticipated. Of events in that quarter of the globe, with which we have so much intercourse and from which we derive our origin, we have always been anxious and interested spectators. The citizens of the United States cherish sentiments the most friendly in favor of the liberty and happiness of their fellow-men on that side of the Atlantic. In the wars of the European powers in matters relating to themselves we have never taken any part, nor does it comport with our policy so to do. It is only when our rights are invaded or seriously menaced that we resent injuries or make preparation for our defense. With the movements in this hemisphere we are of necessity more immediately connected, and by causes which must be obvious to all enlightened and impartial observers. The political system of the allied powers is essentially different in this respect from that of America. This difference proceeds from that which exists in their respective Governments; and to the defense of our own, which has been achieved by the loss of so much blood and treasure, and matured by the wisdom of their most enlightened citizens, and under which we have enjoyed unexampled felicity, this whole nation is devoted. We owe it, therefore, to candor and to the amicable relations existing between the United States and those powers to declare that we should consider any attempt on their part to extend their system to any portion of this hemisphere as dangerous to our peace and safety. With the existing colonies or dependencies of any European power we have not interfered and shall not interfere. But with the Governments who have declared their independence and maintained it, and whose independence we have, on great consideration and on just principles, acknowledged, we could not view any interposition for the purpose of oppressing them, or controlling in any other manner their destiny, by any European power in any other light than as the manifestation of an unfriendly disposition toward the United States. In the war between those new Governments and Spain we declared our neutrality at the time of their recognition, and to this we have adhered, and shall continue to adhere, provided no change shall occur which, in the judgment of the competent authorities of this Government, shall make a corresponding change on the part of the United States indispensable to their security.

The late events in Spain and Portugal shew that Europe is still unsettled. Of this important fact no stronger proof can be adduced than that the allied powers should have thought it proper, on any principle satisfactory to themselves, to have interposed by force in the internal concerns of Spain. To what extent such interposition may be carried, on the same principle, is a question in which all independent powers whose governments differ from theirs are interested, even those most remote, and surely none more so than the United States. Our policy in regard to Europe, which was adopted at an early stage of the wars which have so long agitated that quarter of the globe, nevertheless remains the same, which is, not to interfere in the internal concerns of any of its powers; to consider the government *de facto* as the legitimate government for us; to cultivate friendly relations with it, and to preserve those relations by a frank, firm, and manly policy, meeting in all instances the just claims of every power, submitting to injuries from none. But in regard to those continents circumstances are eminently and conspicuously different. It is impossible that the allied powers should extend their political system to any portion of either continent without endangering our peace and happiness; nor can anyone believe that our southern brethren, if left to themselves, would adopt it of their own accord. It is equally impossible, therefore, that we should behold such interposition in any form with indifference. If we look to the comparative strength and resources of Spain and those new Governments, and their distance from each other, it must be obvious that she can never subdue them. It is still the true policy of the United States to leave the parties to themselves, in the hope that other powers will pursue the same course. . . .

III

Interpreting the Constitution

The Constitution was not precise either as to specific details or to the general nature of the power of the national government. While it affirmed that the Constitution and all laws and treaties made under its authority constituted the supreme law of the land, it also stated that all powers not delegated to the national government nor prohibited to the states were reserved to the states or to the people. This latter provision, added to the Constitution as the tenth amendment, grew out of the debates at the time of the ratifying conventions over the extent of the national government's powers. From the outset it was thus clear that the nature of the new federal union would be greatly determined by the manner in which the Constitution was implemented and interpreted. One of the early questions to arise related to the specified powers of Congress and the interpretation to be given to the provision authorizing Congress to make all laws necessary and proper to carry out these specified powers. In the opinions which they wrote on the constitutionality of the national bank, Jefferson and Hamilton presented two contrary interpretations of this provision and in so doing took the positions that came to be known as "strict construction" and "loose construction."

A key problem underlying the debate over the interpretation of the Constitution was where the line was to be drawn between national and state authority and what was to be done if the national Congress stepped beyond the limits of its power. Who was to determine if Congress had exceeded its authority? Jefferson and Madison in the Kentucky and Virginia Resolutions provided a systematic statement of the compact theory of the formation of the government under the Constitution and the right of the parties to the contract to judge infractions thereof. The fundamental issues raised here were ultimately to be settled only by civil conflict. Under Chief Justice John Marshall, appointed by John Adams in 1801, the Supreme Court went far toward providing a workable interpretation of the Constitution and establishing the supremacy of the national government. In the decision in Marbury v. Madison in 1803, the Supreme Court established the precedent of judicial review by declaring an act of Congress unconstitutional; and in a series of famous decisions Marshall did much to undermine the state-rights interpretation and strengthen national authority. In

McCulloch v. Maryland in 1819 the principle of implied powers was given judicial sanction. At the same time, the doctrines of state rights persisted. They were invoked by New England Federalists after the purchase of Louisiana, and during the War of 1812 they led to the Hartford Convention. With the growing controversy over the protective tariff, the theories of state rights were restated by John C. Calhoun to provide a blueprint for nullification. Thus, the problem of interpreting the Constitution remained a constantly vital issue throughout the early national period.

12. Conflicting Views of the Constitutionality of the Bank of the United States

Although questions of constitutionality had been raised earlier over congressional legislation (e.g., assumption of state debts), the passage of the bill to charter the Bank of the United States in February, 1791, provided the occasion for the first systematic formulation of two sharply divergent positions of constitutional interpretation. Before signing the bill to charter the bank, President Washington asked for written opinions on the constitutionality of the measure from his chief advisers, Secretary of the Treasury Hamilton, Secretary of State Jefferson, and Attorney General Edmund Randolph. Jefferson in his concise brief presented the arguments in support of a strict construction of the Constitution. In a more lengthy opinion, Hamilton formulated the doctrine of implied powers and argued for a loose construction of the Constitution. These documents, as already noted, have become classic expositions of the doctrines of strict and loose construction. In the decision in McCulloch v. Maryland in 1819, the United States Supreme Court gave judicial sanction to Hamilton's interpretation in language strikingly similar to that used by the Secretary of the Treasury in 1791. It should be noted that Hamilton in writing his statement had before him the opinions of both Jefferson and Randolph. Jefferson's opinion is reprinted from Ford (ed.), Writings of Thomas Jefferson, V, 284–289; Hamilton's opinion is from Harold E. Syrett and Jacob E. Cooke (eds.), The Papers of Alexander Hamilton (New York, 1961–   ), VIII, 97–107, 119–122, 124–130.

A. Opinion of Thomas Jefferson, February 15, 1791

. . . I consider the foundation of the Constitution as laid on this ground: That "all powers not delegated to the United States, by the Constitution, nor prohibited by it to the States, are reserved to the States or to the people." To take a single step beyond the boundaries thus specially drawn around the powers of Congress, is to take possession of a boundless field of power, no longer susceptible of any definition.

The incorporation of a bank, and the powers assumed by this bill, have not, in my opinion, been delegated to the United States, by the Constitution.

I. They are not among the powers specially enumerated: for these are: 1st. A power to lay taxes for the purpose of paying the debts of the United States; but no debt is paid by this bill, nor any tax laid. Were it a bill to raise money, its origination in the Senate would condemn it by the Constitution.

2d. "To borrow money." But this bill neither borrows money nor ensures the borrowing it. The proprietors of the bank will be just as free as any other money holders, to lend or not to lend their money to the public. The operation proposed in the bill, first, to lend them two millions, and then to borrow them back again, cannot change the nature of the latter act, which will still be a payment, and not a loan, call it by what name you please.

3. To "regulate commerce with foreign nations, and among the States, and with the Indian tribes." To erect a bank, and to regulate commerce, are very different acts. He who erects a bank, creates a subject of commerce in its bills; so does he who makes a bushel of wheat, or digs a dollar out of the mines; yet neither of these persons regulates commerce thereby. To make a thing which may be bought and sold, is not to prescribe regulations for buying and selling. Besides, if this was an exercise of the power of regulating commerce, it would be void, as extending as much to the internal commerce of every State, as to its external. For the power given to Congress by the Constitution does not extend to the internal regulation of the commerce of a State, (that is to say of the commerce between citizen and citizen,) which remain exclusively with its own legislature; but to its external commerce only, that is to say, its commerce with another State, or with foreign nations, or with the Indian tribes. Accordingly the bill does not propose the measure as a regulation of trade, but as "productive of considerable advantages to trade." Still less are these powers covered by any other of the special enumerations.

II. Nor are they within either of the general phrases, which are the two following:—

1. To lay taxes to provide for the general welfare of the United

States, that is to say, "to lay taxes for *the purpose* of providing for the general welfare." For the laying of taxes is the *power*, and the general welfare the *purpose* for which the power is to be exercised. They are not to lay taxes *ad libitum* for *any purpose they please*; but only to *pay the debts* or *provide for the welfare of the Union*. In like manner, they are not *to do anything they please* to provide for the general welfare, but only to *lay taxes* for that purpose. To consider the latter phrase, not as describing the purpose of the first, but as giving a distinct and independent power to do any act they please, which might be for the good of the Union, would render all the preceding and subsequent enumerations of power completely useless.

It would reduce the whole instrument to a single phrase, that of instituting a Congress with power to do whatever would be for the good of the United States; and, as they would be the sole judges of the good or evil, it would be also a power to do whatever evil they please.

It is an established rule of construction where a phrase will bear either of two meanings, to give it that which will allow some meaning to the other parts of the instrument, and not that which would render all the others useless. Certainly no such universal power was meant to be given them. It was intended to lace them up straitly within the enumerated powers, and those without which, as means, these powers could not be carried into effect. It is known that the very power now proposed as a means was rejected as an end by the Convention which formed the Constitution. A proposition was made to them to authorize Congress to open canals, and an amendatory one to empower them to incorporate. But the whole was rejected, and one of the reasons for rejection urged in debate was, that then they would have a power to erect a bank, which would render the great cities, where there were prejudices and jealousies on the subject, adverse to the reception of the Constitution.

2. The second general phrase is, "to make all laws necessary and proper for carrying into execution the enumerated powers." But they can all be carried into execution without a bank. A bank therefore is not necessary, and consequently not authorized by this phrase.

It has been urged that a bank will give great facility or convenience in the collection of taxes. Suppose this were true: yet the Constitution allows only the means which are "*necessary*," not those which are merely "convenient" for effecting the enumerated powers. If such a latitude of construction be allowed to this phrase as to give any non-enumerated power, it will go to every one, for there is not one which ingenuity may not torture into a *convenience* in some instance or *other, to some one* of so long a list of enumerated powers. It would swallow up all the delegated powers, and reduce the whole to one power, as before observed. Therefore it was that the Constitution restrained them to the *necessary* means, that is to say, to those means without which the grant of power would be nugatory.

But let us examine this convenience and see what it is. The report on this subject, page 3, states the only *general* convenience to be, the preventing the transportation and re-transportation of money between the States and the treasury, (for I pass over the increase of circulating medium, ascribed to it as a want, and which, according to my ideas of paper money, is clearly a demerit). Every State will have to pay a sum of tax money into the treasury; and the treasury will have to pay, in every State, a part of the interest on the public debt, and salaries to the officers of government resident in that State. In most of the States there will still be a surplus of tax money to come up to the seat of government for the officers residing there. The payments of interest and salary in each State may be made by treasury orders on the State collector. This will take up the greater part of the money he has collected in his State, and consequently prevent the great mass of it from being drawn out of the State. If there be a balance of commerce in favor of that State against the one in which the government resides, the surplus of taxes will be remitted by the bills of exchange drawn for that commercial balance. And so it must be if there was a bank. But if there be no balance of commerce, either direct or circuitous, all the banks in the world could not bring up the surplus of taxes but in the form of money. Treasury orders then, and bills of exchange may prevent the displacement of the main mass of the money collected, without the aid of any bank; and where these fail, it cannot be prevented even with that aid.

Perhaps, indeed, bank bills may be a more *convenient* vehicle than treasury orders. But a little *difference* in the degree of *convenience*, cannot constitute the necessity which the Constitution makes the ground for assuming any non-enumerated power.

Besides; the existing banks will, without a doubt, enter into arrangements for lending their agency, and the more favorable, as there will be a competition among them for it; whereas the bill delivers us up bound to the national bank, who are free to refuse all arrangement, but on their own terms, and the public not free, on such refusal, to employ any other bank. That of Philadelphia, I believe, now does this business, by their post-notes, which, by an arrangement with the treasury, are paid by any State collector to whom they are presented. This expedient alone suffices to prevent the existence of that necessity which may justify the assumption of a non-enumerated power as a means for carrying into effect an enumerated one. The thing may be done, and has been done, and well done, without this assumption; therefore, it does not stand on that degree of necessity which can honestly justify it.

It may be said that a bank whose bills would have a currency all over the States, would be more convenient than one whose currency is limited to a single State. So it would be still more convenient that there should be a bank, whose bills should have a currency all over the world. But it does not follow from this superior conveniency, that there exists anywhere a power to establish such a bank; or that the world may not go on very well without it.

Can it be thought that the Constitution intended that for a shade or two of convenience, more or less, Congress should be authorised to break down the most ancient and fundamental laws of the several States; such as those against Mortmain, the laws of Alienage, the rules of descent, the acts of distribution, the laws of escheat and forfeiture, the laws of monopoly? Nothing but a necessity invincible by any other means, can justify such a prostitution of laws, which constitute the pillars of our whole system of jurisprudence. Will Congress be too strait-laced to carry the Constitution into honest effect, unless they may pass over the foundation-laws of the State government for the slightest convenience of theirs?

The negative of the President is the shield provided by the Constitution to protect against the invasions of the legislature: 1. The right of the Executive. 2. Of the Judiciary. 3. Of the States and State legislatures. The present is the case of a right remaining exclusively with the States, and consequently one of those intended by the Constitution to be placed under its protection.

It must be added, however, that unless the President's mind on a view of everything which is urged for and against this bill, is tolerably clear that it is unauthorised by the Constitution; if the pro and the con hang so even as to balance his judgment, a just respect for the wisdom of the legislature would naturally decide the balance in favor of their opinion. It is chiefly for cases where they are clearly misled by error, ambition, or interest, that the Constitution has placed a check in the negative of the President.

B. Opinion of Alexander Hamilton, February 23, 1791

The Secretary of the Treasury having perused with attention the papers containing the opinions of the Secretary of State and Attorney General concerning the constitutionality of the bill for establishing a National Bank proceeds according to the order of the President to submit the reasons which have induced him to entertain a different opinion.

It will naturally have been anticipated that, in performing this task he would feel uncommon solicitude. Personal considerations alone arising from the reflection that the measure originated with him would be sufficient to produce it: The sense which he has manifested of the great importance of such an institution to the successful administration of the department under his particular care; and an expectation of serious ill consequences to result from a failure of the measure, do not permit him to be without anxiety on public accounts. But the chief solicitude arises from a firm persuasion, that principles of construction like those espoused by the Secretary of State and the Attorney General would be fatal to the just & indispensible authority of the United States.

In entering upon the argument it ought to be premised, that the objections of the Secretary of State and Attorney General are founded on a general denial of the authority of the United States to erect corporations. The latter indeed expressly admits, that if there be any thing in the bill which is not warranted by the constitution, it is the clause of incorporation.

Now it appears to the Secretary of the Treasury, that this general principle is inherent in the very definition of Government and essential to every step of the progress to be made by that of the United States; namely—that every power vested in a Government is in its nature sovereign, and includes by force of the term, a right to employ all the means requisite, and fairly applicable to the attainment of the *ends* of such power; and which are not precluded by restrictions & exceptions specified in the constitution; or not immoral, or not contrary to the essential ends of political society.

This principle in its application to Government in general would be admitted as an axiom. And it will be incumbent upon those, who may incline to deny it, to *prove* a distinction; and to shew that a rule which in the general system of things is essential to the preservation of the social order is inapplicable to the United States.

The circumstances that the powers of sovereignty are in this country divided between the National and State Governments, does not afford the distinction required. It does not follow from this, that each of the *portions* of powers delegated to the one or to the other is not sovereign *with regard to its proper objects.* It will only *follow* from it, that each has sovereign power as to *certain things,* and not as to *other things.* To deny that the Government of the United States has sovereign power as to its declared purposes & trusts, because its power does not extend to all cases, would be equally to deny, that the State Governments have sovereign power in any case; because their power does not extend to every case. The tenth section of the first article of the constitution exhibits a long list of very important things which they may not do. And thus the United States would furnish the singular spectacle of a *political society* without *sovereignty,* or of a people *governed* without *government.*

If it would be necessary to bring proof to a proposition so clear as that which affirms that the powers of the federal government, *as to its objects,* are sovereign, there is a clause of its constitution which would be decisive. It is that which declares, that the constitution and the laws of the United States made in pursuance of it, and all treaties made or which shall be made under their authority shall be the supreme law of the land. The power which can create the *Supreme law* of the land, in any case, is doubtless sovereign *as to such case.*

This general & indisputable principle puts at once an end to the *abstract* question—Whether the United States have power to *erect a corporation?* that is to say, to give a *legal* or *artificial capacity* to one or more persons, distinct from the natural. For it is unquestionably incident to *sovereign power* to erect corporations, and consequently to *that* of the United States, in *relation to the objects* intrusted to the management of the government. The difference is this—where the authority of the government is general, it can create corporations in *all cases*; where it is confined to certain branches of legislation, it can create corporations only in those cases. . . .

It is not denied, that there are *implied*, as well as *express* powers, and that the former are as effectually delegated as the latter. And for the sake of accuracy it shall be mentioned, that there is another class of powers, which may be properly denominated *resulting* powers. It will not be doubted that if the United States should make a conquest of any of the territories of its neighbours, they would possess sovereign jurisdiction over the conquered territory. This would rather be a result from the whole mass of the powers of the government & from the nature of political society, than a consequence of either of the powers specially enumerated.

But be this as it may, it furnishes a striking illustration of the general doctrine contended for. It shews an extensive case, in which a power of erecting corporations is either implied in, or would result from some or all of the powers, vested in the National Government. The jurisdiction acquired over such conquered territory would certainly be competent to every species of legislation

To return—It is conceded, that implied powers are to be considered as delegated equally with express ones.

Then it follows, that as a power of erecting a corporation may as well be *implied* as any other thing; it may as well be employed as an *instrument* or *mean* of carrying into execution any of the specified powers, as any other instrument or mean whatever. The only question must be, in this as in every other case, whether the mean to be employed, or in this instance the corporation to be erected, has a natural relation to any of the acknowledged objects or lawful ends of the government. Thus a corporation may not be erected by congress, for superintending the police of the city of Philadelphia because they are not authorised to *regulate* the *police* of that city; but one may be erected in relation to the collection of the taxes, or to the trade with foreign countries, or to the trade between the States, or with the Indian Tribes, because it is the province of the federal government to regulate those objects & because it is incident to a general *sovereign* or *legislative power* to *regulate* a thing, to employ all the means which relate to its regulation to the *best & greatest advantage*. . . .

To this mode of reasoning respecting the right of employing all the means requisite to the execution of the specified powers of the Government, it is objected that none but necessary & proper means are to be employed, & the Secretary of State maintains, that no means are to be considered as necessary, but those without which the grant of the power would be nugatory. Nay so far does he go in his restrictive interpretation of the word, as even to make the case of necessity which shall warrant the constitutional exercise of the power to depend on casual & temporary circumstances, an idea which alone refutes the construction. The expediency of exercising a particular power, at a particular time, must indeed depend on circumstances; but the constitutional right of exercising it must be uniform & invariable—the same to day, as to morrow.

All the arguments therefore against the constitutionality of the bill derived from the accidental existence of certain State-banks: institutions which happen to exist to day, & for ought that concerns the government of the United States, may disappear to morrow, must not only be rejected as fallacious, but must be viewed as demonstrative, that there is a radical source of error in the reasoning.

It is essential to the being of the National government, that so erroneous a conception of the meaning of the word necessary, should be exploded.

It is certain, that neither the grammatical, nor popular sense of the term requires that construction. According to both, necessary often means no more than needful, requisite, incidental, useful, or conducive to. It is a common mode of expression to say, that it is necessary for a government or a person to do this or that thing, when nothing more is intended or understood, than that the interests of the government or person require, or will be promoted, by the doing of this or that thing. The imagination can be at no loss for exemplifications of the use of the word in this sense.

And it is the true one in which it is to be understood as used in the constitution. The whole turn of the clause containing it, indicates, that it was the intent of the convention, by that clause to give a liberal latitude to the exercise of the specified powers. The expressions have peculiar comprehensiveness. They are—"to make all laws, necessary & proper for carrying into execution the foregoing powers & all other powers vested by the constitution in the government of the United States, or in any department or officer thereof." To understand the word as the Secretary of State does, would be to depart from its obvious & popular sense, and to give it a *restrictive* operation; an idea never before entertained. It would be to give it the same force as if the word *absolutely* or *indispensibly* had been prefixed to it.

Such a construction would beget endless uncertainty & embarrassment. The cases must be palpable & extreme in which it could be pronounced with certainty, that a measure was absolutely necessary, or one without which the exercise of a given power would be nugatory. There are few measures of any government, which would stand so severe a test. To insist upon it, would be to make the criterion of the exercise of any implied power a *case of extreme necessity;* which is rather a rule to justify the overleaping of the bounds of constitutional authority, than to govern the ordinary exercise of it.

It may be truly said of every government, as well as of that of the United States, that it has only a right, to pass such laws as are necessary & proper to accomplish the objects intrusted to it. For no government has a right to do *merely what it pleases.* Hence by a process of reasoning similar to that of the Secretary of State, it might be proved, that neither of the State governments has a right to incorporate a bank. It might be shewn, that all the public business of the State, could be performed without a bank, and inferring thence that it was unnecessary it might be argued that it could not be done, because it is against the rule which has been just mentioned. A like mode of reasoning would prove, that there was no power to incorporate the Inhabitants of a town, with a view to a more perfect police: For it is certain, that an incorporation may be dispensed with, though it is better to have one. It is to be remembered, that there is no *express* power in any State constitution to erect corporations.

The *degree* in which a measure is necessary, can never be a test of the *legal* right to adopt it. That must ever be a matter of opinion; and can only be a test of expediency. The *relation* between the *measure* and the *end,* between the *nature of the mean* employed towards the execution of a power and the object of that power, must be the criterion of constitutionality not the more or less of *necessity* or *utility.*

The practice of the government is against the rule of construction advocated by the Secretary of State. Of this the act concerning light houses, beacons, buoys & public piers, is a decisive example. This doubtless must be referred to the power of regulating trade, and is fairly relative to it. But it cannot be affirmed, that the exercise of that power, in this instance, was strictly necessary; or that the power itself would be *nugatory* without that of regulating establishments of this nature.

This restrictive interpretation of the word *necessary* is also contrary to this sound maxim of construction namely, that the powers contained in a constitution of government, especially those which concern the general administration of the affairs of a country, its finances, trade, defence &c ought to be construed liberally, in advancement of the public good. This rule does not depend on the particular form of a government or on the particular demarkation of the boundaries of its powers, but on the nature and objects of government itself. The means by which national exigencies are to be provided for, national inconveniences obviated, national prosperity promoted, are of such infinite variety, extent and complexity, that there must, of necessity, be great latitude of discretion in the selection & application of those means. Hence consequently, the necessity & propriety of exercising the authorities intrusted to a government on principles of liberal construction. . . .

But the doctrine which is contended for is not chargeable with the consequence imputed to it. It does not affirm that the National government is sovereign in all respects, but that it is sovereign to a certain extent: that is, to the extent of the objects of its specified powers.

It leaves therefore a criterion of what is constitutional, and of what is not so. This criterion is the *end* to which the measure relates as a *mean*. If the end be clearly comprehended within any of the specified powers, & if the measure have an obvious relation to that end, and is not forbidden by any particular provision of the constitution—it may safely be deemed to come within the compass of the national authority. There is also this further criterion which may materially assist the decision. Does the proposed measure abridge a preexisting right of any State, or of any individual? If it does not, there is a strong presumption in favour of its constitutionality; & slighter relations to any declared object of the constitution may be permitted to turn the scale. . . .

It is presumed to have been satisfactorily shewn in the course of the preceding observations

1. That the power of the government, *as to* the objects intrusted
   to its management, is in its nature sovereign.

2. That the right of erecting corporations is one, inherent in & inseparable from the idea of sovereign power.

3. That the position, that the government of the United States can exercise no power but such as is delegated to it by its constitution, does not militate against this principle.

4. That the word *necessary* in the general clause can have no *restrictive* operation, derogating from the force of this principle, indeed, that the degree in which a measure is, or is not necessary, cannot be a *test* of *constitutional* right, but of expediency only.

5. That the power to erect corporations is not to be considered, as an *independent* & *substantive* power but as an *incidental* & *auxiliary* one; and was therefore more properly left to implication, than expressly granted.

6. That the principle in question does not extend the power of the government beyond the prescribed limits, because it only affirms a power to *incorporate* for *purposes within the sphere of the specified powers.*

And lastly that the right to exercise such a power, in certain cases, is unequivocally granted in the most *positive* & *comprehensive* terms.

To all which it only remains to be added that such a power has actually been exercised in two very eminent instances: namely in the erection of two governments, One, northwest of the river Ohio, and the other south west—*the last, independent of any antecedent compact.*

And there results a full & complete demonstration, that the Secretary of State & Attorney General are mistaken, when they deny generally the power of the National government to erect corporations.

It shall now be endeavoured to be shewn that there is a power to erect one of the kind proposed by the bill. This will be done, by tracing a natural & obvious relation between the institution of a bank, and the objects of several of the enumerated powers of the government; and by shewing that, *politically* speaking, it is necessary to the effectual execution of one or more of those powers. In the course of this investigation, various instances will be stated, by way of illustration, of a right to erect corporations under those powers.

Some preliminary observations maybe proper.

The proposed bank is to consist of an association of persons for the purpose of creating a joint capital to be employed, chiefly and essentially, in loans. So far the object is not only lawful, but it is the mere exercise of a right, which the law allows to every individual. The bank of New York which is not incorporated, is an example of such an association. The bill proposes in addition, that the government shall become a joint proprietor in this undertaking, and that it shall permit the bills of the company payable on demand to be receivable in its revenues & stipulates that it shall not grant privileges similar to those which are to be allowed to this company, to any others. All this is incontrovertibly within the compass of the discretion of the government. The only question is, whether it has a right to incorporate this company, in order to enable it the more effectually to accomplish ends, which are in themselves lawful.

To establish such a right, it remains to shew the relation of such an institution to one or more of the specified powers of the government.

Accordingly it is affirmed, that it has a relation more or less direct to the power of collecting taxes; to that of borrowing money; to that of regulating trade between the states; and to those of raising, supporting & maintaining fleets & armies. To the two former, the relation may be said to be immediate.

And, in the last place, it will be argued, that it is, clearly, within the provision which authorises the making of all needful rules & regulations concerning the property of the United States, as the same has been practiced upon by the Government.

A Bank relates to the collection of taxes in two ways; indirectly, by increasing the quantity of circulating medium & quickening circulation, which facilitates the means of paying—directly, by creating a convenient species of medium in which they are to be paid.

To designate or appoint the money or thing in which taxes are to be paid, is not only a proper, but a necessary exercise of the power of collecting them. Accordingly congress in the law concerning the collection of the duties on imports & tonnage, have provided that they shall be payable in gold & silver. But while it was an indispensible part of the work to say in what they should be paid, the choice of the specific thing was mere matter of discretion. The payment might have been required in the commodities themselves. Taxes in kind, however ill judged, are not without precedents, even in the United States. Or it might have been in the paper money of the several states; or in the bills of the bank of North America, New York and Massachusetts, all or either of them: or it might have been in bills issued under the authority of the United States.

No part of this can, it is presumed, be disputed. The appointment, then, of the *money* or *thing*, in which the taxes are to be paid, is an incident to the power of collection. And among the expedients which may be adopted, is that of bills issued under the authority of the United States. . . .

A Bank has a direct relation to the power of borrowing money, because it is an usual and in sudden emergencies an essential instrument in the obtaining of loans to Government.

A nation is threatened with a war. Large sums are wanted, on a sudden, to make the requisite preparations. Taxes are laid for the purpose, but it requires time to obtain the benefit of them. Anticipation is indispensible. If there be a bank, the supply can, at once be had; if there be none loans from Individuals must be sought. The progress of these is often too slow for the exigency: in some situations they are not practicable at all. Frequently when they are, it is of great consequence to be able to anticipate the product of them by advances from a bank.

The essentiality of such an institution as an instrument of loans is exemplified at this very moment. An Indian expedition is to be prosecuted. The only fund out of which the money can arise consistently with the public engagements, is a tax which will only begin to be collected in July next. The preparations, however, are instantly to be made. The money must therefore be borrowed. And of whom could it be borrowed; if there were no public banks?

It happens, that there are institutions of this kind, but if there were none, it would be indispensible to create one.

Let it then be supposed, that the necessity existed, (as but for a casualty would be the case) that proposals were made for obtaining a loan; that a number of individuals came forward and said, we are willing to accommodate the government with this money; with what we have in hand and the credit we can raise upon it we doubt not of being able to furnish the sum required: but in order to this, it is indispensible, that we should be incorporated as a bank. This is essential towards putting it in our power to do what is desired and we are obliged on that account to make it the *consideration* or condition of the loan.

Can it be believed, that a compliance with this proposition would be unconstitutional? Does not this alone evince the contrary? It is a necessary part of a power to borrow to be able to stipulate the consideration or conditions of a loan. It is evident, as has been remarked elsewhere, that this is not confined to the mere stipulation of a sum of money by way of interest—why may it not be deemed to extend, where a government is the contracting party, to the stipulation of a *franchise*? If it may, & it is not perceived why it may not, then the grant of a corporate capacity may be stipulated as a consideration of the loan? There seems to be nothing unfit, or foreign from the nature of the thing in giving individuality or a corporate capacity to a number of persons who are willing to lend a sum of money to the government, the better to enable them to do it, and make them an ordinary instrument of loans in future emergencies of the state.

But the more general view of the subject is still more satisfactory. The legislative power of borrowing money, & of making all laws necessary & proper for carrying into execution that power, seems obviously competent to the appointment of the *organ* through which the abilities and wills of individuals may be most efficaciously exerted, for the accommodation of the government by loans. . . .

The institution of a bank has also a natural relation to the regulation of trade between the States: in so far as it is conducive to the creation of a convenient medium of *exchange* between them, and to the keeping up a full circulation by preventing the frequent displacement of the metals in reciprocal remittances. Money is the very hinge on which commerce turns. And this does not mean merely gold & silver, many other things have served the purpose with different degrees of utility. Paper has been extensively employed. . . .

There is an observation of the secretary of state . . . which may require notice in this place. Congress, says he, are not to lay taxes *ad libitum* for any purpose they please, but only to pay the debts, or provide for the *welfare* of the Union. Certainly no inference can be drawn from this against the power of applying their money for the institution of a bank. It is true, that they cannot without breach of trust, lay taxes for any other purpose than the general welfare but so neither can any other government. The welfare of the community is the only legitimate end for which money can be raised on the community. Congress can be considered as under only one restriction, which does not apply to other governments—They cannot rightfully apply the money they raise to any purpose *merely* or purely local. But with this exception they have as large a discretion in relation to the *application* of money as any legislature whatever. The constitutional *test* of a right application must always be whether it be for a purpose of *general* or *local* nature. If the former, there can be no want of constitutional power. The quality of the object, as how far it will really promote or not the welfare of the union, must be matter of conscientious discretion. And the arguments for or against a measure in this light, must be arguments concerning expediency or inexpediency, not constitutional right. Whatever relates to the general order of the finances, to the general interests of trade &c being general objects are constitutional ones for *the application* of *money*.

A Bank then whose bills are to circulate in all the revenues of the country, is *evidently* a general object, and for that very reason a constitutional one as far as regards the appropriation of money to it. Whether it will really be a beneficial one, or not, is worthy of careful examination, but is no more a constitutional point, in the particular referred to; than the question whether the western lands shall be sold for twenty or thirty cents per acre.

A hope is entertained, that it has by this time been made to appear, to the satisfaction of the President, that a bank has a natural relation to the power of collecting taxes; to that of borrowing money; to that of regulating trade; to that of providing for the common defence: and that as the bill under consideration contemplates the government in the light of a joint proprietor of the stock of the bank, it brings the case within the provision of the clause of the constitution which immediately respects the property of the United States.

Under a conviction that such a relation subsists, the Secretary of the Treasury, with all deference conceives, that it will result as a necessary consequence from the position, that all the specified powers of the government are sovereign as to the proper objects;

that the incorporation of a bank is a constitutional measure, and that the objections taken to the bill, in this respect, are ill founded. . . .

13. A Statement of the Compact Theory: The Kentucky Resolutions, 1798, 1799

The enactment of the alien and sedition laws by a Federalist-controlled Congress in 1798 provoked strong protests from the Republican opposition condemning the acts as violations of the constitutional guarantees of freedom of speech, press, and other civil liberties. The most significant of these protests were the resolutions passed by the legislatures of Kentucky and Virginia, originating, unknown to the public, with the Republican party leadership. Keeping their authorships closely guarded secrets, Jefferson wrote the original draft of the Kentucky Resolutions of 1798 and Madison was the author of the Virginia Resolutions. While the immediate importance of the resolutions was more political than constitutional, in the long run the Kentucky and Virginia Resolutions acquired major constitutional significance as the first systematic statement of the compact theory of the formation of the Union under the Constitution and of the doctrine of the right of states to interpose their power against unconstitutional acts of Congress. It should be remembered that, at that time, the Supreme Court had not exercised the power of judicial review to invalidate an act of Congress, and the question of what was to be done in cases where Congress violated the Constitution was an unsettled issue. A number of states replied to the resolutions of Kentucky and Virginia by denying the validity of the arguments advanced, which in turn led both Kentucky and Virginia to reaffirm their positions in 1799. These documents provided an arsenal of arguments for later, more far-reaching, state-rights doctrines. The texts of the Kentucky Resolutions of 1798 and 1799 are taken from the Journal of the House of Representatives . . . of Kentucky, November 10, 1798, and November 14, 1799.

Kentucky Resolutions of 1798

1. Resolved, that the several states composing the United States of America, are not united on the principle of unlimited submission to their general government; but that by compact under the style and title of a constitution for the United States and of amendments thereto, they constituted a general government for

special purposes, delegated to that government certain definitive powers, reserving each state to itself, the residuary mass of right to their own self government; and that whensoever the general government assumes undelegated powers, its acts are unauthoritative, void, and of no force; that to this compact each state acceded, as a state, and is an integral party, its co-states forming as to itself, the other party; that the government created by this compact was not made the exclusive or final *judge* of the extent of the powers delegated to itself; since that would have made its discretion, and not the constitution, the measure of its powers: but that as in all other cases of compact among parties having no common judge, each party has an equal right to judge for itself, as well of infractions as of the mode and measure of redress.

2. Resolved, that the constitution of the United States having delegated to congress a power to punish treason, counterfeiting the securities and current coin of the United States, piracies and felonies committed on the high seas, and offences against the laws of nations, and no other crimes whatever, and it being true as a general principle, and one of the amendments to the constitution having also declared, 'that the powers not delegated to the United States by the constitution, nor prohibited by it to the states, are reserved to the states respectively, or to the people,' therefore, also the same act of congress passed on the fourteenth day of July, 1798, and entitled 'An act in addition to the act entitled an act for the punishment of certain crimes against the United States;' as also the act passed by them on the 27th day of June, 1798, entitled 'an act to punish frauds committed on the bank of the United States,' (and all other their acts which assume to create, define, or punish crimes other then those enumerated in the constitution) are altogether void and of no force, and that the power to create, define and punish such other crimes is reserved, and of right appertains solely and exclusively to the respective states, each within its own territory.

3. Resolved, that it is true, as a general principle, and is also expressly declared by one of the amendments to the constitution, that 'the powers not delegated to the United States by the consitution, nor prohibited by it to the states, are reserved to the states respectively, or to the people;' and that no power over the freedom of religion, freedom of speech, or freedom of the press being delegated to the United States by the constitution, nor pro-

hibited by it to the states, all lawful powers respecting the same did of right remain, and were reserved to the states, or to the people; that thus was manifested their determination to retain to themselves the right of judging how far the licentiousness of speech and of the press may be abridged, without lessening their useful freedom, and how far those abuses which cannot be separated from their use, should be tolerated, rather than the use be destroyed; and thus also they guarded against all abridgement by the United States of the freedom of religious principles and exercises, and retained to themselves the right of protecting the same, as this state by a law passed on the general demand of its citizens, had already protected them from all human restraint or interference: And that in addition to this general principle and express declaration, another and more special provision has been made by one of the amendments to the constitution, which expressly declares, that 'congress shall make no law respecting the establishment of religion, or prohibiting the free exercise thereof, or abridging the freedom of speech, or of the press,' thereby guarding in the same sentence, and under the same words, the freedom of religion, of speech, and of the press, insomuch, that whatever violates either, throws down the sanctuary which covers the others, and that libels, falsehoods, and defamation, equally with heresy and false religion, are withheld from the cognizance of federal tribunals. That, therefore, the act of the congress of the United States passed on the fourteenth day of July, 1798, entitled 'an act in addition to the act for the punishment of certain crimes against the United States,' which does abridge the freedom of the press, is not law, but is altogether void and of no force.

4. Resolved, that alien friends are under the jurisdiction and protection of the laws of the state wherein they are; that no power over them has been delegated to the United States, nor prohibited to the individual states distinct from their power over citizens; and it being true as a general principle, and one of the amendments to the Constitution having also declared, that 'the powers not delegated to the United States by the Constitution nor prohibited by it to the states are reserved to the states respectively or to the people,' the act of congress of the United States passed on the 22nd day of June, 1798, entitled 'an act concerning aliens,' which assumes power over alien friends not delegated by the Constitution, is not law, but is altogether void and of no force.

5. Resolved, that in addition to the general principle as well as the express declaration, that powers not delegated are reserved, another and more special provision inserted in the constitution from abundant caution has declared, 'that the *migration* or importation of such persons as any of the states now existing shall think proper to admit, shall not be prohibited by the congress prior to the year 1808.' That this Commonwealth does admit, the migration of alien friends described as the subject of the said act concerning aliens; that a provision against prohibiting their migration, is a provision against all acts equivalent thereto, or it would be nugatory; that to remove them when migrated is equivalent to a prohibition of their migration, and is therefore contrary to the said provision of the Constitution, and void.

6. Resolved, that the imprisonment of a person under the protection of the Laws of this Commonwealth on his failure to obey the simple order of the president to depart out of the United States, as is undertaken by the said act entitled 'an act concerning aliens,' is contrary to the Constitution, one amendment to which has provided, that 'no person shall be deprived of liberty without due process of law,' and that another having provided 'that in all criminal prosecutions, the accused shall enjoy the right to a public trial by an impartial jury, to be informed of the nature and cause of the accusation, to be confronted with the witnesses against him, to have compulsory process for obtaining witnesses in his favor, and to have the alliance of counsel for his defence,' the same act undertaking to authorize the president to remove a person out of the United States who is under the protection of the law, on his own suspicion, without accusation, without jury, without public trial, without confrontation of the witnesses against him, without having witnesses in his favour, without defence, without counsel, is contrary to these provisions also of the Constitution, is therefore not law but utterly void and of no force.

That transferring the power of judging any person who is under the protection of the laws, from the courts to the president of the United States, as is undertaken by the same act concerning aliens, is against the article of the Constitution which provides that 'the judicial power of the United States shall be vested in courts, the judges of which shall hold their offices during good behaviour,' and that the said act is void for that reason also; and it is further to be noted, that this transfer of judiciary power is to that magistrate of the general government, who already possesses all the executive, and a qualified negative in all the legislative powers.

7. Resolved, that the construction applied by the general government (as is evinced by sundry of their proceedings) to those parts of the constitution of the United States which delegate to congress a power to lay and collect taxes, duties, imposts, and excises to pay the debts, and provide for the common defence and general welfare of the United States, and to make all laws which shall be necessary and proper for carrying into execution the powers vested by the constitution in the government of the United States, or any department thereof, goes to the destruction of all the limits prescribed to their power by the constitution— that words meant by that instrument to be subsidiary only to the execution of the limited powers, ought not to be so construed as themselves to give unlimited powers, nor a part so to be taken, as to destroy the whole residue of the instrument: that the proceedings of the general government, under colour of these articles, will be a fit and necessary subject for revisal and correction at a time of greater tranquility, while those specified in the preceding resolutions call for immediate redress.

8. Resolved, that the preceding resolutions be transmitted to the senators and representatives in congress from this commonwealth, who are hereby enjoined to present the same to their respective houses, and to use their best endeavors to procure at the next session of congress, a repeal of the aforesaid unconstitutional and obnoxious acts.

9. Resolved, lastly, that the governor of this commonwealth be, and is hereby authorised and requested to communicate the preceding resolutions to the legislatures of the several states, to assure them that this commonwealth considers union for specified national purposes, and particularly for those specified in their late federal compact, to be friendly to the peace, happiness and prosperity of all the states: that faithful to that compact, according to the plain intent and meaning in which it was understood and acceded to by the several parties, it is sincerely anxious for its preservation: that it does also believe, that to take from the states all the powers of self government, and transfer them to a general and consolidated government, without regard to the special delegations and reservations solemnly agreed to in that compact, is not for the peace, happiness, or prosperity of these states: and

that therefore, this commonwealth is determined, as it doubts
not its co-states are, tamely to submit to undelegated, and consequently unlimited powers in no man or body of men on earth:
that if the acts before specified should stand, these conclusions
would flow from them: That the general government may place
any act they think proper on the list of crimes, and punish it
themselves, whether enumerated or not enumerated by the constitution as cognizable by them: that they may transfer its cognizance to the president or any other person, who may himself
be the accuser, counsel, judge and jury, whose *suspicions* may be
the evidence, his order the sentence, his officer the executionor,
and his breast the sole record of the transaction: that a very
numerous and valuable description of the inhabitants of these
states, being by this precedent reduced as outlaws to the absolute
dominion of one man, and the barrier of the constitution thus
swept away for us all, no rampart now remains against the passions and the power of a majority of congress, to protect from a
like exportation or other grievous punishment the minority of the
same body, the legislators, judges, governors, and counsellors of
the states, nor their other peaceable inhabitants who may venture
to reclaim the constitutional rights and liberties of the states and
people, or who for other causes, good or bad may be obnoxious to
the views or marked by the suspicions of the president or be
thought dangerous to his or their elections or other interests,
public or personal: that the friendless alien has indeed been selected as the safest subject of a first experiment; but the citizen
will soon follow, or rather has already followed; for, already has
a sedition act marked him as its prey: that these and successive
acts of the same character, unless arrested on the threshold, may
tend to drive these states into revolution and blood, and will
furnish new calumnies against republican governments, and new
pretexts for those who wish it to be believed, that man cannot
be governed but by a rod of iron: that it would be a dangerous
delusion were a confidence in the men of our choice to silence
our fears for the safety of our rights: that confidence is every
where the parent of despotism: free government is founded in
jealousy and not in confidence; it is jealousy and not confidence
which prescribes limited constitutions to bind down those whom
we are obliged to trust with power: that our constitution has
accordingly fixed the limits to which, and no farther, our confi-

dence may go; and let the honest advocate of confidence read the alien and sedition acts, and say if the constitution has not been wise in fixing limits to the government it created, and whether we should be wise in destroying those limits? Let him say what the government is if it be not a tyranny, which the men of our choice have conferred on the president, and the president of our choice has assented to and accepted over the friendly strangers, to whom the mild spirit of our country and its laws had pledged hospitality and protection: that the men of our choice have more respected the bare suspicion of the president, than the solid rights of innocence, the claims of justification, the sacred force of truth, and the forms and substance of law and justice. In questions of power then, let no more be said of confidence in man, but bind him down from mischief, by the chains of the constitution. That this commonwealth does therefore call on its co-states for an expression of their sentiments on the acts concerning aliens, and for the punishment of certain crimes herein before specified, plainly declaring whether these acts are, or are not authorized by the federal compact? And it doubts not, that their sense will be so announced as to prove their attachment to limited government, whether general or particular, and that the rights and liberties of their co-states will be exposed to no dangers by remaining embarked on a common bottom with their own: But they will concur with this commonwealth in considering the said acts as so palpably against the constitution as to amount to an undisguised declaration, that the compact is not meant to be the measure of the powers of the general government, but that it will proceed in the exercise over these states of all power whatsoever: that they will view this as seizing the rights of the states and consolidating them in the hands of the general government with a power assumed to bind the states (not merely in cases made federal) but in all cases whatsoever, by laws made, not with their consent, but by others against their consent: that this would be to surrender the form of government we have chosen, and live under one deriving its powers from its own will, and not from our authority; and that the co-states, recurring to their natural right in cases not made federal, will concur in declaring these acts void, and of no force, and will each unite with this commonwealth in requesting their repeal at the next session of congress.

Kentucky Resolutions of 1799

Resolved, That this commonwealth considers the federal union, upon the terms and for the purposes specified in the late compact, as conducive to the liberty and happiness of the several states: That it does now unequivocally declare its attachment to the union, and to that compact, agreeable to its obvious and real intention, and will be among the last to seek its dissolution: That if those who administer the general government be permitted to transgress the limits fixed by that compact, by a total disregard to the special delegations of power therein contained, an annihilation of the state governments, and the erection upon their ruins, of a general consolidated government, will be the inevitable consequence: That the principle and construction contended for by sundry of the state legislatures, that the general government is the exclusive judge of the extent of the powers delegated to it, stop nothing short of despotism; since the *discretion* of those who administer the government, and not the *constitution,* would be the measure of their powers: That the several states who formed that instrument, being sovereign and independent, have the unquestionable right to judge of its infraction and that a nullification, by those sovereignties, of all unauthorized acts done under colour of that instrument, is the rightful remedy: That this commonwealth does upon the most deliberate reconsideration declare, that the said alien and sedition laws, are in their opinion, palpable violations of the said constitution; and however chearfully it may be disposed to surrender its opinion to a majority of its sister states in matters of ordinary or doubtful policy; yet, in momentous regulations like the present, which so vitally wound the best rights of the citizen, it would consider a silent acquiescence as highly criminal: That although this commonwealth as a party to the federal compact will bow to the laws of the union, yet it does at the same time declare, that it will not now, nor ever hereafter, cease to oppose in a constitutional manner, every attempt from what quarter soever offered, to violate that compact: And finally, in order that no pretexts or arguments may be drawn from a supposed acquiescence on the part of this commonwealth in the constitutionality of those laws, and be thereby used as precedents for similar future violations of the federal compact; this commonwealth does now enter against them, its solemn protest.

14. A Sectional Concern for State Rights: Circular, Hampshire County, Massachusetts, [1814]

The following document illustrates the way in which New England Federalists during the War of 1812 tied their sectional grievances and opposition to the war to alleged violations of the Constitution. The circular, issued from a meeting in Hampshire County in western Massachusetts, proposed a convention of delegates from all the northern and commercial states to consult on measures for securing changes in the federal Constitution. Aside from opposition to the war, particular emphasis was given to the constitutionality of the addition of new states from territory outside the original limits of the United States, to the constitutionality of an embargo, and to the constitutional provision which permitted the inclusion of three fifths of the slave population in determining state representation in the House of Representatives. It was the movement represented by this circular that led to the assemblying of the Hartford Convention in December, 1814, where specific propositions for altering the Constitution were formulated and more drastic measures were threatened if these protests went unheeded. But before the resolutions of the Hartford Convention could be pressed on the national government, the War of 1812 was brought to an end, and the New England movement for altering the Constitution collapsed. While the document below does not expound on constitutional theory, it is illustrative of some of the practical problems to which constitutional theory was always tied. The printed circular, Hampshire County, Massachusetts [1814], is in the Broadside Collection, Rare Book Division, New York Public Library.

[1814]

SIR,

THE multiplied evils, in which the United States have been involved by the measures of the late and present administration, are the subjects of general complaint, and in the opinion of our wisest statesmen, call for some effectual remedy. His Excellency, the Governor of the Commonwealth, in his addresses to the General Court at the last and present Session, has stated, in temperate, but clear and decided language, his opinion of the injustice of the present war, and intimated that measures ought to be adopted by the Legislature to bring it to a speedy close. He also calls the attention of the Legislature to some measures of the General Government, which are believed to be unconstitutional. In all the measures of the General Government, the people of the United States have a common concern; but there are some laws and regulations, which call more particularly for the attention of the Northern States and are deeply interesting to the people of this Commonwealth. Feeling this interest, as it respects the present and future generations, a number of Gentlemen, from various towns in the Old County of Hampshire, have met and conferred on the subject, and upon full conviction that the evils we suffer are not wholly of a temporary nature, springing from the war, but some of them of a permanent character, resulting from a perverse construction of the Constitution of the United States itself, we have thought it a duty we owe to our country, to invite the attention of the good people of the Counties of Hampshire, Hampden and Franklin, to the radical causes of these evils.

We know indeed that a negotiation for peace has been recently set on foot; and peace will remove many public evils. It is an event we ardently desire. But when we consider how often the people of this country have been disappointed in their expectations of peace and of wise measures, and when we consider the terms which our administration has hitherto demanded, some of which it is certain cannot be obtained, and some of which, in the opinion of able statesmen, ought not to be insisted on, we confess our hopes of a speedy peace are not very sanguine.

But still a very serious question occurs—whether without an amendment of the Federal Constitution, the Northern and Commercial States can enjoy the advantages to which their wealth, strength, and white population justly entitle them. By means of the representation of slaves, the Southern States have an influence in our National Councils, altogether disproportioned to their wealth, strength, and resources; and we presume it to be a fact, capable of demonstration, that for about twenty years past, the United States have been governed by a representation of about two fifths of the actual property of the country.

In addition to this, the creation of New States in the South, and out of the original limits of the United States, has increased the Southern interest, which has appeared so hostile to the peace and commercial prosperity of the Northern States. This power assumed by Congress of bringing into the Union new States, not comprehended within the territory of the United States at the time of the Federal Compact, is deemed arbitrary, unjust, and dangerous, and a direct infringement of the Constitution. This is a power that may be hereafter extended; and the evil will not cease with the establishment of peace. We would ask, then, ought the Northern States to acquiesce in the exercise of this power? To what consequences would it lead? How can the people of the Northern States answer to themselves and to their posterity, for an acquiescence in the exercise of a power, that augments an influence already destructive of our prosperity, and will in time annihilate the best interests of the Northern people.

There are other measures of the General Government, which, we apprehend, ought to excite serious alarm. The power assumed to lay a permanent embargo, appears not to be constitutional, but an encroachment upon the rights of our citizens, which calls for decided opposition. It is a power, we believe, never before exercised by a commercial nation; and how can the Northern States, which are habitually commercial, and whose active foreign trade is so necessarily connected with the interest of the farmer and mechanic, sleep in tranquillity under such a violent infringement of their rights? But this is not all. The late act imposing an Embargo is subversive of the first principles of civil liberty. The trade coastwise between different ports *in the same state*, is arbitrarily and unconstitutionally prohibited, and the subordinate officers of government are vested with powers altogether inconsistent with our republican institutions. It arms the President and his Agents with complete control of persons and property, and authorizes the employment of military force to carry its extraordinary provisions into execution.

We forbear to enumerate all the measures of the Federal Government, which we consider as violations of the Constitution, and encroachments upon the rights of the people, and which bear particularly hard upon the commercial people of the North. But we would invite our fellow citizens to consider whether peace will remedy our public evils, without some amendments of the Constitution, which shall secure to the Northern States their due weight and influence in our National Councils.

The Northern States acceded to the representation of slaves as a matter of compromise, upon the express stipulation in the Constitution, that they should be protected in the enjoyment of their commercial rights. These stipulations have been repeatedly violated, and it cannot be expected that the Northern States should be willing to bear their proportion of the burdens of the Federal Government, without enjoying the benefits stipulated.

If our fellow citizens should concur with us in opinion, we would suggest, whether it would not be expedient for the people in Town Meetings to address memorials to the General Court at their present Session, petitioning that honorable body to propose a convention of all the Northern and Commercial States by Delegates to be appointed by their respective Legislatures, to consult upon measures in concert, for procuring such alterations in the Federal Constitution as will give to the Northern States a due proportion of representation, and secure them from the future exercise of powers injurious to their commercial interests;—Or if the General Court shall see fit, that they would pursue such other course, as they, in their wisdom, shall deem best calculated to effect the objects.

The measure is of such magnitude that we apprehend a concert of States will be useful and even necessary to procure the amendments proposed; and should the people of the several towns concur in this opinion, it would be expedient to act on the subject without delay.

We request you, Sir, to consult with your friends on the subject, and if it should be thought advisable, to lay this communication before the people of your town.

In behalf and by direction of the Gentlemen assembled,

JOSEPH LYMAN, *Chairman*

15. Judicial Sanction of Implied Powers: The Decision in McCulloch v. Maryland, 1819

The case of McCulloch v. Maryland resulted from the attempt of Maryland to tax the Baltimore branch of the second Bank of the United States. When the bank refused to pay, the cashier, James W. McCulloch, was sued by the state. In the determination of the case, the Supreme Court decided two major questions: the constitutionality of the act of Congress establishing the bank, and the constitutionality of the tax imposed by Maryland. Even more important than the determination of these two key points at issue was the detailed exposition of the Constitution which Marshall, delivering the opinion for a unanimous court, wrote into the decision. In what was one of Marshall's most far-reaching decisions, the doctrine of implied powers was given judicial approval. In upholding the constitutionality of the bank, Marshall used arguments, and indeed wording, very similar to those used by Hamilton in his opinion written for Washington in 1791. Marshall, a Federalist who had had access to Washington's papers in writing his biography of the first president, was a strong admirer of Hamilton, as his biography of Washington shows. In upholding a loose construction of the necessary and proper clause and denying the power of any state to tax or in any manner impede the operations of constitutional laws enacted by Congress, the decision struck a major blow at the doctrines of state rights. The text of the decision, 4 Wheaton 316 (1819), is reprinted from B. R. Curtis (ed.), Reports of Decisions in the Supreme Court of the United States (6th edn., Boston, 1881), IV, 415–439.

MARSHALL, C. J., delivered the opinion of the court . . .

The first question made in the cause is, has Congress power to incorporate a bank?

It has been truly said, that this can scarcely be considered as an open question, entirely unprejudiced by the former proceedings of the nation respecting it. The principle now contested was introduced at a very early period of our history, has been recognized by many successive legislatures, and has been acted upon by the judicial department, in cases of peculiar delicacy, as a law of undoubted obligation. . . .

In discussing this question, the counsel for the State of Maryland have deemed it of some importance, in the construction of the constitution, to consider that instrument not as emanating from the people, but as the act of sovereign and independent States. The powers of the general government, it has been said, are delegated by the States, who alone are truly sovereign; and must be exercised in subordination to the States, who alone possess supreme dominion.

It would be difficult to sustain this proposition. The convention which framed the constitution was, indeed, elected by the State legislatures. But the instrument, when it came from their hands, was a mere proposal, without obligation, or pretensions to it. It was reported to the then existing congress of the United States, with a request that it might "be submitted to a convention of delegates, chosen in each State, by the people thereof, under the recommendation of its legislature, for their assent and ratification." This mode of proceeding was adopted; and by the convention, by congress, and by the State legislatures, the instrument was submitted to the people. They acted upon it, in the only manner in which they can act safely, effectively, and wisely, on such a subject, by assembling in convention. It is true, they assembled in their several States; and where else should they have assembled? No political dreamer was ever wild enough to think of breaking down the lines which separate the States, and of compounding the American people into one common mass. Of consequence, when they act, they act in their States. But the measures they adopt do not, on that account, cease to be the measures of the people themselves, or become the measures of the State governments.

From these conventions the constitution derives its whole authority. The government proceeds directly from the people; is "ordained and established" in the name of the people; and is declared to be ordained, "in order to form a more perfect union, establish justice, insure domestic tranquillity, and secure the blessings of liberty to themselves and to their posterity." The assent of the States, in their sovereign capacity, is implied in calling a convention, and thus submitting that instrument to the people. But the people were at perfect liberty to accept or reject it; and their act was final. It required not the affirmance, and could not be negatived, by the State governments. The constitution, when thus adopted, was of complete obligation, and bound the State sovereignties. . . .

The government of the Union, then, (whatever may be the influence of this fact on the case), is, emphatically and truly, a government of the people. In form and in substance it emanates from them. Its powers are granted by them, and are to be exercised directly on them, and for their benefit.

This government is acknowledged by all to be one of enumerated powers. The principle, that it can exercise only the powers granted to it, would seem too apparent to have required to be enforced by all those arguments which its enlightened friends, while it was depending before the people, found it necessary to urge. That principle is now universally admitted. But the question respecting the extent of the powers actually granted, is perpetually arising, and will probably continue to arise, as long as our system shall exist.

In discussing these questions, the conflicting powers of the general and State governments must be brought into view, and the supremacy of their respective laws, when they are in opposition, must be settled.

If any one proposition could command the universal assent of mankind, we might expect it would be this: that the government of the Union, though limited in its powers, is supreme within its sphere of action. This would seem to result necessarily from its nature. It is the government of all; its powers are delegated by all; it represents all, and acts for all. Though any one State may be willing to control its operations, no State is willing to allow others to control them. The nation, on those subjects on which it can act, must necessarily bind its component parts. But this question is not left to mere reason: the people have, in express terms, decided it, by saying, "this constitution, and the laws of the United States, which shall be made in pursuance thereof," "shall be the supreme law of the land," and by requiring that the members of the State legislatures, and the officers of the executive and judicial departments of the States, shall take the oath of fidelity to it.

The government of the United States, then, though limited in its powers, is supreme; and its laws, when made in pursuance of the constitution, form the supreme law of the land, "any thing in the constitution or laws of any State, to the contrary, notwithstanding."

Among the enumerated powers, we do not find that of establishing a bank or creating a corporation. But there is no phrase in the instrument which, like the articles of confederation, excludes incidental or implied powers; and which requires that everything granted shall be expressly and minutely described. Even the 10th amendment, which was framed for the purpose of quieting the excessive jealousies which had been excited, omits the word "expressly," and declares only that the powers "not delegated to the United States, nor prohibited to the States, are reserved to the States or to the people;" thus leaving the question, whether the particular power which may become the subject of contest, has been delegated to the one government, or prohibited to the other, to depend on a fair construction of the whole instrument. The men who drew and adopted this amendment, had experienced the embarrassments resulting from the insertion of this word in the articles of confederation, and probably omitted it to avoid those embarrassments. A constitution, to contain an accurate detail of all the subdivisions of which its great powers will admit, and of all the means by which they may be carried into execution, would partake of the prolixity of a legal code, and could scarcely be embraced by the human mind. It would probably never be understood by the public. Its nature, therefore, requires that only its great outlines should be marked, its important objects designated, and the minor ingredients which compose those objects be deduced from the nature of the objects themselves. That this idea was entertained by the framers of the American constitution, is not only to be inferred from the nature of the instrument, but from the language. Why else were some of the limitations, found in the 9th section of the 1st article, introduced? It is also, in some degree, warranted by their having omitted to use any restrictive term which might prevent its receiving a fair and just interpretation. In considering this question, then, we must never forget, that it is a constitution we are expounding.

Although, among the enumerated powers of government, we do not find the word "bank," or "incorporation," we find the great powers to lay and collect taxes; to borrow money; to regulate commerce; to declare and conduct a war, and to raise and support armies and navies. The sword and the purse, all the external relations, and no inconsiderable portion of the industry of the nation, are intrusted to its government. It can never be pretended that these vast powers draw after them others of inferior importance, merely because they are inferior. Such an idea can never be advanced. But it may, with great reason, be contended, that a government, intrusted with such ample powers, on the due execution of which the happiness and prosperity of the nation so vitally depends, must also be intrusted with ample means for their execution. The power being given, it is the interest of the nation to facilitate its execution. It can never be their interest, and cannot be presumed to have been their intention, to clog and embarrass its execution by withholding the most appropriate means. . . .

The government which has a right to do an act, and has imposed on it the duty of performing that act, must, according to the dictates of reason, be allowed to select the means; and those who contend that it may not select any appropriate means, that one particular mode of effecting the object is expected, take upon themselves the burden of establishing that exception.

The creation of a corporation, it is said, appertains to sovereignty. This is admitted. But to what portion of sovereignty does it appertain? Does it belong to one more than to another? In America, the powers of sovereignty are divided between the government of the Union, and those of the States. They are each sovereign, with respect to the objects committed to it, and neither sovereign with respect to the objects committed to the other. We cannot comprehend that train of reasoning which would maintain, that the extent of power granted by the people is to be ascertained, not by the nature and terms of the grant, but by its date. Some state constitutions were formed before, some since that of the United States. We cannot believe that their relation to each other is in any degree dependent upon this circumstance. Their respective powers must, we think, be precisely the same as if they had been formed at the same time. Had they been formed at the same time, and had the people conferred on the general government the power contained in the constitution, and on the States the whole residuum of power, would it have been asserted that the government of the Union was not sovereign with respect to those objects which were intrusted to it, in relation to which its laws were declared to be supreme? If this could not have been asserted, we cannot well comprehend the process of reasoning which maintains, that a power appertaining to sovereignty cannot be connected with that vast portion of it which is granted to the general government, so far as it is calculated to subserve the legitimate objects of that government. The power of creating a corporation, though appertaining to sovereignty, is not, like the power of making war, or levying taxes, or of regulating commerce, a great substantive and independent power, which cannot be implied as incidental to other powers, or used as a means of executing them. It is never the end for which other powers are exercised, but a means by which other objects are accomplished. No contributions are made to charity for the sake of an incorporation, but a corporation is created to administer the charity; no seminary of learning is instituted in order to be incorporated, but the corporate character is conferred to subserve the purposes of education. No city was ever built with the sole object of being incorporated, but is incorporated as affording the best means of being well governed. The power of creating a corporation is never used for its own sake, but for the purpose of effecting something else. No sufficient reason is, therefore, perceived, why it may not pass as incidental to those powers which are expressly given, if it be a direct mode of executing them.

But the constitution of the United States has not left the right of congress to employ the necessary means, for the execution of the powers conferred on the government, to general reasoning. To its enumeration of powers is added that of making "all laws which shall be necessary and proper, for carrying into execution the foregoing powers, and all other powers vested by this constitution, in the government of the United States, or in any department thereof."

The counsel for the State of Maryland have urged various arguments, to prove that this clause, though in terms a grant of power, is not so in effect; but is really restrictive of the general right, which might otherwise be implied, of selecting means of executing the enumerated powers. . . .

But the argument on which most reliance is placed, is drawn from the peculiar language of this clause. Congress is not empowered by it to make all laws, which may have relation to the powers conferred on the government, but such only as may be "necessary and proper" for carrying them into execution. The word "necessary" is considered as controlling the whole sentence, and as limiting the right to pass laws for the execution of the granted powers, to such as are indispensable, and without which the power would be nugatory. That it excludes the choice of means, and leaves to congress, in each case, that only which is most direct and simple.

Is it true, that this is the sense in which the word "necessary" is always used? Does it always import an absolute physical necessity, so strong, that one thing, to which another may be termed necessary cannot exist without that other? We think it does not. If reference be had to its use, in the common affairs of the world, or in approved authors, we find that it frequently imports no more than that one thing is convenient, or useful, or essential to another. To employ the means necessary to an end, is generally understood as employing any means calculated to produce the end, and not as being confined to those single means, without which the end would be entirely unattainable. Such is the character of human language, that no word conveys to the mind, in all situations, one single definite idea; and nothing is more common than to use words in a figurative sense. Almost all compositions contain words, which, taken in their rigorous sense, would convey a meaning different from that which is obviously intended. It is essential to just construction, that many words which import something excessive, should be understood in a more mitigated sense—in that sense which common usage justifies. The word "necessary" is of this description. It has not a fixed character peculiar to itself. It admits of all degrees of comparison; and is often connected with other words, which increase or diminish the impression the mind receives of the urgency it imports. A thing may be necessary, very necessary, absolutely or indispensably necessary. To no mind would the same idea be conveyed, by these several phrases. . . . This word, then, like others, is used in various senses; and, in its construction, the subject, the context, the intention of the person using them, are all to be taken into view.

Let this be done in the case under consideration. The subject is the execution of those great powers on which the welfare of a nation essentially depends. It must have been the intention of those who gave these powers, to insure, as far as human prudence could insure, their beneficial execution. This could not be done by confiding the choice of means to such narrow limits as not to leave it in the power of congress to adopt any which might be appropriate, and which were conducive to the end. This provision is made in a constitution intended to endure for ages to come, and, consequently, to be adapted to the various crises of human affairs. To have prescribed the means by which government should, in all future time, execute its powers, would have been to change, entirely, the character of the instrument, and give it the properties of a legal code. It would have been an unwise attempt to provide, by immutable rules, for exigencies which, if foreseen at all, must have been seen dimly, and which can be best provided for as they occur. To have declared that the best means shall not be used, but those alone without which the power given would be nugatory, would have been to deprive the legislature of the capacity to avail itself of experience, to exercise its reason, and to accommodate its legislation to circumstances. . . .

The result of the most careful and attentive consideration bestowed upon this clause is, that if it does not enlarge, it cannot be construed to restrain the powers of congress, or to impair the right of the legislature to exercise its best judgment in the selection of measures, to carry into execution the constitutional powers of the government. If no other motive for its insertion can be suggested, a sufficient one is found in the desire to remove all doubts respecting the right to legislate on that vast mass of incidental powers which must be involved in the constitution, if that instrument be not a splendid bauble.

We admit, as all must admit, that the powers of the government are limited, and that its limits are not to be transcended. But we think the sound construction of the constitution must allow to the national legislature that discretion, with respect to the means by which the powers it confers are to be carried into execution, which will enable that body to perform the high duties assigned to it, in the manner most beneficial to the people. Let the end be legitimate, let it be within the scope of the constitution, and all means which are appropriate, which are plainly adapted to that end, which are not prohibited, but consist with the letter and spirit of the constitution, are constitutional. . . .

If a corporation may be employed indiscriminately with other means to carry into execution the powers of the government, no particular reason can be assigned for excluding the use of a bank, if required for its fiscal operations. To use one, must be within the discretion of congress, if it be an appropriate mode of executing the powers of government. That it is a convenient, a useful, and essential instrument in the prosecution of its fiscal operations, is not now a subject of controversy. . . .

But were its necessity less apparent, none can deny its being an appropriate measure; and if it is, the degree of its necessity as has been very justly observed, is to be discussed in another place. Should congress, in the execution of its powers, adopt measures which are prohibited by the constitution; or should congress, under the pretext of executing its powers, pass laws for the accomplishment of objects not intrusted to the government, it would become the painful duty of this tribunal, should a case requiring such a decision come before it, to say that such an act was not the law of the land. But where the law is not prohibited, and is really calculated to effect any of the objects intrusted to the government, to undertake here to inquire into the degree of its necessity, would be to pass the line which circumscribes the judicial department, and to tread on legislative ground. This court disclaims all pretensions to such a power. . . .

After the most deliberate consideration, it is the unanimous and decided opinion of this court, that the act to incorporate the Bank of the United States is a law made in pursuance of the constitution, and is a part of the supreme law of the land. . . .

It being the opinion of the Court, that the act incorporating the bank is constitutional; and that the power of establishing a branch in the State of Maryland might be properly exercised by the bank itself, we proceed to inquire:—

2. Whether the State of Maryland may, without violating the constitution, tax that branch?

That the power of taxation is one of vital importance; that it is retained by the States; that it is not abridged by the grant of a similar power to the government of the Union; that it is to be concurrently exercised by the two governments; are truths which have never been denied. But, such is the paramount character of the constitution, that its capacity to withdraw any subject from the action of even this power, is admitted. The States are expressly forbidden to lay any duties on imports or exports, except what may be absolutely necessary for executing their inspection laws. If the obligation of this prohibition must be conceded—if it may restrain a State from the exercise of its taxing power on imports and exports, the same paramount character would seem to restrain, as it certainly may restrain, a State from such other exercise of this power, as is in its nature incompatible with, and repugnant to, the constitutional laws of the Union. A law, absolutely repugnant to another, as entirely repeals that other as if express terms of repeal were used.

On this ground the counsel for the bank place its claim to be exempted from the power of a State to tax its operations. There is no express provision for the case; but the claim has been sustained on a principle which so entirely pervades the constitution, is so intermixed with the materials which compose it, so interwoven with its web, so blended with its texture, as to be incapable of being separated from it, without rending it into shreds.

This great principle is, that the constitution and the laws made in pursuance thereof are supreme; that they control the constitution and laws of the respective States, and cannot be controlled by them. From this, which may be almost termed an axiom, other propositions are deduced as corollaries, on the truth or error of which, and on their application to this case, the cause has been supposed to depend. These are, 1. That a power to create implies a power to preserve. 2. That a power to destroy, if wielded by a different hand, is hostile to, and incompatible with, these powers to create and preserve. 3. That where this repugnancy exists, that authority which is supreme must control, not yield to that over which it is supreme. . . .

The power of congress to create, and of course to continue, the bank, was the subject of the preceding part of this opinion; and is no longer to be considered as questionable.

That the power of taxing it by the States may be exercised so as to destroy it, is too obvious to be denied. But taxation is said to be an absolute power, which acknowledges no other limits than those expressly prescribed in the constitution, and like sovereign power of every other description, is trusted to the discretion of those who use it. . . .

The argument on the part of the State of Maryland, is, not that the states may directly resist a law of congress, but that they may exercise their acknowledged powers upon it, and that the constitution leaves them this right in the confidence that they will not abuse it. . . .

That the power to tax involves the power to destroy; that the power to destroy may defeat and render useless the power to create; that there is a plain repugnance, in conferring on one government a power to control the constitutional measures of another, which other, with respect to those very measures, is declared to be supreme over that which exerts the control, are propositions not to be denied. But all inconsistencies are to be reconciled by the magic of the word confidence. Taxation, it is said, does not necessarily and unavoidably destroy. To carry it to the excess of destruction would be an abuse, to presume which, would banish that confidence which is essential to all government.

But is this a case of confidence? Would the people of any one State trust those of another with a power to control the most insignificant operations of their state government? We know they would not. Why, then, should we suppose that the people of any one State should be willing to trust those of another with a power to control the operations of a government to which they have confided their most important and most valuable interests? In the legislature of the Union alone, are all represented. The legislature of the Union alone, therefore, can be trusted by the people with the power of controlling measures which concern all, in the confidence that it will not be abused. This, then, is not a case of confidence, and we must consider it as it really is.

If we apply the principle for which the State of Maryland contends, to the constitution generally, we shall find it capable of changing totally the character of that instrument. We shall find it capable of arresting all the measures of the government, and of prostrating it at the foot of the States. The American people have declared their constitution, and the laws made in pursuance thereof, to be supreme; but this principle would transfer the supremacy, in fact, to the States.

If the States may tax one instrument, employed by the government in the execution of its powers, they may tax any and every other instrument. They may tax the mail; they may tax the mint; they may tax patent rights; they may tax the papers of the customhouse; they may tax judicial process; they may tax all the means employed by the government, to an excess which would defeat all the ends of government. This was not intended by the American people. They did not design to make their government dependent on the States. . . .

. . . The question is, in truth, a question of supremacy; and if the right of the States to tax the means employed by the general government be conceded, the declaration that the constitution, and the laws made in pursuance thereof, shall be the supreme law of the land, is empty and unmeaning declamation. . . .

It has also been insisted, that, as the power of taxation in the general and state governments is acknowledged to be concurrent, every argument which would sustain the right of the general government to tax banks chartered by the States, will equally sustain the right of the States to tax banks chartered by the general government.

But the two cases are not on the same reason. The people of all the States have created the general government, and have conferred upon it the general power of taxation. The people of all the States, and the State themselves, are represented in congress, and, by their representatives, exercise this power. When they tax the chartered institutions of the States, they tax their constituents; and these taxes must be uniform. But when a State taxes the operations of the government of the United States, it acts upon institutions created, not by their own constituents, but by people over whom they claim no control. It acts upon the measures of a government created by others as well as themselves, for the benefit of others in common with themselves. The difference is that which always exists, and always must exist, between the action of the whole on a part, and the action of a part of the whole—between the laws of a government declared to be supreme, and those of a government which, when in opposition to those laws, is not supreme. . . .

The Court has bestowed on this subject its most deliberate consideration. The result is a conviction that the States have no power, by taxation or otherwise, to retard, impede, burden, or in any manner control, the operations of the constitutional laws enacted by congress to carry into execution the powers vested in the general government. This is, we think, the unavoidable consequence of that supremacy which the constitution has declared.

We are unanimously of opinion, that the law passed by the legislature of Maryland, imposing a tax on the Bank of the United States, is unconstitutional and void. . . .

16. The Survival of State-Rights Doctrine: The South Carolina Exposition, 1828

Although John C. Calhoun as a young Republican after the War of 1812 had supported a protective tariff, internal improvements, and other nationalistic measures, by the mid-1820's he was following the changing sentiment of his native South Carolina and standing against protective tariffs. In 1827 Vice President Calhoun cast the deciding vote in the Senate against the tariff bill to grant additional protection. In response to the so-called "Tariff of Abominations" passed by Congress in 1828, Calhoun wrote the South Carolina Exposition, which though not adopted by the state legislature was published in February, 1829, by order of the lower house of the Assembly and thus had the appearance of authority. Calhoun's authorship was not publicly known at that time. More important than the protest against the tariff were the arguments of constitutional interpretation advanced by the document. In a detailed treatise on the Constitution, Calhoun restated the doctrines of state rights and argued the case for the right of a state to interpose its authority to block the execution of federal laws deemed unconstitutional; he also outlined the process by which nullification could be carried out. The close thought to the problems of interpreting the Constitution and determining the nature of the federal union displayed by Calhoun make the South Carolina Exposition a major document in American constitutional history. This excerpt is from Richard K. Crallé (ed.), The Works of John C. Calhoun (6 vols., New York, 1888), VI, 36–51.

. . . Our system, then, consists of two distinct and independent Governments. The general powers, expressly delegated to the General Government, are subject to its sole and separate control; and the States cannot, without violating the constitutional compact, interpose their authority to check, or in any manner to counteract its movements, so long as they are confined to the proper sphere. So, also, the peculiar and local powers reserved to the States are subject to their exclusive control; nor can the General Government interfere, in any manner, with them, without violating the Constitution.

In order to have a full and clear conception of our institutions, it will be proper to remark that there is, in our system, a striking distinction between Government and Sovereignty. The separate governments of the several States are vested in their Legislative, Executive, and Judicial Departments; while the sovereignty resides in the people of the States respectively. The powers of the General Government are also vested in its Legislative, Executive, and Judicial Departments, while the sovereignty resides in the people of the several States who created it. But, by an express provision of the Constitution, it may be amended or changed by three fourths of the States; and thus each State, by assenting to the Constitution with this provision, has modified its original right as a sovereign, of making its individual consent necessary to any change in its political condition; and, by becoming a member of the Union, has placed this important power in the hands of three fourths of the States,—in whom the highest power known to the Constitution actually resides. Not the least portion of this high sovereign authority resides in Congress, or any of the departments of the General Government. They are but the creatures of the Constitution, and are appointed but to execute its provisions; and, therefore, any attempt by all, or any of these departments, to exercise any power which, in its consequences, may alter the nature of the instrument, or change the condition of the parties to it, would be an act of usurpation.

It is thus that our political system, resting on the great principle involved in the recognized diversity of geographical interests in the community, has, in theory, with admirable sagacity, provided the most efficient check against their dangers. Looking to facts, the Constitution has formed the States into a community only to the extent of their common interests; leaving them distinct and independent communities as to all other interests, and drawing the line of separation with consummate skill, as before stated. It is manifest that, so long as this beautiful theory is adhered to in practice, the system, like the atmosphere, will press equally on all the parts. But reason and experience teach us that theory of itself, however excellent, is nugatory, unless there be means of efficiently enforcing it in practice;—which brings under consideration the highly important question—What means are provided by the system for enforcing this fundamental provision?

If we look to the history and practical operation of the system, we shall find, on the side of the States, no means resorted to in order to protect their reserved rights against the encroachments of the General Government; while the latter has, from the beginning, adopted the most efficient to prevent the States from encroaching on those delegated to them. The 25th section of the Judiciary Act, passed in 1789,—immediately after the Constitution went into operation,—provides for an appeal from the State courts to the Supreme Court of the United States in all cases, in the decision of which, the construction of the Constitution,—the laws of Congress, or treaties of the United States may be involved; thus giving to that high tribunal the right of final interpretation, and the power, in reality, of nullifying the acts of the State Legislatures whenever, in their opinion, they may conflict with the powers delegated to the General Government. A more ample and complete protection against the encroachments of the governments of the several States cannot be imagined; and to this extent the power may be considered as indispensable and constitutional. But, by a strange misconception of the nature of our system,—and, in fact, of the nature of government,—it has been regarded as the ultimate power, not only of protecting the General Government against the encroachments of the governments of the States, but also of the encroachments of the former on the latter;—and as being, in fact, the only means provided by the Constitution of confining all the powers of the system to their proper constitutional spheres; and, consequently, of determining the limits assigned to each. Such a construction of its powers would, in fact, raise one of the departments of the General Government above the parties who created the constitutional compact, and virtually invest it with the authority to alter, at its pleasure, the relative powers of the General and State Governments, on the distribution of which, as established by the Constitution, our whole system rests;—and which, by an express provision of the instrument, can only be altered by three fourths of the States, as has already been shown. It would go farther. Fairly considered, it would, in effect, divest the people of the States of the sovereign authority, and clothe that department with the robe of supreme power. A position more false and fatal cannot be conceived. . . .

If it be conceded, as it must be by every one who is the least conversant with our institutions, that the sovereign powers delegated are divided between the General and State Governments, and that the latter hold their portion by the same tenure as the former, it would seem impossible to deny to the States the right of deciding on the infractions of their powers, and the proper remedy to be applied for their correction. The right of judging, in such cases, is an essential attribute of sovereignty,—of which the States cannot be divested without losing their sovereignty itself,—and being reduced to a subordinate corporate condition. In fact, to divide power, and to give to one of the parties the exclusive right of judging of the portion allotted to each, is, in reality, not to divide it at all; and to reserve such exclusive right to the General Government (it matters not by what department to be exercised), is to convert it, in fact, into a great consolidated government, with unlimited powers, and to divest the States, in reality, of all their rights. It is impossible to understand the force of terms, and to deny so plain a conclusion. The opposite opinion can be embraced only on hasty and imperfect views of the relation existing between the States and the General Government. But the existence of the right of judging of their powers, so clearly established from the sovereignty of the States, as clearly implies a veto or control, within its limits, on the action of the General Government, on contested points of authority; and this very control is the remedy which the Constitution has provided to prevent the encroachments of the General Government on the reserved rights of the States; and by which the distribution of power, between the General and State Governments, may be preserved for ever inviolable, on the basis established by the Constitution. It is thus effectual protection is afforded to the minority, against the oppression of the majority. Nor does this important conclusion stand on the deduction of reason alone. It is sustained by the highest contemporary authority. Mr. Hamilton, in the number of the Federalist already cited, remarks that,—"in a single republic, all the power surrendered by the people is submitted to the administration of a single government; and usurpations are guarded against, by a division of the government into distinct and separate departments. In the compound republic of America, the power surrendered by the people is first divided between two distinct governments, and then the portion allotted to each subdivided among distinct and separate departments. Hence a double security arises to the rights of the people. The different governments will control each other; at the same time that each will be controlled by itself." He thus clearly affirms the control of the States over the General Government, which he traces to the division in the exercise of the sovereign powers under our political system; and by comparing this control to the veto, which the departments in most of our constitutions respectively exercise over the acts of each other, clearly indicates it as his opinion, that the control between the General and State Governments is of the same character. Mr. Madison is still more explicit. In his report, already alluded to, in speaking on this subject, he remarks;—"The resolutions, having taken this view of the Federal compact, proceed to infer that, in cases of a deliberate, palpable, and dangerous exercise of other powers, not granted by the said compact, the States, who are parties thereto, have the right, and are in duty bound to interpose to arrest the evil, and for maintaining, within their respective limits, the authorities, rights, and liberties appertaining to them. It appears to your committee to be a plain principle, founded in common sense, illustrated by common practice, and essential to the nature of compacts, that where resort can be had to no tribunal superior to the rights of the parties, the parties themselves must be the rightful judges, in the last resort, whether the bargain made has been pursued or violated. The Constitution of the United States was formed by the sanction of the States, given by each in its sovereign capacity. It adds to the stability and dignity, as well as to the authority of the Constitution, that it rests on this solid foundation. The States, then, being parties to the constitutional compact, and in their sovereign capacity, it follows of necessity that there can be no tribunal above their authority to decide, in the last resort, whether the compact made by them be violated; and, consequently, as parties to it, they must themselves decide, in the last resort, such questions as may be of sufficient magnitude to require their interposition." To these the no less explicit opinions of Mr. Jefferson may be added; who, in the Kentucky resolutions on the same subject, which have always been attributed to him, states that—"The Government, created by this compact, was not made the exclusive or final judge of the extent of the powers delegated to itself; since that would have made its discretion, and not the Constitution, the measure of its powers;—but, as in all other cases of compact between parties having no common judge, each party has an equal right to judge for itself, as well of infractions as of the mode and measure of redress."

To these authorities, which so explicitly affirm the right of the States, in their sovereign capacity, to decide, in the last resort, on the infraction of their rights and the remedy, there may be added the solemn decisions of the Legislatures of two leading States— Virginia and Kentucky—that the power in question rightfully belongs to the States,—and the implied sanction which a majority of the States gave, in the important political revolution which shortly followed, and brought Mr. Jefferson into power. It is scarcely possible to add to the weight of authority by which this fundamental principle in our system is sustained. . . .

The committee, having thus established the constitutional right of the States to interpose, in order to protect their reserved powers, it cannot be necessary to bestow much time or attention, in order to meet possible objections;—particularly as they must be raised, not against the soundness of the arguments, by which the position is sustained, and which they deem unanswerable,—but against apprehended consequences, which, even if well founded, would be an objection, not so much to the conclusions of the committee, as to the Constitution itself. They are persuaded that, whatever objection may be suggested, it will be found, on investigation, to be destitute of solidity. Under these impressions, the committee propose to discuss such as they suppose may be urged, with all possible brevity.

It may be objected, then,— in the first place, that the right of the States to interpose rests on mere inference, without any express provision in the Constitution; and that it is not to be supposed—if the Constitution contemplated the exercise of powers of such high importance—that it would have been left to inference alone. In answer, the committee would ask, whether the power of the Supreme Court to declare a law unconstitutional is not among the very highest and most important that can be exercised by any department of the Government,—and if any express provision can be found to justify its exercise? Like the power in question, it also rests on mere inference;—but an inference so clear, that no express provision could render it more certain. The simple fact, that the Judges must decide according to law, and that the Constitution is paramount to the acts of Congress, imposes a necessity on the court to declare the latter void whenever, in its opinion, they come in conflict, in any particular case, with the former. So, also, in the question under consideration. The right of the States, —even supposing it to rest on inference, stands on clearer and stronger grounds than that of the Court. In the distribution of powers between the General and State Governments, the Constitution professes to enumerate those assigned to the former, in whatever department they may be vested; while the powers of the latter are reserved in general terms, without attempt at enumeration. It may, therefore, constitute a presumption against the former,—that the Court has no right to declare a law unconstitutional, because the power is not enumerated among those belonging to the Judiciary;—while the omission to enumerate the power of the States to interpose in order to protect their rights,—being strictly in accord with the principles on which its framers formed the Constitution, raises not the slightest presumption against its existence. Like all other reserved rights, it is to be inferred from the simple fact that it is not delegated,—as is clearly the case in this instance.

Again—it may be objected to the power, that it is inconsistent with the necessary authority of the General Government,—and, in its consequences, must lead to feebleness, anarchy, and finally disunion.

... it is, indeed, strange that any intelligent citizen should consider limitations on the authority of government incompatible with its nature;—or should fear danger from any check properly lodged, which may be necessary to guard against usurpation or abuse, and protect the great and distinct interests of the country. That there are such interests represented by the States, and that the States are the only competent powers to protect them, has been sufficiently established; and it only remains, in order to meet the objection, to prove that, for this purpose, the States may be safely vested with the right of interposition.

If the committee do not greatly mistake, the checking or veto power never has, in any country, or under any institutions, been lodged where it was less liable to abuse. The great number, by whom it must be exercised, of the people of a State,—the solemnity of the mode,—a Convention specially called for the purpose, and representing the State in her highest capacity,—the delay,—the deliberation,—are all calculated to allay excitement,—to impress on the people a deep and solemn tone, highly favorable to calm investigation and decision. Under such circumstances, it would be impossible for a mere party to maintain itself in the State, unless the violation of its rights be palpable, deliberate, and dangerous. The attitude in which the State would be placed in relation to the other States,—the force of public opinion which would be brought to bear on her,—the deep reverence for the General Government,—the strong influence of all public men who aspire to office or distinction in the Union,—and, above all, the local parties which must ever exist in the State, and which, in this case, must ever throw the powerful influence of the minority on the side of the General Government,—constitute impediments to the exercise of this high protective right of the State, which must render it safe. So powerful, in fact, are these difficulties, that nothing but truth and a deep sense of oppression on the part of the people of the State, will ever sustain the exercise of the power;—and if it should be attempted under other circumstances, it must speedily terminate in the expulsion of those in power, to be replaced by others who would make a merit of closing the controversy, by yielding the point in dispute.

But, in order to understand more fully what its operation really would be in practice, we must take into the estimate the effect which a recognition of the power would have on the tone of feeling, both of the General and State Governments. On the part of the former, it would necessarily produce, in the exercise of doubtful powers, the most marked moderation. In the discussion of measures involving such powers, the argument would be felt with decisive weight, that the State, also, had the right of judging of the constitutionality of the power; which would cause an abandonment of the measure,—or, at least, lead to such modifications as would make it acceptable. On the part of the State, a feeling of conscious security, depending on herself,—with the effect of moderation and kindness on the part of the General Government, would effectually put down jealousy, hatred, and animosity,—and thus give scope to the natural attachment to our institutions, to expand and grow into the full maturity of patriotism. But withhold this protective power from the State, and the reverse of all these happy consequences must follow;—which the committee will not undertake to describe, as the living example of discord, hatred, and jealousy,—threatening anarchy and dissolution, must impress on every beholder a more vivid picture than any they could possibly draw. The continuance of this unhappy state must lead to the loss of all affection;—when the Government must be sustained by force instead of *patriotism*. In fact, to him who will duly reflect, it must be apparent that, where there are important separate interests, there is no alternative but a veto to protect them, or the military to enforce the claims of the majority interests.

If these deductions be correct,—as can scarcely be doubted,— under that state of moderation and security, followed by mutual kindness, which must accompany the acknowledgment of the right, the necessity of exercising the veto would rarely exist, and the possibility of its abuse, on the part of the State, would be almost wholly removed. Its acknowledged existence would thus supersede its exercise. But suppose in this the committee should be mistaken, —still there exists a sufficient security. As high as this right of interposition on the part of a State may be regarded in relation to the General Government, the constitutional compact provides a remedy against its abuse. There is a higher power,—placed above all by the consent of all,—the creating and preserving power of the system,—to be exercised by three fourths of the States,—and which, under the character of the amending power, can modify the whole system at pleasure,—and to the acts of which none can object. Admit, then, the power in question to belong to the States,—and admit its liability to abuse,—and what are the utmost consequences, but to create a presumption against the constitutionality of the power exercised by the General Government,—which, if it be well founded, must compel them to abandon it;—or, if not, to remove the difficulty by obtaining the contested power in the form of an amendment to the Constitution. If, on an appeal for this purpose, the decision be favorable to the General Government, a disputed power will be converted into an expressly granted power;—but, on the other hand, if it be adverse, the refusal to grant will be tantamount to an inhibition of its exercise: and thus, in either case, the controversy will be determined. And ought not a sovereign State, as a party to the constitutional compact, and as the guardian of her citizens and her peculiar interests, to have the power in question? Without it, the amending power must become obsolete, and the Constitution, through the exercise of construction, in the end utterly subverted. Let us examine the case. The disease is, that a majority of the States, through the General Government, by construction, usurp powers not delegated, and by their exercise, increase their wealth and authority at the expense of the minority. How absurd, then, to expect the injured States to attempt a remedy by proposing an amendment to be ratified by three fourths of the States, when, by supposition, there is a majority opposed to them? Nor would it be less absurd to expect the General Government to propose amendments, unless compelled to that course by the acts of a State. The Government can have no inducement. It has a more summary mode,—the assumption of power by construction. The consequence is clear;—neither would resort to the amending power;—the one, because it would be useless,—and the other, because it could effect its purpose without it;—and thus the highest power known to the Constitution,—on the salutary influence of which, on the operations of our political institutions, so much was calculated, would become, in practice, obsolete, as stated; and in lieu of it, the will of the majority, under the agency of construction, would be substituted, with unlimited and supreme power. On the contrary, giving the right to a State to compel the General Government to abandon its pretensions to a constructive power, or to obtain a positive grant of it, by an amendment to the Constitution, would call efficiently into action, on all important disputed questions, this highest power of the system,—to whose controlling authority no one can object, and under whose operation all controversies between the States and General Government would be adjusted, and the Constitution gradually acquire all the perfection of which it is susceptible. It is thus that the *creating* becomes the *preserving* power; and we may rest assured it is no less true in politics than in theology, that the power which creates can alone preserve,—and that preservation is perpetual creation. Such will be the operation and effect of State interposition. . . . .

IV

Shaping National Economic Policy

Since many of the problems in establishing the new government related in some way to economic considerations, the documents in earlier sections have illustrated a number of the problems involved in working out the young nation's economic policies. The assumption of state debts, the chartering of a national bank, the national debt, taxes, governmental expenditures—these and other matters were at the center of political controversy. The determination of national economic policy was always related to political and constitutional considerations, to local, state, and regional differences, and to world conditions, especially those of war or peace. During two key periods of the early republic, the office of Secretary of the Treasury was held by men who were able to think in broad terms, to look ahead to the future, and to formulate their recommendations with long-term goals in view. In the first crucial years of Washington's presidency, Alexander Hamilton as Secretary of the Treasury from 1789 to 1795 provided the president and the Congress with a steady stream of broad ideas and specific proposals. In the years immediately following the first party changeover in the administration of the national government in 1801, Albert Gallatin as Secretary of the Treasury—throughout the entire eight years of Jefferson's presidency and for five years under Madison—demonstrated a broad understanding of economic problems and a capacity for long-range planning. Both Hamilton and Gallatin were intimately involved in partisan politics; neither was removed from the pressures of his immediate circumstances. Yet in the state papers they prepared can be seen the immense capacity of each man to relate the solution of the immediate problems of his day to the future development of the nation. The documents grouped in this section illustrate the scope and character of major proposals for guiding the direction of the nation's economy, as well as something of the nature of the arguments in the broad debate over national economic policy. They also suggest that the nation as a whole moved cautiously behind the recommendations of its most advanced economic planners and that the issues raised by Hamilton and Gallatin, and later by Henry Clay and John C. Calhoun, were not settled during the period of the Federalists and the Jeffersonians.

17. Alexander Hamilton's Report on Manufactures, December 5, 1791

The "Report on the Subject of Manufactures," which Secretary of the Treasury Hamilton submitted to Congress on December 5, 1791, has generally been regarded as Hamilton's most important state paper. It was his only major report that failed to generate favorable action by Congress, yet it displayed Hamilton at his best as an economic planner and practical statesman. Although not original in economic theory, it illustrated his knowledge of American economic data and of the thought of leading European economists. The excerpt given here, from the introduction to Hamilton's detailed report, reflects particularly his use of the writings of Adam Smith and Jacques Necker among the sources drawn upon in preparing the statement. In apologizing for the length of the preliminary discussion, Hamilton observed that "it appeared proper to investigate principles, to consider objections, and to endeavour to establish the utility of the thing proposed to be encouraged." In his specific proposals the secretary recommended protective tariffs, government bounties for the establishment of new industries, awards for inventions, and exemptions of essential raw materials from import duties. This selection is reprinted from Syrett and Cooke (eds.), The Papers of Alexander Hamilton, X, 230–261.

The Secretary of the Treasury in obedience to the order of ye House of Representatives, of the 15th day of January 1790, has applied his attention, at as early a period as his other duties would permit, to the subject of Manufactures; and particularly to the means of promoting such as will tend to render the United States, independent on foreign nations, for military and other essential supplies. And he there[upon] respectfully submits the following Report.

The expediency of encouraging manufactures in the United States, which was not long since deemed very questionable, appears at this time to be pretty generally admitted. The embarrassments, which have obstructed the progress of our external trade, have led to serious reflections on the necessity of enlarging the sphere of our domestic commerce: the restrictive regulations, which in foreign markets abrige the vent of the increasing surplus of our Agricultural produce, serve to beget an earnest desire, that a more extensive demand for that surplus may be created at home: And the complete success, which has rewarded manufacturing enterprise, in some valuable branches, conspiring with the promising symptoms, which attend some less mature essays, in others, justify a hope, that the obstacles to the growth of this species of industry are less formidable than they were apprehended to be; and that it is not difficult to find, in its further extension; a full indemnification for any external disadvantages, which are or may be experienced, as well as an accession of resources, favourable to national independence and safety. . . .

It ought readily to be conceded, that the cultivation of the earth —as the primary and most certain source of national supply—as the immediate and chief source of subsistence to man—as the principal source of those materials which constitute the nutriment of other kinds of labor—as including a state most favorable to the freedom and independence of the human mind—one, perhaps, most conducive to the multiplication of the human species—has intrinsically a strong claim to pre-eminence over every other kind of industry.

But, that it has a title to any thing like an exclusive predilection, in any country, ought to be admitted with great caution. That it is even more productive than every other branch of Industry requires more evidence, than has yet been given in support of the position. That its real interests, precious and important as without the help of exaggeration, they truly are, will be advanced, rather than injured by the due encouragement of manufactures, may, it is believed, be satisfactorily demonstrated. And it is also believed that the expediency of such encouragement in a general view may be shewn to be recommended by the most cogent and persuasive motives of national policy.

It has been maintained, that Agriculture is, not only, the most productive, but the only productive species of industry. The reality of this suggestion in either aspect, has, however, not been verified by any accurate detail of facts and calculations; and the general arguments, which are adduced to prove it, are rather subtil and paradoxical, than solid or convincing. . . .

But without contending for the superior productiveness of Manufacturing Industry, it may conduce to a better judgment of the policy, which ought to be pursued respecting its encouragement, to contemplate the subject, under some additional aspects, tending not only to confirm the idea, that this kind of industry has been improperly represented as unproductive in itself; but [to] evince in addition that the establishment and diffusion of manufactures have the effect of rendering the total mass of useful and productive labor in a community, *greater than it would otherwise be*. In prosecuting this discussion, it may be necessary briefly to resume and review some of the topics, which have been already touched.

To affirm, that the labour of the Manufacturer is unproductive, because he consumes as much of the produce of land, as he adds value to the raw materials which he manufactures, is not better founded, than it would be to affirm, that the labour of the farmer, which furnishes materials to the manufacturer, is unproductive, *because he consumes an equal value of manufactured articles*. Each furnishes a certain portion of the produce of his labor to the other, and each destroys a correspondent portion of the produce of the labour of the other. In the mean time, the maintenance of two Citizens, instead of one, is going on; the State has two members instead of one; and they together consume twice the value of what is produced from the land.

If instead of a farmer and artificer, there were a farmer only, he would be under the necessity of devoting a part of his labour to the fabrication of cloathing and other articles, which he would procure of the artificer, in the case of there being such a person; and of course he would be able to devote less labor to the cultivation of his farm; and would draw from it a proportionably less product. The whole quantity of production, in this state of things, in provisions, raw materials and manufactures, would certainly not exceed in value the amount of what would be produced in provisions and raw materials only, if there were an artificer as well as a farmer.

Again—if there were both an artificer and a farmer, the latter would be left at liberty to pursue exclusively the cultivation of his farm. A greater quantity of provisions and raw materials would of course be produced—equal at least—as has been already observed, to the whole amount of the provisions, raw materials and manufactures, which would exist on a contrary supposition. The artificer, at the same time would be going on in the production of manufactured commodities; to an amount sufficient not only to repay the farmer, in those commodities, for the provisions and materials which were procured from him, but to furnish the Artificer himself with a supply of similar commodities for his own use. Thus, then, there would be two quantities or values in existence, instead of one; and the revenue and consumption would be double in one case, what it would be in the other.

If in place of both these suppositions, there were supposed to be two farmers, and no artificer, each of whom applied a part of his labour to the culture of land, and another part to the fabrication of Manufactures—in this case, the portion of the labour of both bestowed upon land would produce the same quantity of provisions and raw materials only, as would be produced by the intire sum of the labour of one applied in the same manner, and the portion of the labour of both bestowed upon manufactures, would produce the same quantity of manufactures only, as would be produced by the intire sum of the labour of one applied in the same manner. Hence the produce of the labour of the two farmers would not be greater than the produce of the labour of the farmer and artificer; and hence, it results, that labour of the artificer is as possitively productive as that of the farmer, and, as positively, augments the revenue of the Society.

The labour of the Artificer replaces to the farmer that portion of his labour, with which he provides the materials of exchange with the Artificer, and which he would otherwise have been compelled to apply to manufactures: and while the Artificer thus enables the farmer to enlarge his stock of Agricultural industry, a portion of which he purchases for his own use, *he also supplies himself with the manufactured articles of which he stands in need.*

He does still more—Besides this equivalent which he gives for the portion of Agricultural labour consumed by him, and this supply of manufactured commodities for his own consumption—he furnishes still a surplus, which compensates for the use of the Capital advanced either by himself or some other person, for carrying on the business. This is the ordinary profit of the Stock employed in the manufactory, and is, in every sense, as effective an addition to the income of the Society, as the rent of land.

The produce of the labour of the Aritificer consequently, may be regarded as composed of three parts; one by which the provisions for his subsistence and the materials for his work are purchased of the farmer, one by which he supplies himself with manufactured necesssaries, and a third which constitutes the profit on the Stock employed. The two last portions seem to have been overlooked in the system, which represents manufacturing industry as barren and unproductive.

In the course of the preceding illustrations, the products of equal quantities of the labour of the farmer and artificer have been treated as if equal to each other. But this is not to be understood as intending to assert any such precise equality. It is merely a manner of expression adopted for the sake of simplicity and perspicuity. Whether the value of the produce of the labour of the farmer be somewhat more or less, than that of the artificer, is not material to the main scope of the argument, which hitherto has only aimed at shewing, that the one, as well as the other, occasions a possitive augmentation of the total produce and revenue of the Society.

It is now proper to proceed a step further, and to enumerate the principal circumstances, from which it may be inferred—That manufacturing establishments not only occasion a possitive augmentation of the Produce and Revenue of the Society, but that they contribute essentially to rendering them greater than they could possibly be, without such establishments. These circumstances are—

1. The division of Labour.
2. An extension of the use of Machinery.
3. Additional employment to classes of the community not ordinarily engaged in the business.
4. The promoting of emigration from foreign Countries.
5. The furnishing greater scope for the diversity of talents and dispositions which discriminate men from each other.
6. The affording a more ample and various field for enterprize.
7. The creating in some instances a new, and securing in all, a more certain and steady demand for the surplus produce of the soil.

Each of these circumstances has a considerable influence upon the total mass of industrious effort in a community. Together, they add to it a degree of energy and effect, which are not easily conceived. Some comments upon each of them, in the order in which they have been stated, may serve to explain their importance.

I. As to the Division of Labour.

It has justly been observed, that there is scarcely any thing of greater moment in the economy of a nation, than the proper division of labour. The separation of occupations causes each to be carried to a much greater perfection, than it could possibly acquire, if they were blended. This arises principally from three circumstances.

1st—The greater skill and dexterity naturally resulting from a constant and undivided application to a single object. It is evident, that these properties must increase, in proportion to the separation and simplification of objects and the steadiness of the attention devoted to each; and must be less, in proportion to the complication of objects, and the number among which the attention is distracted.

2nd. The economy of time—by avoiding the loss of it, incident to a frequent transition from one operation to another of a different nature. This depends on various circumstances—the transition itself —the orderly disposition of the impliments, machines and materials employed in the operation to be relinquished—the preparatory steps to the commencement of a new one—the interruption of the impulse, which the mind of the workman acquires, from being engaged in a particular operation—the distractions hesitations and reluctances, which attend the passage from one kind of business to another.

3rd. An extension of the use of Machinery. A man occupied on a single object will have it more in his power, and will be more naturally led to exert his imagination in devising methods to facilitate and abrige labour, than if he were perplexed by a variety of independent and dissimilar operations. Besides this, the fabrication of Machines, in numerous instances, becoming itself a distinct trade, the Artist who follows it, has all the advantages which have been enumerated, for improvement in his particular art; and in both ways the invention and application of machinery are extended.

And from these causes united, the mere separation of the occupation of the cultivator, from that of the Artificer, has the effect of augmenting the *productive powers* of labour, and with them, the total mass of the produce or revenue of a Country. In this single view of the subject, therefore, the utility of Artificers or Manufacturers, towards promoting an increase of productive industry, is apparent.

II. As to an extension of the use of Machinery a point which though partly anticipated requires to be placed in one or two additional lights.

The employment of Machinery forms an item of great importance in the general mass of national industry. 'Tis an artificial force brought in aid of the natural force of man; and, to all the purposes of labour, is an increase of hands; an accession of strength, *unincumbered too by the expense of maintaining the laborer.* May it not therefore be fairly inferred, that those occupations, which give greatest scope to the use of this auxiliary, contribute most to the general Stock of industrious effort, and, in consequence, to the general product of industry?

It shall be taken for granted, and the truth of the position referred to observation, that manufacturing pursuits are susceptible in a greater degree of the application of machinery, than those of Agriculture. If so all the difference is lost to a community, which, instead of manufacturing for itself, procures the fabrics requisite to its supply from other Countries. The substitution of foreign for domestic manufactures is a transfer to foreign nations of the advantages accruing from the employment of Machinery, in the modes in which it is capable of being employed, with most utility and to the greatest extent.

The Cotton Mill invented in England, within the last twenty years, is a signal illustration of the general proposition, which has been just advanced. In consequence of it, all the different processes for spinning Cotton are performed by means of Machines, which are put in motion by water, and attended chiefly by women and Children; [and by a smaller] number of [persons, in the whole, than are] requisite in the ordinary mode of spinning. And it is an advantage of great moment that the operations of this mill continue with convenience, during the night, as well as through the day. The prodigious affect of such a Machine is easily conceived. To this invention is to be attributed essentially the immense progress, which has been so suddenly made in Great Britain in the various fabrics of Cotton.

III. As to the additional employment of classes of the community, not ordinarily engaged in the particular business.

This is not among the least valuable of the means, by which manufacturing institutions contribute to augment the general stock of industry and production. In places where those institutions prevail, besides the persons regularly engaged in them, they afford occasional and extra employment to industrious individuals and families, who are willing to devote the leisure resulting from the intermissions of their ordinary pursuits to collateral labours, as a resource of multiplying their acquisitions or [their] enjoyments. The husbandman himself experiences a new source of profit and support from the encreased industry of his wife and daughters; invited and stimulated by the demands of the neighboring manufactories.

Besides this advantage of occasional employment to classes having different occupations, there is another of a nature allied to it [and] of a similar tendency. This is—the employment of persons who would otherwise be idle (and in many cases a burthen on the community), either from the byass of temper, habit, infirmity of body, or some other cause, indisposing, or disqualifying them for the toils of the Country. It is worthy of particular remark, that, in general, women and Children are rendered more useful and the latter more early useful by manufacturing establishments, than they would otherwise be. Of the number of persons employed in the Cotton Manufactories of Great Britain, it is computed that $\frac{4}{7}$ nearly are women and children; of whom the greatest proportion are children and many of them of a very tender age.

And thus it appears to be one of the attributes of manufactures, and one of no small consequence, to give occasion to the exertion of a greater quantity of Industry, even by the *same number* of persons, where they happen to prevail, than would exist, if there were no such establishments.

IV. As to the promoting of emigration from foreign Countries.

Men reluctantly quit one course of occupation and livelihood for another, unless invited to it by very apparent and proximate advantages. Many, who would go from one country to another, if they had a prospect of continuing with more benefit the callings, to which they have been educated, will often not be tempted to change their situation, by the hope of doing better, in some other way. Manufacturers, who listening to the powerful invitations of a better price for their fabrics, or their labour, of greater cheapness of provisions and raw materials, of an exemption from the chief part of the taxes burthens and restraints, which they endure in the old world, of greater personal independence and consequence, under the operation of a more equal government, and of what is far more precious than mere religious toleration—a perfect equality of religious privileges; would probably flock from Europe to the United States to pursue their own trades or professions, if they were once made sensible of the advantages they would enjoy, and were inspired with an assurance of encouragement and employment, will, with difficulty, be induced to transplant themselves, with a view to becoming Cultivators of Land.

If it be true then, that it is the interest of the United States to open every possible [avenue to] emigration from abroad, it affords a weighty argument for the encouragement of manufactures; which for the reasons just assigned, will have the strongest tendency to multiply the inducements to it.

Here is perceived an important resource, not only for extending the population, and with it the useful and productive labour of the country, but likewise for the prosecution of manufactures, without deducting from the number of hands, which might otherwise be drawn to tillage; and even for the indemnification of Agriculture for such as might happen to be diverted from it. Many, whom Manufacturing views would induce to emigrate, would afterwards yield to the temptations, which the particular situation of this Country holds out to Agricultural pursuits. And while Agriculture would in other respects derive many signal and unmingled advantages, from the growth of manufactures, it is a problem whether it would gain or lose, as to the article of the number of persons employed in carrying it on.

V. As to the furnishing greater scope for the diversity of talents and dispositions, which discriminate men from each other.

This is a much more powerful mean of augmenting the fund of national Industry than may at first sight appear. It is a just observation, that minds of the strongest and most active powers for their proper objects fall below mediocrity and labour without effect, if confined to uncongenial pursuits. And it is thence to be inferred, that the results of human exertion may be immensely increased by diversifying its objects. When all the different kinds of industry obtain in a community, each individual can find his proper element, and can call into activity the whole vigour of his nature. And the community is benefitted by the services of its respective members, in the manner, in which each can serve it with most effect.

If there be anything in a remark often to be met with—namely that there is, in the genius of the people of this country, a peculiar aptitude for mechanic improvements, it would operate as a forcible reason for giving opportunities to the exercise of that species of talent, by the propagation of manufactures.

VI. As to the affording a more ample and various field for enterprise.

This also is of greater consequence in the general scale of national exertion, than might perhaps on a superficial view be supposed, and has effects not altogether dissimilar from those of the circumstance last noticed. To cherish and stimulate the activity of the human mind, by multiplying the objects of enterprise, is not among the least considerable of the expedients, by which the wealth of a nation may be promoted. Even things in themselves not positively advantageous, sometimes become so, by their tendency to provoke exertion. Every new scene, which is opened to the busy nature of man to rouse and exert itself, is the addition of a new energy to the general stock of effort.

The spirit of enterprise, useful and prolific as it is, must necessarily be contracted or expanded in proportion to the simplicity or variety of the occupations and productions, which are to be found in a Society. It must be less in a nation of mere cultivators, than in a nation of cultivators and merchants; less in a nation of cultivators and merchants, than in a nation of cultivators, artificers and merchants.

VII. As to the creating, in some instances, a new, and securing in all a more certain and steady demand, for the surplus produce of the soil.

This is among the most important of the circumstances which have been indicated. It is a principal mean, by which the establishment of manufactures contributes to an augmentation of the produce or revenue of a country, and has an immediate and direct relation to the prosperity of Agriculture.

It is evident, that the exertions of the husbandman will be steady or fluctuating, vigorous or feeble, in proportion to the steadiness or fluctuation, adequateness, or inadequateness, of the markets on which he must depend, for the vent of the surplus, which may be produced by his labour; and that such surplus in the ordinary course of things will be greater or less in the same proportion.

For the purpose of this vent, a domestic market is greatly to be preferred to a foreign one; because it is in the nature of things, far more to be relied upon.

It is a primary object of the policy of nations, to be able to supply themselves with subsistence from their own soils; and manufacturing nations, as far as circumstances permit, endeavor to procure, from the same source, the raw materials necessary for their own fabrics. This disposition, urged by the spirit of monopoly, is sometimes even carried to an injudicious extreme. It seems not always to be recollected, that nations, who have neither mines nor manufactures, can only obtain the manufactured articles, of which they stand in need, by an exchange of the products of their soils; and that, if those who can best furnish them with such articles are unwilling to give a due course to this exchange, they must of necessity make every possible effort to manufacture for themselves, the effect of which is that the manufacturing nations abrige the natural advantages of their situation, through an unwillingness to permit the Agricultural countries to enjoy the advantages of theirs, and sacrifice the interests of a mutually beneficial intercourse to the vain project of *selling every thing* and *buying nothing*.

But it is also a consequence of the policy, which has been noted, that the foreign demand for the products of Agricultural Countries, is, in a great degree, rather casual and occasional, than certain or constant. To what extent injurious interruptions of the demand for some of the staple commodities of the United States, may have been experienced, from that cause, must be referred to the judgment of those who are engaged in carrying on the commerce of the country; but it may be safely assumed, that such interruptions are at times very inconveniently felt, and that cases not unfrequently occur, in which markets are so confined and restricted, as to render the demand very unequal to the supply.

Independently likewise of the artificial impediments, which are created by the policy in question, there are natural causes tending to render the external demand for the surplus of Agricultural nations a precarious reliance. The differences of seasons, in the countries, which are the consumers make immense differences in the produce of their own soils, in different years; and consequently in the degrees of their necessity for foreign supply. Plentiful harvests with them, especially if similar ones occur at the same time in the countries, which are the furnishers, occasion of course a glut in the markets of the latter.

Considering how fast and how much the progress of new settlements in the United States must increase the surplus produce of the soil, and weighing seriously the tendency of the system, which prevails among most of the commercial nations of Europe; whatever dependence may be placed on the force of natural circumstances to counteract the effects of an artificial policy; there appear strong reasons to regard the foreign demand for that surplus as too uncertain a reliance, and to desire a substitute for it, in an extensive domestic market.

To secure such a market, there is no other expedient, than to promote manufacturing establishments. Manufacturers who constitute the most numerous class, after the Cultivators of land, are for that reason the principal consumers of the surplus of their labour.

This idea of an extensive domestic market for the surplus produce of the soil is of the first consequence. It is of all things, that which most effectually conduces to a flourishing state of Agriculture. If the effect of manufactories should be to detach a portion of the hands, which would otherwise be engaged in Tillage, it might possibly cause a smaller quantity of lands to be under cultivation but by their tendency to procure a more certain demand for the surplus produce of the soil, they would, at the same time, cause the lands which were in cultivation to be better improved and more productive. And while, by their influence, the condition of each individual farmer would be meliorated, the total mass of Agricultural production would probably be increased. For this must evidently depend as much, if not more, upon the degree of improvement; than upon the number of acres under culture.

It merits particular observation, that the multiplication of manufactories not only furnishes a Market for those articles, which have been accustomed to be produced in abundance, in a country; but it likewise creates a demand for such as were either unknown or produced in inconsiderable quantities. The bowels as well as the surface of the earth are ransacked for articles which were before neglected. Animals, Plants and Minerals acquire an utility and value, which were before unexplored.

The foregoing considerations seem sufficient to establish, as general propositions, That it is the interest of nations to diversify the industrious pursuits of the individuals, who compose them— That the establishment of manufactures is calculated not only to increase the general stock of useful and productive labour; but even to improve the state of Agriculture in particular; certainly to advance the interests of those who are engaged in it. . . .

18. Albert Gallatin's Report on Internal Improvements, April 4, 1808

The first commitment of Jefferson's Secretary of the Treasury. Albert Gallatin, was to paying off the national debt. After this indebtedness had been substantially reduced and provisions made for the orderly retirement of the entire debt, Gallatin directed his attention to a plan for building roads, canals, and other internal improvements at the expense of the national government. Such a program, he believed, would serve a great national purpose in binding together the different sections of the country. Responding to a suggestion that originated with Gallatin, the Senate in 1807 called upon the Secretary of the Treasury to submit a plan for internal improvements, which, after an exhaustive study, he presented to the Senate on April 6, 1808. The program, at an estimated cost of $20 million, proposed a network of roads, canals, and river improvements interlacing the country, North and South, East and West. All improvements would be made only with the consent of the states through which they passed, unless an amendment were added to the Constitution. Gallatin's bold program ranks with Hamilton's Report on Manufactures in its farsightedness and in its practical vision of serving the national purpose. Congress failed to enact Gallatin's plan, but his recommendations served as the inspiration for later proposals. The excerpts below are the introductory and concluding sections of the detailed report, which is published in full in American State Papers, Miscellaneous, *I, 724–741.*

The SECRETARY OF THE TREASURY, in obedience to the resolution of the Senate of the 2d March, 1807, respectfully submits the following report on roads and canals:

The general utility of artificial roads and canals is at this time so universally admitted, as hardly to require any additional proofs. It is sufficiently evident that, whenever the annual expense of transportation on a certain route, in its natural state, exceeds the interest on the capital employed in improving the communication, and the annual expense of transportation (exclusively of the tolls,) by the improved route, the difference is an annual additional income to the nation. Nor does in that case the general result vary, although the tolls may not have been fixed at a rate sufficient to pay to the undertakers the interest on the capital laid out. They, indeed, when that happens, lose; but the community is nevertheless benefited by the undertaking. The general gain is not confined to the difference between the expense of the transportation of those articles which had been formerly conveyed by that route, but many which were brought to market by other channels will then find a new and more advantageous direction; and those which on account of their distance or weight could not be transported in any manner whatever, will acquire a value, and become a clear addition to the national wealth. Those and many other advantages have become so obvious, that in countries possessed of a large capital, where property is sufficiently secure to induce individuals to lay out that capital on permanent undertakings, and where a compact population creates an extensive commercial intercourse, within short distances, those improvements may often, in ordinary cases, be left to individual exertion, without any direct aid from Government.

There are, however, some circumstances, which, whilst they render the facility of communication throughout the United States an object of primary importance, naturally check the application of private capital and enterprise to improvements on a large scale.

The price of labor is not considered as a formidable obstacle, because whatever it may be, it equally affects the expense of transportation, which is saved by the improvement, and that of effecting the improvement itself. The want of practical knowledge is no longer felt; and the occasional influence of mistaken local interests, in sometimes thwarting or giving an improper direction to public improvements, arises from the nature of man, and is common to all countries. The great demand for capital in the United States, and the extent of territory compared with the population, are, it is believed, the true causes which prevent new undertakings, and render those already accomplished less profitable than had been expected.

1. Notwithstanding the great increase of capital during the last fifteen years, the objects for which it is required continue to be more numerous, and its application is generally more profitable than in Europe. A small portion therefore is applied to objects which offer only the prospect of remote and moderate profit. And it also happens that a less sum being subscribed at first than is actually requisite for completing the work, this proceeds slowly; the capital applied remains unproductive for a much longer time than

was necessary, and the interest accruing during that period becomes, in fact, an injurious addition to the real expense of the undertaking.

2. The present population of the United States, compared with the extent of territory over which it is spread, does not, except in the vicinity of the seaports, admit that extensive commercial intercourse within short distances, which, in England and some other countries, forms the principal support of artificial roads and canals. With a few exceptions, canals particularly cannot, in America, be undertaken with a view solely to the intercourse between the two extremes of, and along the intermediate ground which they occupy. It is necessary, in order to be productive, that the canal should open a communication with a natural extensive navigation which will flow through that new channel. It follows that whenever that navigation requires to be improved, or when it might at some distance be connected by another canal to another navigation, the first canal will remain comparatively unproductive until the other improvements are effected, until the other canal is also completed. Thus the intended canal between the Chesapeake and Delaware, will be deprived of the additional benefit arising from the intercourse between New York and the Chesapeake, until an inland navigation shall have been opened between the Delaware and New York. Thus the expensive canals completed around the falls of Potomac will become more and more productive in proportion to the improvement, first, of the navigation of the upper branches of the river, and then of its communication with the Western waters. Some works already executed are unprofitable; many more remain unattempted, because their ultimate productiveness depends on other improvements, too extensive or too distant to be embraced by the same individuals.

The General Government can alone remove these obstacles.

With resources amply sufficient for the completion of every practicable improvement, it will always supply the capital wanted for any work which it may undertake, as fast as the work itself can progress; avoiding thereby the ruinous loss of interest on a dormant capital, and reducing the real expense to its lowest rate.

With these resources, and embracing the whole Union, it will complete on any given line all the improvements, however distant, which may be necessary to render the whole productive, and eminently beneficial.

The early and efficient aid of the *Federal* Government is recommended by still more important considerations. The inconveniences, complaints, and perhaps dangers, which may result from a vast extent of territory, can no otherwise be radically removed or prevented than by opening speedy and easy communications through all its parts. Good roads and canals will shorten distances, facilitate commercial and personal intercourse, and unite, by a still more intimate community of interests, the most remote quarters of the United States. No other single operation, within the power of Government, can more effectually tend to strengthen and perpetuate that Union which secures external independence, domestic peace, and internal liberty.

With that view of the subject the facts respecting canals, which have been collected in pursuance of the resolution of the Senate, have been arranged under the following heads:

1. Great canals, from north to south, along the Atlantic seacoast.

2. Communications between the Atlantic and Western waters.

3. Communications between the Atlantic waters, and those of the great lakes, and river St. Lawrence.

4. Interior canals. . . .

The improvements which have been respectfully suggested as most important in order to facilitate the communication between the great geographical divisions of the United States, will now be recapitulated; and their expense compared with the resources applicable to that object.

I. From north to south, in a direction parallel to the seacoast.

1. Canals opening an inland navigation for sea vessels from Massachusetts to North Carolina, being more than two-thirds of the Atlantic seacoast of the United States, and across all the principal capes, Cape Fear excepted, $3,000,000

2. A great turnpike road from Maine to Georgia along the whole extent of the Atlantic seacoast,   4,800,000

$ 7,800,000

II. From east to west, forming communications across the mountains between the Atlantic and western rivers.
  1. Improvement of the navigation of
     four great Atlantic rivers, including
     canals parallel to them,   1,500,000
  2. Four firstrate turnpike roads from
     those rivers across the mountains, to
     the four corresponding western rivers,   2,800,000
  3. Canal around the falls of the Ohio,   300,000
  4. Improvement of roads to Detroit, St.
     Louis and New Orleans,   200,000
                                                              4,800,000

III. In a northern and northwestwardly
direction, forming inland navigations
between the Atlantic seacoast, and
the great lakes and the St. Lawrence.
  1. Inland navigation between the North
     river and Lake Champlain,   800,000
  2. Great inland navigation opened the
     whole way by canals from the North
     river to Lake Ontario,   2,200,000
  3. Canal around the falls and rapids of
     Niagara, opening a sloop navigation
     from Lake Ontario to the upper
     lakes as far as the extremities of
     Lake Michigan,   1,000,000
                                                              4,000,000
              Making, together, $16,600,000

IV. The great geographical features of the country have been
solely adhered to in pointing out those lines of communication;
and these appear to embrace all the great interests of the Union,
and to be calculated to diffuse and increase the national wealth in
a very general way, by opening an intercourse between the remotest extremes of the United States. Yet it must necessarily
result from an adherence to that principle, that those parts of
the Atlantic States through which the great western and north-
west communications will be carried, must, in addition to the
general advantages in which they will participate, receive from

those communications greater local and immediate benefits than the Eastern and perhaps Southern States. As the expense must be defrayed from the general funds of the Union, justice, and, perhaps, policy not less than justice, seems to require that a number of local improvements, sufficient to equalize the advantages, should also be undertaken in those States, parts of States, or districts which are less immediately interested in those inland communications. Arithmetical precision cannot, indeed, be attained in objects of that kind; nor would an apportionment of the moneys applied according to the population of each State be either just or practicable, since roads and particularly canals are often of greater utility to the States which they unite; than to those through which they pass. But a sufficient number of local improvements, consisting either of roads or canals may, without any material difficulty, be selected, so as to do substantial justice and give general satisfaction. Without pretending to suggest what would be the additional sum necessary for that object, it will, for the sake of round numbers, be estimated at $ 3,400,000

Which, added to the sum estimated for general improvements, 16,600,000

Would make an aggregate of $20,000,000

An annual appropriation of two millions of dollars would accomplish all those great objects in ten years, and may, without inconvenience, be supplied in time of peace by the existing revenues and resources of the United States. This may be exemplified in several ways.

The annual appropriation, on account of the principal and interest of the public debt, has, during the last six years, amounted to eight millions of dollars. After the present year, or, at furthest, after the ensuing year, the sum which, on account of the irredeemable nature of the remaining debt, may be applied to that object cannot, in any one year, exceed four million six hundred thousand dollars; leaving, therefore, from that source alone, an annual surplus of three million four hundred thousand dollars applicable to any other object.

From the 1st January, 1801, to the 1st January, 1809, a period of eight years, the United States shall have discharged about thirty-four millions of the principal of the old debt, or deducting the Louisiana debt incurred during the same period and not yet discharged, about twenty-three millions of dollars. They may, with equal facility, apply, in a period of ten years, a sum of twenty millions of dollars to internal improvements.

The annual permanent revenue of the United States, calculated on a state of general peace, and on the most moderate estimate, was, in a report made to Congress on the 6th day of December, 1806, computed for the years 1809, 1815, at fourteen millions of dollars. The annual expenses on the peace establishment, and including the four million six hundred thousand dollars on account of the debt, and four hundred thousand dollars for contingencies, do not exceed eight millions and a half, leaving an annual surplus of five millions and a half of dollars. To provide for the protection and defence of the country is undoubtedly the object to which the resources of the United States must, in the first instance, be applied, and to the exclusion of all others, if the times shall require it. But it is believed that, in times of peace, and to such period only are these remarks applicable; the surplus will be amply sufficient to defray the expenses of all the preparatory measures of a permanent nature which prudence may suggest, and to pay the sum destined for internal improvements. Three millions annually applied during the same period of ten years, would arm every man in the United States, fill the public arsenals and magazines, erect every battery and fortification which could be manned, and even, if thought eligible, build a navy. That the whole surplus would be inadequate to the support of any considerable increase of the land or naval force kept in actual service in time of peace, will be readily admitted. But such a system is not contemplated; if ever adopted, the objects of this report must probably be abandoned; for it has not heretofore been found an easy task for any Government to indulge in that species of expense, which, leaving no trace behind it, adds nothing to the real strength of the country, and, at the same time, to provide for either its permanent defence or improvement.

It must not be omitted that the facility of communications constitutes, particularly in the United States, an imporant branch of national defence. Their extensive territory opposes a powerful obstacle to the progress of an enemy; but, on the other hand, the number of regular forces which may be raised, necessarily limited by the population, will, for many years, be inconsiderable when compared with that extent of territory. That defect cannot otherwise be supplied than by those great national improvements, which will afford the means of a rapid concentration of that regular force, and of a formidable body of militia on any given point.

Amongst the resources of the Union, there is one which, from its nature, seems more particularly applicable to internal improvements. Exclusively of Louisiana, the General Government possesses, in trust for the people of the United States, about one hundred millions of acres fit for cultivation, north of the river Ohio, and near fifty millions south of the State of Tennessee. For the disposition of these lands a plan has been adopted, calculated to enable every industrious citizen to become a freeholder, to secure indisputable titles to the purchasers, to obtain a national revenue, and, above all, to suppress monopoly. Its success has surpassed that of every former attempt, and exceeded the expectations of its authors. But a higher price than had usually been paid for waste lands by the first inhabitants of the frontier became an unavoidable ingredient of a system intended for general benefit, and was necessary, in order to prevent the public lands being engrossed by individuals possessing greater wealth, activity, and local advantages. It is believed that nothing could be more gratifying to the purchasers, and to the inhabitants of the Western States generally, or better calculated to remove popular objections, and to defeat insidious efforts, than the application of the proceeds of the sales to improvements conferring general advantages on the nation, and an immediate benefit on the purchasers and inhabitants themselves. It may be added, that the United States, considered merely as owners of the soil, are also deeply interested in the opening of those communications which must necessarily enhance the value of their property. Thus the opening an inland navigation from tide water to the great lakes, would immediaately give to the great body of lands bordering on those lakes as great value as if they were situated at the distance of one hundred miles by land from the seacoast. And if the proceeds of the first ten millions of acres which may be sold were applied to such improvements, the United States would be amply repaid in the sale of the other ninety millions.

The annual appropriation of two millions of dollars drawn from the general revenues of the Union, which has been suggested, could operate to its full extent only in times of peace and under prosperous circumstances. The application of the proceeds of the sales of the public lands, might, perhaps, be made permanent until it had amounted to a certain sum, and until the most important improvements had been effected. The fund created by those improvements, the expense of which has been estimated at twenty millions of dollars, would afterwards become itself a perpetual resource for further improvements. Although some of those first communications should not become immediately productive; and although the same liberal policy, which dictated the measure, would consider them less as objects of revenue to Government, than of increased wealth and general convenience to the nation, yet they would all, sooner or later, acquire, as productive property, their par value. Whenever that had taken place in relation to any of them, the stock might be sold to individuals or companies, and the proceeds applied to a new improvement. And by persevering in that plan, a succession of improvements would be effected until every portion of the United States should enjoy all the advantages of inland navigation and improved roads, of which it was susceptible. To effect that great object, a disbursement of twenty millions of dollars, applied with more or less rapidity, according to the circumstances of the United States, would be amply sufficient.

The manner in which the public moneys may be applied to such objects remains to be considered.

It is evident that the United States cannot, under the constitution, open any road or canal, without the consent of the State through which such road or canal must pass. In order, therefore, to remove every impediment to a national plan of internal improvements, an amendment to the constitution was suggested by the Executive when the subject was recommended to the consideration of Congress. Until this be obtained, the assent of the State being necessary for each improvement, the modifications under which that assent may be given, will necessarily control the manner of applying the money. It may be, however, observed that in relation to the specific improvements which have been suggested, there is hardly any which is not either already authorized by the States respectively, or so immediately beneficial to them, as to render it highly probable that no material difficulty will be experienced in that respect.

The moneys may be applied in two different manners. The

United States may, with the assent of the States, undertake some of the works at their sole expense, or they may subscribe a certain number of shares of the stock of companies incorporated for the purpose. Loans might also, in some instances, be made to such companies. The first mode would, perhaps, by effectually controlling local interests, give the most proper general direction to the work. Its details would probably be executed on a more economical plan by private companies. Both modes may, perhaps, be blended together so as to obtain the advantages pertaining to each. But the modifications of which the plan is susceptible must vary according to the nature of the work, and of the charters, and seem to belong to that class of details which are not the immediate subject of consideration.

At present the only work undertaken by the United States at their sole expense, and to which the assent of the States has been obtained, is the road from Cumberland to Brownsville; an appropriation may, for that purpose, be made at any time. In relation to all other works, the United States have nothing at this time in their power but to assist those already authorized, either by loans, or by becoming stockholders; and the last mode appears the most eligible. The only companies incorporated for effecting some of the improvements, considered in this report as of national and firstrate importance, which have applied for such assistance, are the Chesapeake and Delaware Canal, the Susquehannah Canal, and the Dismal Swamp companies; and authority might be given to subscribe a certain number of shares to each on condition that the plan of the work to be executed should be approved by the General Government. A subscription to the Ohio Canal, to the Pittsburg Road, and perhaps to some other objects not fully ascertained, is also practicable at this time. As an important basis of the general system, an immediate authority might also be given to take the surveys and levels of the routes of the most important roads and canals which are contemplated: a work always useful, and by which the practicability and expense of the undertakings would be ascertained with much more correctness than in this report. . . .

ALBERT GALLATIN, *Secretary of the Treasury*
TREASURY DEPARTMENT, *April 4, 1808*

19. John C. Calhoun's Support of the Tariff, April 4, 1816

In the immediate years after the War of 1812, the infant industries born of wartime conditions sought protection to survive against British importations, and they found support in Congress among young Republicans who voiced arguments similar to those of Hamilton two decades earlier. One of the spokesmen in Congress in support of a policy of protection was Representative John C. Calhoun of South Carolina, who supported the bill in 1816 to levy duties high enough to be protective on certain manufactures, particularly on cotton cloth. The following selection is an excerpt from the speech made by Calhoun on April 4, 1816, during the congressional debate on the tariff measure which passed the house, April 8, 1816, by a vote of 88 to 54. Robert L. Meriwether and W. Edwin Hemphill (eds.), The Papers of John C. Calhoun (Columbia, S.C., 1959–   ), I, 347–356.

. . . Neither agriculture, manufactures or commerce, taken separately, is the cause of wealth; it flows from the three combined; and cannot exist without each. The wealth of any single nation or an individual, it is true, may not *immediately* depend on the three, but such wealth always presupposes their existence. He viewed the words in the most enlarged sense. Without commerce, industry would have no stimulus; without manufactures, it would be without the means of production; and without agriculture, neither of the others can subsist. When separated entirely and permanently, they perish. War in this country produces, to a great extent, that effect; and hence, the great embarrassment which follows in its train. The failure of the wealth and resources of the nation necessarily involved the ruin of its finances and its currency. It is admitted by the most strenuous advocates, on the other side, that no country ought to be dependent on another for its means of defence; that, at least, our musket and bayonet, our cannon and ball, ought to be of domestic manufacture. But what, he asked, is more necessary to the defence of a country than its currency and finance? Circumstanced as our country is, can these stand the shock of war? Behold the effect of the late war on them. When our manufactures are grown to a certain perfection, as they soon will under the fostering care of government, we will no longer experience these evils. The farmer will find a ready market for his surplus produce; and what is almost of equal consequence, a certain and cheap supply of all his wants. His prosperity will diffuse itself to every class in the community; and instead of that languor of industry and individual distress now incident to a state of war, and suspended commerce, the wealth and vigor of the community will not be materially impaired. The arm of government will be nerved, and taxes in the hour of danger, when essential to the independence of the nation, may be greatly increased; loans, so uncertain and hazardous, may be less relied on; thus situated, the storm may beat without, but within all will be quiet and safe.

To give perfection to this state of things, it will be necessary to add, as soon as possible, a system of internal improvements, and at least such an extension of our navy, as will prevent the cutting off our coasting trade. The advantage of each is so striking, as not to require illustration, especially after the experience of the recent war. It is thus the resources of this government and people would be placed beyond the power of a foreign war materially to impair. But it may be said that the derangement then experienced, resulted not from the cause assigned, but from the errors or the weakness of the government. He admitted, that many financial blunders were committed, for the subject was new to us; that the taxes were not laid sufficiently early, or to as great an extent as they ought to have been; and that the loans were in some instances injudiciously made; but he ventured to affirm, that had the greatest foresight and fortitude been exerted, the embarrassment would have been still very great; and that even under the best management, the total derangement which was actually felt, would not have been postponed eighteen months, had the war so long continued. How could it be otherwise? A war, such as this country was then involved in, in a great measure dries up the resources of individuals, as he had already proved; and the resources of the government are no more than the aggregate of the surplus incomes of individuals called into action by a system of taxation. It is certainly a great political evil, incident to the character of the industry of this country, that, however prosperous our situation when at peace, with an uninterrupted commerce, and nothing then could exceed it, the moment that we were involved in war the whole is reversed. When resources are most needed; when indispensible to maintain the honor; yes, the very existence of the nation, then they desert us. Our currency is also sure to experience the shock; and becomes so deranged as to prevent us from calling out fairly whatever of means is left to the country. The result of a war in the present state of our naval power is the blockade of our coast, and consequent destruction of our trade. The wants and habits of the country, founded on the use of foreign articles, must be gratified; importation to a certain extent continues, through the policy of the enemy, or unlawful traffic; the exportation of our bulky articles is prevented too, the specie of the country is drawn to pay the balance perpetually accumulating against us; and the final result is a total derangement of our currency.

To this distressing state of things there were two remedies, and only two; one in our power immediately, the other requiring much time and exertion; but both constituting, in his opinion, the essential policy of this country; he meant the navy, and domestic manufactures. By the former, we could open the way to our markets; by the latter we bring them from beyond the ocean, and naturalize them. Had we the means of attaining an immediate naval ascendancy, he acknowledged that the policy recommended by this bill, would be very questionable; but as that is not the fact—as it is a period remote, with any exertion, and will be probably more so, from that relaxation of exertion, so natural in peace, when necessity is not felt, it became the duty of this House to resort, to a considerable extent, at least as far as is proposed, to the only remaining remedy. But to this it has been objected, that the country is not prepared, and that the result of our premature exertion would be to bring distress on it, without effecting the intended object. Were it so, however urgent the reasons in its favor, we ought to desist, as it is folly to oppose the laws of necessity. But he could not for a moment yield to the assertion; on the contrary, he firmly believed that the country is prepared, even to maturity, for the introduction of manufactures. We have abundance of resources, and things naturally tend at this moment in that direction. A prosperous commerce has poured an immense amount of commercial capital into this country. This capital has, till lately, found occupation in commerce; but that state of the world which transferred it to this country, and gave it active employment, has passed away, never to return. Where shall we now find full employment for our prodigious amount of tonnage; where markets for the numerous and abundant products of our country? This great body of active capital, which for the moment has found sufficient employment in supplying our markets, exhausted by the war, and measures preceding it, must find a new direction; it will not be idle. What channel can it take, but that of manufactures? This, if things continue as they are, will be its direction. It will introduce a new era in our affairs, in many respects highly advantageous, and ought to be countenanced by the government.

Besides, we have already surmounted the greatest difficulty that has even been found in undertakings of this kind. The cotton and woollen manufactures are not to be *introduced*—they are *already* introduced to a great extent; freeing us entirely from the hazards, and, in a great measure the sacrifices experienced in giving the capital of the country a new direction. The restrictive measures and the war, though not intended for that purpose, have, by the necessary operation of things, turned a large amount of capital to this new branch of industry. He had often heard it said, both in and out of Congress, that this effect alone would indemnify the country for all of its losses. So high was this tone of feeling, when the want of these establishments were practically felt, that he remembered, during the war, when some question was agitated respecting the introduction of foreign goods, that many then opposed it on the ground of injuring our manufactures. He then said, that war alone furnished sufficient stimulus, and perhaps too much, as it would make their growth unnaturally rapid; but, that on the return of peace, it would then be time to show our affection for them. He at that time did not expect an apathy and aversion to the extent which is now seen. But it will no doubt be said, if they are so far established, and if the situation of the country is so favorable to their growth, where is the necessity of affording them protection? It is to put them beyond the reach of contingency. Besides, capital is not yet, and cannot, for some time, be adjusted to the new state of things. There is, in fact, from the operation of temporary causes, a great pressure on these establishments. They had extended so rapidly during the late war, that many, he feared, were without the requisite surplus capital, or skill to meet the present crisis. Should such prove to be the fact, it would give a back set, and might, to a great extent, endanger their ultimate success. Should the present owners be ruined, and the workmen dispersed and turn to other pursuits, the country would sustain a great loss. Such would, no doubt, be the fact to a considerable extent, if not protected. Besides, circumstances, if we act with wisdom, are favorable to attract to our country much skill and industry. The country in Europe, having the most skilful workmen, is broken up. It is to us, if wisely used, more valuable than the repeal of the Edict of Nantz was to England. She had the prudence to profit by it—let us not discover less political sagacity. Afford to ingenuity and industry immediate and ample protection, and they will not fail to give a preference to this free and happy country. . . .

Other objections of a political character were made to the encouragement of manufactures. It is said they destroy the moral and physical power of the people. This might formerly have been true to a considerable extent, before the perfection of machinery, and when the success of the manufactures depended on the minute subdivision of labor. At that time it required a large portion of the population of a country to be engaged in them; and every minute sub-division of labor is undoubtedly unfavorable to the intellect; but the great perfection of machinery has in a considerable degree obviated these objections. In fact it has been stated that the manufacturing districts in England furnish the greatest number of recruits to her army, and that, as soldiers, they are not materially inferior to the rest of her population. It has been further asserted that manufactures are the fruitful cause of pauperism; and England has been referred to as furnishing conclusive evidence of its truth. For his part, he could perceive no such tendency in them, but the exact contrary, as they furnished new stimulus and means of subsistence to the laboring classes of the community. We ought not to look to the cotton and woollen establishments of Great Britain for the prodigious numbers of poor with which her population was disgraced. Causes much more efficient exist. Her poor laws and statutes regulating the price of labor with heavy taxes, were the real causes. But if it must be so, if the mere fact that England manufactured more than any other country, explained the cause of her having more beggars, it is just as reasonable to refer her courage, spirit, and all her masculine virtues, in which she excels all other nations, with a single exception; he meant our own; in which we might without vanity challenge a pre-eminence.

Another objection had been made, which he must acknowledge was better founded, that capital employed in manufacturing produced a greater dependance on the part of the employed, than in commerce, navigation or agriculture. It is certainly an evil and to be regretted; but he did not think it a decisive objection to the system; especially when it had incidental political advantages which in his opinion more than counterpoised it. It produced an interest strictly American, as much so as agriculture; in which it had the decided advantage of commerce or navigation. The country will from this derive much advantage. Again, it is calculated to bind together more closely our widely-spread Republic. It will greatly increase our mutual dependence and intercourse; and will as a necessary consequence, excite an increased attention to internal improvement, a subject every way so intimately connected with the ultimate attainment of national strength and the perfection of our political institutions. He regarded the fact that it would make the parts adhere more closely, that it would form a new and most powerful cement, far out-weighing any political objections that might be urged against the system. In his opinion the liberty and the union of this country were inseparably united! That as the destruction of the latter would most certainly involve the former; so its maintenance will with equal certainty preserve it. He did not speak lightly. He had often and long revolved it in his mind; and he had critically examined into the causes that destroyed the liberty of other states. There are none that apply to us, or apply with a force to alarm. The basis of our Republic is too broad and its structure too strong to be shaken by them. Its extension and organization will be found to afford effectual security against their operation; but let it be deeply impressed on the heart of this House and country, that while they guarded against the old they exposed us to a new and terrible danger, disunion. This single word comprehended almost the sum of our political dangers; and against it we ought to be perpetually guarded.

20. David Trimble's Defense of the American System, February 28, 1827

The "American System" of protective tariffs, internal improvements, and a national bank, whose best-known advocate was Henry Clay, em-

braced the key issues of national economic policy in the years between the end of the War of 1812 and the election of Jackson. Indeed, since none of these issues was settled during this period, they provided the major issues of Jackson's presidency. The American System as it related to internal improvements built at the expense of the national government was defended by David Trimble, a representative in Congress from Kentucky, who emphasized the importance of internal improvements to agriculture and argued the case for the constitutionality of the building of roads and canals by the national government. Trimble, who had been in Congress since 1817, had been defeated for re-election in 1826 and was serving in his last session when he wrote this address on February 28, 1827, To the People of the First Congressional District, Ky. The excerpt is taken from the original pamphlet in the Library Company of Philadelphia.

WASHINGTON, February 28th, 1827

FELLOW CITIZENS:

It is agreed by every one, that the interests of agriculture and manufactures may be promoted or discouraged by the measures of policy adopted by the National Legislature; and experience has proven that the same interests may be deeply injured by the reaction of foreign systems of policy upon our trade and intercourse with foreign nations. The colonial policy of England is at this time, and always has been, highly injurious to the agricultural interests of this country: The same may be said of her Home system; and it is now, more than ever, necessary for us to defend ourselves against her restrictive and prohibitory regulations. The American system of policy was adopted by Congress to counteract the British system, and, if persevered in, will certainly have that effect. The measures brought before Congress for the protection of household and domestic manufactures; and those in favour of roads, canals, and other internal improvements are parts of the American system. . . .

Is it sound policy in the General Government to encourage agriculture, by making internal improvements? Experience answers in the affirmative. Society, we know, may live and prosper without them, but we know also, that it will prosper more and faster with them. It has been established again and again by actual experiments in our own country and out of it, that the interests of agriculture are promoted, and the general profits of the farmer greatly increased, by the cheap and easy transportation of his products to market upon canals and turnpike roads. Strike out the roads and canals in England, and the nation would become insolvent, and its Treasury bankrupt in less than twelve months: strike out the Ohio and Mississippi Rivers, and the roads leading to them, and what would be our condition in the West? Certainly worse than it is at present. And would it not as certainly be better, if the roads were turnpiked, and the navigation of those streams made safe and easy. Is not this manifest. In fact, roads and canals are a part of every man's farm, and ought to be considered so, in all the estimates of loss and profit upon capital employed in tillage. The first care of a farmer should be to put his farm in good condition, and the next, to make canals or turnpike roads, or both, and thereby ensure the safe and easy transportation of his surplus crop to market at the cheapest rate. It is too plain for argument that the interests of commerce and manufactures are also promoted in the same way, and probably in an equal ratio. If any portion of our countrymen could do entirely without these facilities, it would seem to be those who live on the sea-board, and enjoy all the advantages of tide water navigation; and yet, instead of opposing roads and canals as useless, they are making every possible effort to establish and construct them. How much stronger are the reasons why our western farmers should adopt the same system of policy, posted as they are in the interior of the country, with heavy articles and a long hazardous expensive journey to the sea coast. Of what avail is it that we have fertile lands, unless we have cheap and easy transportation for our products? Men may think and speak as they please about this matter, but the truth is, that we shall remain poor, compared with the people east of the Alleghany Mountains, so long as we are without roads and canals. We shall never prosper as they do— nor enjoy the fruits of our toil as they do—nor receive the same equal value for our products—nor realize equal agricultural profits —nor enjoy the blessings of ease and affluence as they do, until roads and canals are brought in aid of agricultural labour. Nor can our articles compete with theirs in market upon equal terms until we follow their example, and take the same mode of reducing the price of transportation.

An example may throw some light upon the subject. A single glance at a national map, will satisfy us, that any scheme of international improvement will include a post road from the City of Washington by way of Wheeling, in Virginia, to some point in Ohio; say Zanesville, where it will branch, one fork of it keeping

Westward through Ohio, Indiana, and Illinois to Missouri; and the other turning Southward through Ohio, Kentucky, Tennessee, and Mississippi, to New Orleans. The space between Maysville and Lexington, will be a section of this great national highway. The Cumberland road is part and parcel of it. That road was begun in 1807, under the auspices and sanction of Mr. Jefferson. It is now in process of extension from Wheeling, Virginia, to Zanesville, in Ohio, and at the proper time, an effort will be made in Congress, to obtain appropriations for the Southern route through Kentucky to New Orleans. Can any man in his sober senses doubt the utility of this as a national road: and yet an obstinate, deadly opposition to the road exists in Congress, and will probably continue to exist, until public opinion shall react upon it and put it down. . . .

If I am rightly informed, it was General Washington who first proposed a scheme of internal improvement to the American people. It is certain that his zeal in favour of the subject gave the first impulse to it. As early as 1784, he made a tour to the West as far as Pittsburg, for the general purpose of devising a *system* to begin with, and for the special purpose of ascertaining the practicability of making canals and turnpike roads from the navigable waters of the Ohio to those of the Atlantic. It was his opinion "that all the doors of trade and intercourse between the East and West should be thrown wide open." He pressed the subject in letters, upon the members of the old Congress, and upon the Governor and Legislature of Virginia; and urged it upon his friends every where. It is desirable that some one should collect and print his letters; they would form a valuable document. In fact, and in a few words, he was the father of internal improvements as well as the father of his country. His zeal and weight of character made the system popular among the leading Statesmen of the time; but unhappily, neither the States, nor the old Congress, had the command of funds to begin the work. The revolutionary debt lay too heavy on them, and had first to be provided for. From that time until the death of Washington, and for some years after, there was no opposition in or out of Congress, to his plans of international improvement.

On the 23d of June, 1807, the British ship of war Leopard, insulted our national flag on the high seas. I allude to the attack upon the frigate Chesapeake, Captain Barron. From that time

Congress began to foresee the necessity of a war with Great Britain. To avoid it an embargo was laid; and to prepare for it, and make ourselves independent of foreign nations during its continuance, became matters of serious concernment to the nation generally. The necessity of encouraging domestic manufactures was manifest to every one; and the necessity of improving the country by roads and canals, was not less apparent. National independence, internal improvements, domestic industry, home manufactures, and home made clothing, were among the countersigns and watch words of the day. Mr. Jefferson asked Congress for an appropriation to make the Cumberland road. The money was granted, and the work commenced. No serious question was raised about the power of Congress on the subject. After a time the war came on, and lessons of experience came with it, and followed after it, which have not been lost upon the Western people.

The transition of Society from war to peace, is a painful operation. All history proves that wars, especially long ones, when they terminate, are followed by periods of embarrassment and pressure. The price of every thing is enhanced by war: peace brings them down again to the fair peace standard; war is a sort of social revolution; and society, at the return of peace, is compelled to resolve itself back again into its old habits, and re-organize its business and pursuits. It is a period of pressure and distress. Every one knows that the price of American imports and exports had been greatly enhanced by the long wars in Europe, and we all know that a further enhancement took place in some things, with a corresponding depression in others, soon after we were drawn into the contest. It was foreseen that a return from war to peace prices, would be followed by the usual derangement and severe distress; and it was easy to foreknow that the western states, owing to their distance from market, would feel the pressure much more severely than those bordering on the sea coast. The rise in price of cotton left the cotton States in ease and affluence; but all other portions of the union suffered, and Kentucky more than any of the rest. How far the impending pressure and distress was mitigated by the introduction of steam boats upon our western waters, is for you to estimate. I am sure you will agree with me that our condition would have been much worse, if steam boat navigation had remained unknown, and our products left to pay the former heavy burthens incident to transportation. Is it not manifest that the best preventative for all these pressures and distresses would have been timely protection and effective encouragement of agriculture and domestic manufactures, by an increase of duties upon foreign imports, and by making roads and canals to give us cheap and easy access to market with our agricultural commodities. Convinced of this, and knowing the disadvantages under which we labour in the west, the western members in Congress, with a few exceptions, have concurred in their support of measures favourable to these objects. . . .

Has Congress power to Legislate upon these subjects?

The framers of the Constitution, with perhaps a single exception, if just conclusions may be drawn from what they said and did, were certainly of opinion that the National Government had power to make great national improvements. The States surrendered to Congress the power of taxing imports; and the right to tax exports is totally prohibited. They gave up the only profitable source of revenue equal to such undertakings. And surely the States, when they surrendered the money power, had a right to expect that Congress would employ it in making such internal improvements as they would have undertaken with the same means. The revenue became common property, and it is reasonable to contend that it shall be disbursed upon objects of common interest and utility. Take the case of post roads, and the question may well be asked, shall the States make post roads for the General Government, or shall the General Government make its own roads?

The Constitution was not made for a day; nor were its powers limited to things present. It looks to the future. It was ordained and established "to secure the blessings of liberty," to those for whom it was made, and to their posterity. Such is its language, and we are the immediate posterity of its framers, and of the generation of men then living. It made provision for things present, and for events to come. It established a political futurity for the people of the United States in federation. They entered upon the new and untried system, with the full knowledge that human institutions are not perfect. They had the lights of reason, not experience, to guide them. The scheme was new to themselves, and to the whole world. "If the enumerated powers, and the auxiliary powers, necessary and proper to carry these into execution, had been expressed in language plain, clear, and determinate, susceptible of only one sense, and attended in application with no doubt or difficulty, there would have been no room for comment or interpretation: but such is not the fact. The extent of the powers actually granted, is perpetually arising, and will continue to arise, as long as our system shall exist." The practical application of them to our international concerns and interests, has furnished many questions, doubtful enough to puzzle the best and wisest heads among us, as well as among those who went before us. Particular cases may be found in which each of our Ex-Presidents have mistaken the true spirit and meaning of the Constitution. They, like other men, were not infallible, and we shall look in vain for infallible successors. Some of these contested questions have been settled finally, and put at rest; and others are in process of adjustment. A history of the rise, progress, and termination of some of them would be both curious and instructive. Looking entirely to the Halls of Congress, we should find that each question brought forth an array of parties. That some of them were debated from year to year, with great heat and violence, each party believing honestly that a decision against it would be destructive of federal or State rights, and ruinous to the country, and the great cause of freedom and free government. A cool observer would have concluded that the only way left to save the nation, and preserve our happy institutions, would have been, to prorogue the argument, and suspend forever the adjustment of the matter in dispute. We should find the writers and presses of the day as active and as honest as they can be now, in sounding the alarm, and publishing their evil omens: but the councils of wisdom and the spirit of moderation were usually successful. Question after question was settled and carried into practical operation, and the country continued to increase in prosperity and happiness. The nation saw in the useful and fortunate results, that the fears of the alarmists and the forebodements of presagers were equally idle and unfounded. As it was in time past, so it is now, and will be in the future. Those who first moot a question are the last to give it up. The pride of opinion lives after the occasion which gave birth to it is forgotten, and therefore it is, that contested powers are often finally decided and carried into full effect long before the opposition to them ceases on the floor of Congress. This is exactly the case with the power to construct post roads and other internal improvements.

I could name fifty instances in which the power has been exercised, and yet the opposition to it is as fierce as ever.

It would be well for the country if these obstinate contentions could be brought within some limitation. The adhesion of individuals to their self-sufficient notions and opinions, is of little consequence, so long as the questions are at issue, and before the people; but so soon as public opinion has awarded its decision on the matter in dispute, it would seem to be the duty of those who differ from the body of the nation, to suspend their opposition. When the majority, after full consideration, gives its approving voice in favour of constructions put upon the Constitution, it would be well to let the contest end. When the people are satisfied, their agents might in reason be contented. Where both the policy of a measure, and the power to execute it are contested, we might expect to find protracted opposition; but where all admit the policy, and the existence of the power has been often and again asserted and maintained by large majorities in Legislation; and where, as in the present case of roads and canals, all the co-ordinate branches of Government have concurred in the opinion, it would seem that opposition might well cease from the minority. Such ill-timed obstinate hostility, to the measures called for by the embodied will of the nation, must always be, as it always has been, detrimental to the public service. Perpetual opposition is perpetual madness. Things fairly settled should remain at rest. Mutual deference, and mutual concessions, are more necessary in the management of our public than our private interests. Some flexibility of character, united with forbearing diffidence and modest toleration, is essentially necessary in the affairs of free government, where the majority must always rule. . . .

V

Developing the Art of Politics

The party system of the Federalists and the Republicans formed in the 1790's did not survive, but the basic rules for the operation of American politics established during the period did in large part endure. It became respectable to campaign for office, to work to influence voters in their choices at the polls, to organize campaign committees and formal party machinery, to vote the straight party ticket, and to work behind the scenes to bring about victory at the polls. Although the Jeffersonian Republicans were the innovators of much party organization and many new political techniques, the Federalists commonly followed Republican examples. The documents in this section illustrate an approach to politics that was not confined to any particular party but displayed an American style of politics that, despite an obsoleteness of literary expression, will hardly seem alien to the twentieth-century reader. In the instructions from party managers, the confidential letters that passed between party leaders, the reports of political meetings, and similar documents can be seen the process through which a workable political structure was established and American political life maintained its vitality.

21. Conducting an Election in Virginia: The Contested Election of Congressman Francis Preston, 1793

The way in which elections were held and the conduct of candidates seeking office varied from state to state depending on state laws, traditions, and local practices. Campaigning for office was earlier more direct and vigorous in the South than in any other region. The custom of candidates in Virginia of treating the voters on election days to refreshments, usually rum punch, turned polling places at times into scenes of near riot. Contemporary newspapers, while reporting the issues and rhetoric of campaigns and the results of elections, rarely described exactly how the electorate was polled since this was, of course, common knowledge to those who participated. Some of the best sources of information on the conduct of elections are found in records relating to contested elections, for here details were brought out that otherwise would have escaped recording. This document records the case of Francis Preston, elected as a representative from Virginia to the Third Congress in 1793. Preston's election was contested by Abram Trigg, who complained of the actions of the sheriffs in conducting the poll and of the undue influence of federal troops, commanded by Preston's brother, present at the poll in one county. Although the Committee of Elections recommended that a new election be held, the house, after a debate which provoked some very outspoken comments on the conduct of elections, upheld the right of Preston to his seat in Congress. The report is taken from M. St. Clair Clarke and David A. Hall (eds.), Cases of Contested Elections in Congress (Washington, D.C., 1834), pp. 78–84.

Francis Preston being returned as one of the members of the House from Virginia, his seat was contested by Abram Trigg, upon whose petition the Committee of Elections, on the 17th April, 1794, made report as follows:

"That, upon examining the evidence in this case, it appears that in the county of Lee, in the said State, the poll was closed, after due proclamation by the sheriff, at or about three o'clock P.M.: that application was afterwards made to the sheriff to open the poll for several voters who appeared, which the sheriff refused. On recurring to the election law of Virginia, the sheriff appears to be vested with discretionary power to close the poll at any time of the day after three proclamations made, and no voters appearing. The committee are, therefore, of opinion that the election was conducted according to law in the said county.

"It appears that the sheriff of Washington county, in consequence of rain, adjourned the poll to the second day; and that, from the latitude of discretion vested in him by law, he was fully authorized so to do.

"No evidence having been produced in support of the charge that persons were polled in Washington county who live in the territory south of the Ohio, and in Kentucky, the petitioner has abandoned that charge.

"The evidence, with regard to Montgomery county, being very voluminous, and in some respects contradictory, the committee have found some difficulty in forming an opinion in relation to that county. The following facts, however, appear to be well established, viz.

"That Capt. William Preston, brother, and agent at the election, of the sitting member, was quartered near Montgomery court-house with about 60 or 70 federal troops, of which he had the command. That, on the day of election, the said troops were marched, in a body, twice or three times round the court-house, and paraded in front of and close to the door thereof. That, towards the close of the election, the said troops were polled generally in favor of the sitting member; but their votes were put down on a separate paper, and, after the election, at the comparison of the polls of the respective counties, were rejected by the returning officers. That some of them threatened to beat any person who should vote in favor of the petitioner. That one of the soldiers struck and knocked down a magistrate who was attending at the said election. That three soldiers stood at the door of the court-house, and refused to admit a voter because he declared he would vote for the petitioner. That many of the country people were dissatisfied with the conduct of the soldiers, which produced altercations at the election between the soldiers and the country people, the former being generally for the sitting member, and the latter for the petitioner, and terminated in a violent affray between them after the poll was closed. That some of the soldiers being afterwards interrogated why they said they would beat any man who voted for Trigg, replied, "they who are bound must obey." That, though it is doubtful whether any of the soldiers were armed at the court-house, yet it appears that at the time of the affray, after the election, Capt. Preston had a sword and dagger; and that, when the soldiers, being overpowered by the country people, retreated to their barracks, some guns were fired by the soldiers towards the country people.

"The committee, on full consideration of all the evidence in relation to Montgomery county, from which the foregoing facts result, are of opinion that, notwithstanding the soldiers were not disfranchised of the right of voting, merely as such, yet their conduct, as well as that of their commander, was inconsistent with that freedom and fairness which ought to prevail at elections; and that although it does not appear, from any other than hearsay testimony, that any voter was actually prevented from voting, yet there is every reasonable ground to believe that some were, and that the election was unduly and unfairly biassed by the turbulent and menacing conduct of the military; and that the petitioner, who only lost his election by a majority of ten votes, has not had that fair opportunity of obtaining the suffrages of the people of that district to which every candidate is entitled. The committee, therefore, viewing the precedent as a dangerous one, and considering the inestimable privilege of free suffrage ought never to be violated by any military interposition; that the sitting member may have obtained a majority by improper influence, and that the petitioner ought to have a chance of obtaining a seat on equal terms, are of opinion that Francis Preston is not duly elected a member of this House."

In support of the reasoning and conclusion of this report, the petitioner submitted a paper containing, at great length, his observations on the depositions and other exhibits connected with this case.

The report being before the House for consideration, a debate arose thereon, which was sustained for three days: such speeches as were reported are subjoined.

Mr. SMITH, of South Carolina, said he considered it a very clear point that the election was not a fair one, because it was evident that the petitioner had not enjoyed an equally fair chance with the sitting member. It was true that some facts in the petition had not been substantiated, but many had. The House had been told that hearsay testimony was unworthy of attention, but he wished to remind them that they were not, like a court of law, restricted to proceed upon regular proof, and not to go beyond the letter of it: they were entitled to hear and weigh every thing advanced, and to form their opinion from the general conviction arising upon the whole circumstances. Some facts, of the most unwarrantable kind, had come out. Three of Capt. Preston's soldiers guarded the door of the court-house, where the election was held: when a person, since examined as an evidence, wanted to go in, they stopped him with this question, "are you to vote for Trigg?" Upon answering yes, they replied "by Jesus, then, you shall not!" and though he was fifty-eight years of age, two of them laid hold upon him and cast him to the ground: when he got up again, he went off. Mr. SMITH said there was a clear collusion between Capt. Preston and the soldiery. [Here Mr. PRESTON interrupted him by declaring that there was no such thing in the evidence. Mr. S. affirmed that there was. The Clerk was then directed to read part of the examination of the witnesses. The particulars above-stated appeared in proof.] And Mr. S. insisted that they contained a demonstration of the collusive measures between the sitting member, and his brother, Capt. Preston, and the military. It was objected to, said Mr. S., on the part of the soldiers, that they only said that they *could*, not that they *would*, knock down Mr. Trigg's voters. But Mr. S. considered this critical distinction as minute and trifling from the lips of a soldier in liquor. He did not understand its accuracy, and he imagined that his own nerves must have been as much affected by the *could* as the *would*. Many of the country people had expressed much dissatisfaction with the soldiers. It was proved that when the fray began, Capt. Preston had wished to have twenty of his soldiers there; and this hint was no sooner given than a person ran off, and immediately returned with a party of them.

Mr. SHERBURNE was for supporting the sitting member. He wished that the time of the House might not be squandered in a useless display of eloquence; it was, to be sure, agreeable to the speaker himself, but at the same time very superfluous in regard to his audience.

The Clerk was again ordered to read some passages in the proof as far as they respected the behavior of Capt. Preston.

Mr. W. SMITH then rose a second time. As a member of the committee that had been chosen upon this business, he was entitled to vindicate their report, of which he read some extracts very unfavorable to the behavior of the soldiers.

Mr. SMITH observed that Mr. Preston, in his defence, had been extremely profuse of his censure on the committee for doing what they considered to be their duty. Mr. SMITH, referring to the observations of Mr. SHERBURNE, said that he was perfectly in order for defending the report of the committee, because it was justified by the facts.

Though the quarrel between the soldiers and the country people did not happen till after the poll, yet it was from bad blood before the poll began, and therefore a reference to it was strictly in order. Mr. S. said it was no part of his intention to injure the character of Capt. Preston, who, when the tumult began, took off his sword and gave it to some person to hold. For this moderation Capt. Preston deserved credit; but still Mr. S. considered himself justified in opposing the election, since it was not conducted with that fairness, that regularity, and that equality of chances, requisite upon republican principles. He read a quotation from Blackstone as to elections. "Violent interposition," says that writer, "what is it but to cut Government up by the roots, and poison the foundations of public security?" He dwelt at some length on this idea, and the peculiar impropriety of military interposition. He said that, upon the whole, Mr. Preston had only a majority of ten votes, and when the circumstance of sixty or seventy soldiers driving off the voters of Mr. Trigg was opposed to such a narrow majority, could any body call the transaction legal? [At the words "*ten votes*," Mr. S. was twice interrupted, first by Mr. MACON, and then by Mr. SMITH, of Maryland, but he persisted in his assertion.] He had stated facts; the premises were obvious. Shall the House suffer an officer, the brother of a candidate, to seize the door of the court-house, and turn away the voters against his brother? It had been said that it was customary for a candidate in that part of the country to collect his friends and block up doors, but surely it was an improper custom. The sitting member had said that if his brother had taken any wrong course, he should have been prosecuted in a court of law. Mr. S. did not mean to say that Capt. Preston had committed any offence worthy of that; he did not, perhaps, imagine that he was doing wrong at all. It had been asked if it was possible that sixty or seventy soldiers could overawe two or three hundred people. He thought it possible.

Mr. SMITH, of Maryland, defended Mr. Preston. He said, that in forming an impartial judgment on this question, various circumstances must be taken into consideration besides the facts in evidence before the House. In the elections in the Eastern States, the citizens met in small bodies, and they conducted the business with that order and decency which became the true republican character; but it was the misfortune of the Southern States that their citizens assembled in large bodies; the electors of a county meet altogether before the sheriff, and give their votes at the same time. Hence it appears, as the matter was described by Mr. S., that an election in the Southern States is nothing but a nursery of superlative mischief. He said that he was somewhat surprised at hearing another member express so much resentment at an *election riot*. The gentleman had access to the history of a *certain election*, where the very chancellor of a court of justice bred a riot in his own court for the express purpose of serving his party. Much had been said about the enormity of knocking down a justice of the peace; and, in the report, the affair was stated as if the magistrate had been at the court-house in his official capacity. Now sir, said Mr. SMITH, in this part of it the report is not fair: the justice of the peace was not there in his official capacity, he was there *drunk*, sir, and he gave the first blow to the man who knocked him down. Mr. SMITH had, by the first accounts of this affair, been very much prejudiced against the election of the sitting member, but when he came to examine closely into the business, he declared that he had never known an election in the Southern States where there was so little mischief. He was sorry, for the honor of his part of the country, to give this account of it to the Eastern members, but, in point of common justice to Mr. Preston, they ought to be informed that a Southern election was quite a different sort of transaction from one of theirs. In the evidence before the House, it had been stated that one person had been seen at the court-house with a club under his coat. But, sir, said Mr. SMITH, I suppose that five hundred of my constituents had clubs under their coats; so that if this be a sufficient reason for putting an end to an election, the committee may begin by dissolving mine. If the committee are to break up every election where persons were seen drunk, they will have a great deal of work upon hand, sir. In what way were elections for Southern members carried on? A man of influence came to the place of election with two or three hundred of his friends; and, to be sure, they would not, if they could help it, suffer any body on the other side to give a vote as long as they were there. It was certainly a very bad custom, and must very much surprise an Eastern member, but it was the custom, and perfectly known to be so, and therefore it was very injurious to hold up the character of Capt. Preston as a pretence for dissolving the election. The behavior of that young gentleman, when insulted, had been exemplary: in the midst of a riotous mob, he gave away his sword, that he might do no mischief in that way. This was a great instance of moderation and presence of mind. The aspersions cast upon the character of this officer, Mr. S. regarded as highly unjust, and they might, if not properly taken notice of, be extremely injurious to his hopes of advancing in the service. Capt. Preston had gone to the court-house as a private citizen, and he had a right to be there. As to the menace of the soldiers, that they *could* knock down one of Col. Trigg's voters, this was very different from asserting that they *would* do it. Were a man to have come up to Mr. S. in the street, and say "I will knock you down, sir," Mr. S. would be for giving the first blow; but were he only to say "I can knock you down, sir," the expression would be quite different. But as to the affray that fell out after the election was over, Mr. S. asserted that if the soldiers had killed all the country people, or the country people had killed all the soldiers, this had nothing to do with the merits of the election itself. And as to this quarrel, few men had the temper of this young officer, (Capt. Preston,) in ordering off his soldiers; so that, instead of the censure of that House, he deserved their praise. At his age, Mr. S. would not have ordered his men off; and as to the censure on the military, inserted in the report, he did not agree with it. It would be a very fine reason, to be sure, to vacate a seat in this House because one of the electors had been seen with a club under his coat! Mr. S. was sorry to give such a description to the Eastern members of the manners of his country, but he did so that he might hinder them from being hurt at the facts brought forward in the evidence. He concluded by reminding the House that it would be perfectly ridiculous to measure one thing by another which was perfectly opposite, or to judge of a Southern by an Eastern election.

Mr. CLARK said that three days had now been spent upon this business. Long speeches did not alter the way in which members were to give their votes, and they were, therefore, nothing but a loss of time; he wished for the question.

Mr. MACON said that there was no law to hinder the militia from attending elections as well as any body else.

Mr. GILLON spoke for a few minutes. He saw no reason why another member (Mr. W. SMITH, of S. C.) should be so much hurt by the circumstance of an election riot. Referring to the speech of Mr. S. SMITH, he observed that there was a riot at the gentleman's own election, and in his own favor; and still worse, this riot was in a church; the riot was raised by a magistrate, who with his own hand dragged one of the opposite party out of the church. And if you want evidence of all this, said Mr. GILLON, I myself was present, and can be a witness. Mr. GILLON saw, therefore, no reason why there should be such a noise about this election, in particular, when others were just as bad, or a great deal worse.

After the reading of the proofs and the petitioner's written observations thereon, and after the sitting member had been fully heard in his defence, the parties retired from the bar, and the House proceeded to a decision on the case; and the question being put on the resolution reported by the Committee of Elections, to wit: "Resolved, That Francis Preston is not duly elected a member of this House;" it passed in the negative. The resolution in this negative form having failed, the sitting member was, by consequence, confirmed in his seat.

22. Plotting Federalist Strategy: Letter of Robert Goodloe Harper, September 25, 1812

In 1804 Federalist candidate Charles C. Pinckney lost to Jefferson by an electoral vote of 14 to 162; in 1808 he lost to Madison, 47 to 122. As difficulties with Great Britain over neutral rights mounted, Federalist strength revived, and the dominant Republican party became increasingly split. With public opinion divided over the declaration of war in June, 1812, Federalist party leaders gathered in New York in September to plan their tactics in the presidential campaign. President Madison had been nominated for re-election by the Republican nominating caucus, but dissident Republicans in New York were supporting the candidacy of DeWitt Clinton. In the letter given below, Robert Goodloe Harper of Maryland, a former Federalist congressman from South Carolina, reports on the Federalists' decision not to nominate their own candidate but to support Clinton. The letter is particularly revealing of the way in which party leaders weighed election prospects, counted safe and doubtful states, evaluated the public pulse, and decided on party strategy. Harper's speculation on election prospects was well informed. As he predicted, Clinton carried New York, New Hampshire, Rhode Island, Connecticut, Delaware, and five of the six electoral votes of Maryalnd. As Harper had hoped, Clinton also carried Massachusetts and New Jersey, but he failed to win Pennsylvania or votes elsewhere and lost to Madison 89 to 128 in the closest contest for the presidency between 1800 and 1824. Harper's letter, addressed to Clement Dorsey, Port Tobacco, Maryland, is in the Robert Goodloe Harper Papers, Library of Congress.

Baltimore Sept. 25th 1812

My Dear Sir,

At the request of some of our friends in this State, I lately attended a meeting of federal Gentlemen at New-York, assembled from all the States north and east of Virginia, to deliberate on the conduct which it may be proper for the federal party to pursue, in the approaching election of President. The meeting was very full and respectable. It was attended by Delegates from all the States north of the Potomac, and from South Carolina.

After a very full and free communication of sentiment and information, we found no hope nor chance of electing a federal President. Vermont is lost to us. It is quite certain that we could not get the votes of Massachusetts. Those of New-York are very doubtful, and Pennsylvania desperate. We might hope for five or six votes in Maryland, but cannot rely on more than three. As to North Carolina, tho we learn that very considerable changes have taken place, yet there does not appear, from any facts known to us, any reason to expect that the votes of that State could be obtained for a federal candidate.

The choice of a president of our own being thus desperate, nothing remains for us, but to acquiesce in the reelection of Mr. Madison, or take the chance of getting rid of him and his political system, the worst parts of it at least, by giving our aid to Clinton.

In favour of this policy the meeting was almost unanimous. It consisted of more than sixty persons, of whom Mr. King and Mr. Radcliffe of New-York, and Mr. Sitgreaves of Pennsylvania, were the only dissentients. Mr. Sitgreaves rather disapproved the policy than opposed it. His opinion was that it would be better to take all the hazards of Mr. Madison's reelection, including that of separation and french alliance, than to endanger, as he thought, our own honour union and existence as a party, by giving our aid to Mr. Clinton. This opinion he expressed in conversation, but took no part in the debate. Mr. King warmly and very eloquently supported it in the debate. With these three exceptions the meeting was, I believe, unanimously of opinion, that we ought to support Clinton in preference and opposition to Madison; as the only means now in our power, of averting the evils which have assailed and still threaten us.

The expectation that Mr. Clinton, if elected, will change the present course of measures, in all essential points, rests much more on his position, geographical and political than in his professions and assurances. But they have been ample and positive. They were made without reserve, and repeated while I was in New-York. In substance they amount to this: that Mr. Clinton looks with abhorrence on a french alliance, in any form and under any circumstances: that he holds Buonaparte and his views and system in such detestation, as to be willing to bear a great deal from England, rather than throw the least weight into the french scale: that he thinks a peace with England, upon honourable terms, is easily attainable, and ought to be made as soon as possible: that he is opposed to the whole restrictive system, and thinks that commerce ought to be fostered and protected; to which end a navy, fully commensurate with the resources of the nation, ought to be immediately provided, and constantly maintained; and that while the present war continues the honour of the nation ought to be supported, by a vigorous and manly exertion of its force.

If Mr. Clinton relied on federalists alone for success, these sentiments ought to be and no doubt would be published. But he cannot be elected without the aid of a large portion of the Democratic party; which the avowal of such opinions, or the knowledge that any explanations had been made by him to the federal party, would certainly in a great measure and perhaps entirely alienate from his cause. We must therefore consider the communications as strictly confidential, and take every precaution to prevent them from becoming public. His sentiments are no doubt known to his confidential friends. But we have all seen the grounds on which they have thought it best to rest his pretensions. The general probability, arising from his character situation and connexions, that he will pursue a more correct course than Mr. Madison, is a sufficient justification to us, in giving him the preference.

The hope of electing Mr. Clinton rests on this. We can certainly give him New-York, New-Hampshire, Rhode-Island, Connecticut, Delaware and part of Maryland. There is great probability that we may, in conjunction with his supporters among the democrats, give him Massachusetts, Jersey, Pennsylvania, and the greater part, if not the whole of Maryland. We entertain the same expectation of North Carolina; and his friends expect to carry Vermont and part of Ohio.

The meeting did not resolve to recommend the support of Mr. Clinton. It was thought best to take a course somewhat different. They resolved that it appeared impracticable to elect, and was therefore inexpedient to propose, a federal candidate; and that it should be recommended to the federalists throughout the United States, to exert themselves in the approaching election of electors, to procure the choice of such persons, as will be most likely to effect by their votes a change in the present course of public measures. They then appointed a Committee, to collect and disseminate information on the subject. The committee sits in Philadelphia. Three of its members, Mr. Hopkinson, Mr. Binny and Mr. Meredith reside there. The other two are Mr. Sitgreaves and Mr. Duncan of Pennsylvania.

The plan of operations which appeared best to the meeting, and which they resolved to recommend to their friends generally, is to let the Clintonian democrats take the lead, in all the democratic States and districts and to support them silently with our votes; while we every where exert ourselves to the utmost, to place federalists in the house of Representatives, and the State Legislatures. That seemed to be the best mode of keeping Clinton right, and of restraining Madison in his mischievous course, should we be forced to bear him four years longer.

The plan adopted at New-York leaves us at large to profit by favourable events. With as many Clintonian electors as we can carry, where there are no hopes or but very faint ones of carrying federalists, and with all the federal electors that we can get, we may hold the fate of the candidates in our own hands, and at the decisive moment take the course which we may deem best for the public safety. We do not stand committed to Mr. Clinton. He and his friends must therefore do all in their power to convince us that he deserves the preference, in other words, that we may expect from him a different course of measures, or else we may drop him, and try the effect of submitting four years longer to Madison, in hopes of a complete cure in that time. We may even bring forward a federal Candidate, should any thing occur to warrant the attempt.

I am Dear Sir, with very great regard,
Yours most truly.
Robt: G: Harper

23. Getting Out the Vote: A Republican Circular, February 27, 1819

Numerous party circulars and handbills survive to testify to the attention which active party workers gave to getting out the vote at elections and to making preparations to secure the full force of the party's strength at the polls. In elections where ballots were used, the voter was commonly required to submit a handwritten one. A frequent technique of party leaders, therefore, was to arrange to have handwritten ballots prepared in advance for distribution to the voters. This and other party techniques are illustrated in the following Republican party circular sent out in preparation for the elections for the state legislature in Connecticut held in April, 1819. This document also suggests that the one-party character of national politics during the "era of good feelings" did not hold true in state politics. The original printed sheet is in the Broadside Collection, New-York Historical Society.

Hartford, February 27 1819

SIR,

On the first Monday of April next, the Electors will meet in the several towns for the choice of their rulers for the year ensuing; and it is a duty enjoined upon me to communicate with gentlemen in this County on that important subject—to you I direct by advice of Republican friends—It is hoped and confidently expected, that you will immediately consult with the most influential and active Republicans, and cause such arrangements to be made as will bring to the Polls all the Electors in your town, and also every candidate qualified to receive the oath—Do not fail to suggest to them the necessity of a prompt and early attendance at the meeting and of their continuing at their posts until the business of the day is finished—Urge the great importance of a united exertion in voting for every candidate on our general Ticket, more particularly for the SENATE. In choosing the Senate each Elector has a right to vote for twelve persons only, & their names must be fairly written on one piece of paper—have such arrangements made as will insure a full supply of votes.—We should be pleased if every Elector would write his own votes, but that cannot be relied upon. Few will carry their votes written to the meeting—and fewer still will have pen, ink, and paper to write them there—unless votes for the Senate are previously written, and ready to be delivered to those who may want them, many of the electors will leave the meeting without voting—we know that to have been the case in a great many towns last fall.

If our ticket is supported by the whole strength of the party, our success is certain—but should we from personal or other considerations neglect to vote for the republican candidates, or scatter our votes, we hazard having their places filled with federalists, for they will unite to a man on their ticket. In those towns where there are but few republicans, they are too apt to neglect attending the electoral meetings—they ought to reflect that their votes are very important on the general ticket, and at the present crisis it is the indispensible duty of every man to come forward in support of his principles.

Your own judgment together with the advice of such friends as you may confer with on the subject, will dictate to you the most efficient measures to call forth your whole strength. Permit me however to suggest to you the expediency of a general meeting of our friends in your town, and sectional meetings in each School district—and that large committees be appointed to make arrangements in their several districts—by which a correct knowledge of your strength may be obtained, and the best arrangements made to call forth and concentrate your force—(a similar course has been for several years adopted in this town, and has been attended with very great success.)

The order of the business at the Proxies will somewhat differ from former practice, and it is desirable that this order should be well understood previous to the meeting. To this understanding, and to a union of sentiment and action, frequent meetings will essentially contribute. To be correct you will refer to the Election law passed at the last session of the General Assembly—extracts of which will be seasonably published in the newspapers.

The federalists will undoubtedly make a desperate effort to regain their lost power—and their newspapers will be filled with false electioneering tales—they will use every exertion to alarm your fears, and sow the seeds of jealousy and discord in the republican ranks—"*divide and conquer is their motto.*" They are and ever have been the office-seekers. They are not willing that the republicans should participate in the honors and emoluments of office, they grasp at the whole. They agreed upon a ticket last fall, at New Haven, for the Senate, the names of their candidates are known, though they have not yet been published; they are nearly to a man, lawyers; and generally of the true "*blue light stamp.*" That ticket, however, they are using every possible exertion to induce their party to support—It becomes our indispensible duty to counteract them—the Judges of the Superior and other courts—Sheriffs for the several counties, and many other important appointments conformable to the Constitution are to be made this spring, and our opponents have their eyes upon them—Fidelity to ourselves, and the good of the public demands our most active exertions to prevent our enemies having it in their power to controul those appointments.

You may rest assured that the federalists are now, and have been for several months past actively engaged throughout the State, in organizing themselves for the April election—They have appointed county, town, and school-district committees, &c. for that purpose—they have generally thus far been very cautious to keep their movements from the view of the republicans—they hoped in that way to lull us into security, and at the polls to rush forward and take us by stratagem—but in some instances their friends have betrayed them, and disclosed their plans.

We ought to be on the alert—watch the movements of our enemies and counteract them—come forward at the polls with our full strength, do our duty there, and our triumph is certain.

Should your business lead you to town, please to call; and should any thing important occur, please to write your friend

JOHN RUSS

24. Challenging the Caucus: A Jackson Circular, April 20, 1824

From 1800 to 1824, Republican presidential candidates were nominated by the congressional caucus composed of Republican members of Congress. Each time the caucus met it aroused controversy, the system was attacked as being undemocratic, and members of Congress were reminded that they were not chosen to select presidents. Much of the criticism came from Federalists, who in 1800 had held a caucus but had abandoned the practice as Federalist strength in Congress dwindled. The caucus was attacked also from time to time by dissident Republicans who disapproved of the caucus nominee; for example, John Randolph of Roanoke in opposing the nomination of Madison in 1808 centered his attack on the caucus. Thus, the 1824 assault was not unusual; the new condition was the inability of the caucus to enforce its decision. For the first time since 1800, the nominee of the Republican nominating caucus did not win election. Part of the explanation for this can be seen in the following circular originating in Winchester, Virginia. It not only challenged the caucus nomination of William H. Crawford but also initiated efforts to advance the can-

didacy of Andrew Jackson. Crawford carried Virginia in 1824, but his
41 electoral votes placed him in a distant third place behind Jackson
with 99 electoral votes and John Quincy Adams with 84. Although
Jackson won the largest electoral vote, it was not a majority, and the
election went to the House of Representatives, where John Quincy
Adams was elected president. The circular also furnishes evidence of
the methods of politics inherited from the Jeffersonian era that would
be found useful in the age of Jackson. The original document is in
the Broadside Collection, Virginia Historical Society.

WINCHESTER, APRIL 20, 1824

SIR,—With the hope that you approve of the accompanying
resolutions, I beg leave, on behalf of the Winchester corresponding committee, named in one of them, to address you. If your
views do not accord with those resolutions, I hope you will excuse the liberty. It is believed, by that committee, that General
Jackson is *decidedly the man of the people*; that faith, zeal, and a
fair interchange of thought, are alone necessary to develope *this
truth*; that industry, system, and concert, can devise a plan, by
which a ticket, favorable to the object in view, can be formed
immediately from the people. The committee for themselves
concur with the meeting in preferring General Jackson and John
C. Calhoun to any men in public view. The committee are
also persuaded that neither of the other aspirants can in Virginia oppose the caucus nomination with success. It is therefore hoped that even those who are more inclined towards others
would surrender their predilections on the altar of the public good;
and unite with the friends of the object of this meeting, in en-
deavoring to restore to the people once more the exercise of the
right of choosing their chief rulers. It will take some time to ascertain an expression of public sentiment on this subject; but it is
hoped there is ample time to effect this object. If you should not
be disposed to co-operate with the friends of the people's ticket,
to be formed at a future day, in favor of General Jackson and John
C. Calhoun, we trust your candour will induce you to hand this
letter to some one who may be so inclined. It is expected that
meetings will be held in every county in the state, by the friends
of the people's ticket. That the cause has advocates every where,
cannot be doubted. In some counties, it may at first seem that it
has but few. Even there, if *they* are not lukewarm and wavering,
they will soon find many ardent friends to join them. In many

counties in the state, the committee venture to predict there will be overwhelming majorities; and that the result will be, when public opinion is ascertained, that GENERAL JACKSON and JOHN C. CALHOUN are the men to whom the PEOPLE of Virginia now look as the men most worthy to be exalted to the highest stations under the government. Any communication you can make to the committee here, calculated to promote the object of the late meeting at Winchester, will be thankfully received.

> Yours respectfully,
> ROBERT B. WHITE,
> On behalf of the committee

At a meeting of a large and respectable number of the free-holders of Frederick county, held at the Town Hall in Winchester, on Monday, the 5th day of April, 1824, in pursuance of previous notice, given in the public papers on Saturday last, *On motion*, Doct. JOHN HEDGES was called to the chair, and A. S. TIDBALL appointed secretary. The following Preamble and Resolutions were offered by *Robert B. White*, Esq. and unanimously adopted:

WE regard the people as the fountain of all legitimate authority, and think that it is consonant with our free and representative system of government, that by a fair expression of their choice, they should elect the President and Vice-President of the United States. We deprecate any policy, measure, or influence, calculated to defeat or even render doubtful the people's will, on so interesting a subject. Any attempt to trench on this sacred right of the people, or to divert this important power from its proper channel, or in any way to frustrate or impede the due exercise of it, should, in our opinion, be viewed with alarm and distrust. Abuses, long tolerated, are apt to grow into precedent, and precedent to be taken for authority. Power usurped, and usurpation long acquiesced in, are often mistaken for right. We believe the crisis has arrived, when it becomes the duty of the independent freeholders of Virginia, to inquire, whether the general ticket system, combined with the influence of congressional and legislative caucuses, and other causes now existing at Washington, are not likely to divest them of one of the most important rights they have retained. Such a result will be inevitable, if it be true (as it certainly is in the opinion of this meeting) that Mr. Crawford and Mr. Gallatin are not the men that Virginia would most delight to honor at this time, and if the people, heedless of the exercise of so valuable a right, should supinely acquiesce in the late caucus nominations at Washington and Richmond. It is not our purpose to censure the motives of the respectable gentlemen who composed those caucuses; but it is due to truth to say, that the nomination was made, and the electoral ticket formed, in Richmond, without any power delegated for the purpose—without any accurate estimate of public sentiment—without instructions from the people; and as to the will of Virginia on the subject, *that nomination* is at best but *uncertain* and *conjectural*. For ourselves, we protest against that nomination, and appeal to the people.

If early and uniform devotion to the cause of American freedom; if faithful and important services, both in civil and military life; if talents, useful knowledge, energy of character and integrity, united with a clear hand, a sound mind, a prompt judgment, and long experience; if patriotism and illustrious services in the cause of our country,—are still to be revered and honored, as they were in the days of WASHINGTON,—we confidently believe that Gen. ANDREW JACKSON is now, what the immortal WASHINGTON was when he lived, "first in war, first in peace, and first in the hearts of his countrymen."

If ability, fidelity, zeal and firmness, in the discharge of the arduous duties of an exalted and highly responsible station, during a trying and eventful period of our history, are to be remembered and rewarded, we consider JOHN C. CALHOUN as second only to Gen. Andrew Jackson.

Resolved therefore, That this meeting will support an Electoral Ticket, hereafter to be formed by the people of Virginia, in favor of Gen. ANDREW JACKSON as President, and JOHN C. CALHOUN as Vice-President.

Resolved, That we respectfully recommend it to the independent freeholders in the different electoral districts in Virginia, to co-operate with us in forming and in supporting such a ticket.

Resolved, That Robert B. White, Geo. Orrick, William S. Jones, Alexander S. Tidball, John W. Baylis, George Linn, Henry W. Baker, Baylis Davis, William M. Barton, Province M'Cormick, Edward M'Guire, John W. Miller, John Baker, and Josiah Lockhart, be a committee of correspondence, whose duty it will be, to correspond with a committee appointed for the like purpose by some of the people of Fredericksburg, and with all other committees that have been or may hereafter be appointed to promote the object of this meeting; and that the said committees be instructed to answer any communications they may receive from any individual or individuals in the state, well disposed towards the success of the People's Ticket.

Resolved, That when this meeting adjourns, it will adjourn until the 5th of July next.

Resolved, That the committee of correspondence be instructed to report such measures as they may have taken, and such information as they may have acquired, touching the object of this meeting, to the adjourned meeting on the 5th of July.

Resolved, That the editors of the different papers in Virginia be requested to insert in their papers the proceedings of this meeting.

JOHN HEDGES, Chairman

A. S. TIDBALL, Secretary

VI

Building a New Society

Americans in the formative years of the republic were conscious of being involved in the process of shaping a new society. Some thought not merely in terms of the American nation but also of providing a model for mankind. While the formation of the constitutional and political structure of the United States and the development of its economic foundations remained of paramount concern, many Americans addressed themselves to the broader problems of society. The place of education and the means of providing it in a republic attracted considerable thought. Jefferson regarded his role in the establishment of the University of Virginia as one of the most significant accomplishments of his life. The age was an optimistic one, in which many men thought in terms of shaping both their own world and the society of the future for the betterment of mankind. Discussions of education or the speculations of Jefferson and Adams on aristocracy were as fundamental a part of the time as the debates on state rights or Hamiltonian finance. But it was not a period of great achievement in arts and letters, and some men, including architect Benjamin Henry Latrobe, sought to awaken Americans to the importance of the fine arts to society. For all its defects, American society with its youth and vigor and its optimistic vision of the future was able to inspire confidence in the success of the American experiment.

25. Education in a Republic: *Remarks on Education* by Samuel Harrison Smith, 1798

The American Philosophical Society in 1797 offered a prize of $100 for "the best System of liberal Education and literary instruction, adapted to the genius of the Government of the United States; comprehending also a plan for instituting and conducting public schools in this country, on principles of the most extensive utility." The prize was shared by Samuel Knox and Samuel Harrison Smith, two essayists whose influences upon Jefferson's educational thought can be observed. Smith's essay was published under the title Remarks on Education: Illustrating the Close Connection Between Virtue and Wisdom, To

Which Is Annexed a System of Liberal Education (*Philadelphia: printed for John Ormrod, 1798*). His plan was grounded upon the importance to both the individual and the republic of the "diffusion of knowledge," the acquisition of which was "open to all." Smith, who had graduated from the University of Pennsylvania at the age of fifteen, was twenty-four when he wrote this essay and just beginning the career for which he would become known, that of newspaper editor. In 1800 he moved from Philadelphia to Washington to establish the National Intelligencer. This was the newspaper that became the major Republican party organ during the administration of Jefferson, who had been president of the American Philosophical Society when Smith won the prize for his essay. The selections below summarize the main arguments of Smith's essay and his plan for a national system of education. They are reprinted from the 1798 Philadelphia edition cited above, pp. 36–37, 40–50, 66–71, 79–86.

. . . The diffusion of knowledge, co-extensive with that of virtue, would seem to apply with close precision to a republican system of education, because;

1. An enlightened nation is always most tenacious of its rights.

2. It is not the interest of such a society to perpetuate error; as it undoubtedly is the interest of many societies differently organized.

3. In a republic, the sources of happiness are open to all without injuring any.

4. If happiness be made at all to depend on the improvement of the mind, and the collision of mind with mind, the happiness of an individual will greatly depend upon the general diffusion of knowledge and a capacity to think and speak correctly.

5. Under a Republic, duly constructed, man feels as strong a bias to improvement, as under a despotism he feels an impulse to ignorance and depression.

We have now reached the goal of the preceding speculations. The necessary limits to an essay of this nature have prohibited minute illustration; but it has, we hope, been made to appear, with sufficient perspicacity, that human happiness depends upon the possession of virtue and wisdom; that virtue cannot be too highly cultivated; that it is only secure when allied with knowledge; and of consequence that knowledge itself cannot possibly be too extensively diffused. It follows that the great object of a liberal plan of education should be the almost universal diffusion of knowledge. . . .

It is necessary that the principle of a universal diffusion of knowledge should be in the highest degree energetic. This is a principle which cannot be too extensively embraced; for it is too true, that all the efforts of an enlightened zeal will never make a whole nation as well informed as its interests would prescribe.

But this necessary limit forms no objection to every practicable extension of it. We shall be furnished with irrefragable evidence of its beneficial tendency, on considering that knowledge has only produced injurious effects when it has been the subject of monopoly. The efforts of ignorance to oppress science have excited a spirit of retaliation, which we must not be surprised at beholding, in its turn, its own avenger. The moment, however, which marks the universal diffusion of science, by withdrawing the temptation to, as well as the means of, injury, will restore knowledge to its original purity and lustre. It is with knowledge, as with every other thing which influences the human mind. It acts precisely in proportion to the force of the object acted upon. As the beggar cannot corrupt by gold the beggar; so neither can opulence corrupt opulence. In the same manner, equality of intellectual attainments is a foe to oppression; and just as mankind shall advance in its possession, the means as well as the inducement to oppress will be annihilated. We are correct, therefore, in declaring a diffusion of knowledge, the best, perhaps the only, pledge of virtue, of equality, and of independence.

Let us, then, with mental inflexibility, believe that though all men will never be philosophers, yet that all men may be enlightened; and that folly, unless arising from physical origin, may be banished from the society of men.

The ideas already expressed, and those which succeed, must be understood as applicable to a system of general education. They only prescribe what it is necessary every man should know. They do not attempt to limit his acquisitions. Wealth and genius will always possess great advantages. It will be their prerogatives, if properly directed, to carry improvement to its highest eminences.

In forming a system of liberal education, it is necessary to avoid ideas of too general a character, as well as those which involve too minute a specification. Considerable latitude must be allowed for the different degrees of natural capacity, and the varying shades of temper and bias. It seems, therefore, fit to lay down principles which possess properties common to every mind, and which will, of course, in their application, admit of few, if any, exceptions.

The first great object of a liberal system of education should be the admission into the young mind of such ideas only as are either absolutely true, or in the highest degree probable; and the cautious exclusion of all error. . . .

Let then those truths in which all men agree be firmly impressed; let those which are probable be inculcated with caution, and let doubt always hang over those respecting which the good and the wise disagree. Above all things let the infant mind be protected from conviction without proof.

But it will be said that in almost all the departments of a general plan of education, the perusal of approved books must be chiefly relied on. The indispensable economy of arrangements which are to pervade a whole society, will prohibit the employment of preceptors of either great or original talents. It will therefore be fit that the preceptor, instead of inculcating his own immature ideas, should be guided by prescribed works. It is asked, where performances explaining and enforcing plain and undeniable truths, and avoiding prejudices or falsehoods, are to be found? Such productions are acknowledged to be rare. It is also granted that this difficulty presents one of the most serious obstacles to successful education. But it is not insurmountable. It is attempted to be removed, as will appear hereafter, by offering large rewards for books of this nature, and by inciting the learned by other inducements to embark in so noble a service. At present we must be satisfied in giving the preference to those works which abound most with truth and are the most exempt from error.

The elements of education, viz. reading and writing, are so obviously necessary that it is useless to do more than enumerate them.

Of nearly equal importance are the first principles of mathematics, as at present almost universally taught.

A tolerably correct idea of Geography would seem, in a Republic especially, to involve great advantages. The interest of the mercantile part of the community is closely connected with correct geographical knowledge. Many important departments of science include an accurate knowledge of it. But the most important consideration is that which contemplates the United States as either allied in friendship, or arrayed in hostility, with the other nations of the earth. In both which cases, it becomes the duty of the citizen to have just ideas of the position, size, and strength of nations, that he may as much as possible confide in his own judgment in forming an opinion of our foreign relations, instead of yielding his mind to a dangerous credulity. A most interesting part of Geography relates to a knowledge of our own country. Correct information on this subject will always conduce to strengthen the bands of friendship, and to dissipate the misrepresentations of party prejudice.

The cultivation of natural philosophy, particularly so far as it relates to agriculture and manufactures, has been heretofore almost entirely neglected. The benefits, however, which it would produce, are great, both as they regard the happiness of the individual, and as they regard national wealth. Many of the labours of the farmer and the mechanic, so far from forbidding reflection, invite it. Thus the constant development of new beauties in nature, and the almost as constant production of new wonders in art, extort admiration from the most ignorant, and even impress their minds with considerable delight. And yet how little do they know of the energies of nature or art? Lost in the contemplation of effects, the tribute of a grateful mind finds vent in simple wonder.

If we reverse the scene and behold the farmer enlightened by the knowledge of chemistry, how wide a field of reflection and pleasure, as well as profit, would acknowledge his empire?

The ingenuity of the mechanic would not long remain passive. Repeated efforts at improvement would often prove successful, and be the source of new and rapid wealth. At any rate, in all these cases, whether prospered with the expected success or not, an adequate compensation would be conferred on the mind thus employed, whose thoughts generally bring with them their own reward.

The circumscribed advantages, attending Geographical knowledge, will be greatly enlarged by a liberal acquaintance with History. In proportion as this branch of education shall be cultivated, men will see the mighty influence of moral principle, as well on the private individuals of a community, as on those who are called to preside over its public concerns. It will be distinctly seen that ambition has generally risen on a destruction of every sentiment of virtue, and that it much oftener merits execration than applause. Power, long enjoyed, will appear to be hostile to the happiness and subversive of the integrity, of the individual in whom it centers. Fanaticism and superstition will appear surrounded with blood and torture. War will stand forth with the boldest prominence of vice and folly, and make it, for a while, doubtful whether man is most a villain or a fool. In short the mirror which history presents will manifest to man what, it is probable, he will become, should he surrender himself up to those selfish pursuits, which centering in his own fame alone, have enabled him without horror to wade through the blood and tears of millions.

This horrid truth, confirmed by every page of history, will restrain, as it undoubted has restrained, the indulgence of furious passion. The immortal admiration attached to great and disinterested virtue, the immortal detestation inseparable from great and selfish vice, will furnish the mind at once with the strongest incentives to the one, and the liveliest abhorrence of the other.

The second leading object of education, should be to inspire the mind with a strong disposition to improvement.

It is acknowledged that science is still in its infancy. The combination of knowledge is enlarged, and of course, the sphere of happiness extended. At present science is only cultivated by a few recluse students, too apt to mingle the illusions of imagination with the results of indistinct observation. Hence the reproach that theory and practice oppose each other. But no sooner shall a whole nation be tributary to science, than it will dawn with new lustre. To adopt a physical illustration, its rays may be expected to meet with little absorption from ignorance, but to be reflected with additional lustre from every object they strike.

The most splendid discoveries have not been made by philosophers of profound erudition and abstracted reflection, but by men of moderate attainments and correct observation. They have proceeded from steady and patient observation. . . .

All science ought to derive its rank from its utility. The real good which it actually does, or is capable of doing, is the only genuine criterion of its value. Man may indulge himself in sublime reveries, but the world will forever remain uninterested in them. It is only when he applies the powers of his mind to objects of general use, that he becomes their benefactor; until he does this he is neither entitled to their gratitude or applause.

He is the best friend of man, who makes discoveries involving effects which benefit mankind the most extensively. Moral truths are therefore of importance but little short of infinite. For they apply to numbers which almost evade enumeration, and to time which loses itself in eternity. These truths, all agree, are not to be sought in the cloister. They are only acquired by uniting the calm and patient reflection of retirement, with the bold and penetrating observation of active life. . . .

Before a detail is given of the course of education proposed, it may be proper concisely to state the points which it has been the object of the preceding remarks to establish.

In the first place, virtue and wisdom have been deemed to possess an inseparable connection, and the degree and efficiency of the one has been decided to depend on the measure and vigor of the other. From this proposition the inference is deduced that a nation cannot possibly be too enlightened, and that the most energetic zeal is necessary to make it sufficiently so for the great interests of virtue and happiness.

Secondly. That it is the duty of a nation to superintend and even to coerce the education of children, and that high considerations of expediency not only justify, but dictate the establishment of a system, which shall place under a control, independent of, and superior to, parental authority, the education of children.

Thirdly. The preference has been given at a certain age to public education over domestic education.

Fourthly. The period of education recommended has been fixed at an age so early, as to anticipate the reign of prejudice, and to render the first impressions made on the mind subservient to virtue and truth.

Guided by these principles it is proposed:

I. That the period of education be from 5 to 18.

II. That every male child, without exception, be educated.

III. That the instructor in every district be directed to attend to the faithful execution of this injunction. That it be made punishable by law in a parent to neglect offering his child to the preceptor for instruction.

IV. That every parent, who wishes to deviate in the education of his children from the established system, be made responsible for devoting to the education of his children as much time as the established system precribes.

V. That a fund be raised from the citizens in the ratio of their property.

VI. The the system be composed of primary schools; of colleges; and of a University.

VII. That the primary schools be divided into two classes;

the first consisting of boys from 5 to 10 years old; the second consisting of boys from 10 to 18. And that these classes be subdivided, if necessary, into smaller ones.

VIII. That the instruction given to the first class be the rudiments of the English Language, Writing, Arithmetic, the commission to memory and delivery of select pieces, inculcating moral duties, describing natural phenomena, or displaying correct fancy.

IX. Though this class is formed of boys between the age of 5 and 10 years, yet should rapid acquisitions be made in the above branches of knowledge at an earlier age than that of 10, the boy is to be promoted into the second class.

X. The most solemn attention must be paid to avoid instilling into the young mind any ideas or sentiments whose truth is not unequivocally established by the undissenting suffrage of the enlightened and virtuous part of mankind.

XI. That the instruction given to the second class be an extended and more correct knowledge of Arithmetic; of the English language, comprising plain rules of criticism and composition; the concise study of General History and a more detailed acquaintance with the history of our own country; of Geography; of the laws of nature, practically illustrated. That this practical illustration consist in an actual devotion of a portion of time to agriculture and mechanics, under the superintendence of the preceptor. That it be the duty of this class to commit to memory, and frequently to repeat, the constitution and the fundamental laws of the United States.

XII. That each primary school consist of 50 boys.

XIII. That such boys be admitted into the college as shall be deemed by the preceptor to be worthy, from a manifestation of industry and talents, of a more extended education. That one boy be annually chosen out of the second class of each primary school for this preferment.

XIV. That the students at college so promoted be supported at the public expense, but that such other students may be received, as shall be maintained by their parents.

XV. That the studies of the college consist in a still more extended acquaintance with the above stated branches of knowledge, together with the cultivation of polite literature.

XVI. That each college admit 200 students.

XVII. That an opportunity be furnished to those who have the ability, without interfering with the established studies, of acquiring a knowledge of the modern languages, music, drawing, dancing, and fencing; and that the permission to cultivate these accomplishments be held forth as the reward of diligence and talents.

XVIII. That a National University be established, in which the highest branches of science and literature shall be taught. That it consist of students promoted from the colleges. That one student out of ten be annually chosen for this promotion by a majority of the suffrages of the professors of the college to which he may belong.

XIX. That the student so promoted be supported at the public expense, and be lodged within the walls of the University; remaining so long as he please on a salary, in consideration of his devoting his time to the cultivation of science or literature, in which last case he shall become a fellow of the University.

XX. The number of professors in the College and the University is not fixed; but it is proposed that the last contain a professor of every branch of useful knowledge.

XXI. It is proposed that the professors be in the first instance designated by law; that afterwards, in all cases of vacancy, the professors of the college choose the preceptors of the primary schools, and that the professors of the University choose the professors of the colleges.

XXII. For the promotion of literature and science, it is proposed that a board of literature and science be established on the following principles:

It shall consist of fourteen persons skilled in the several branches of, 1. Languages. 2. Mathematics. 3. Geography and History. 4. Natural Philosophy in general. 5. Moral Philosophy. 6. English Language, Belle Lettres, and Criticism. 7. Agriculture. 8. Manufactures. 9. Government and Laws. 10. Medicine. 11. Theology. 12. Elements of taste, including principles of Music, Architecture, Gardening, Drawing, &c. 13. Military Tactics. And in addition, 14. A person eminently skilled in Science, who shall be President of the board. . . .

Notwithstanding the universal agreement of all men in this country as to the necessity of a reform in education, so essentially do their professions disagree with their actions that nothing short of the commanding eloquence of truth, without cessation thundered on their ears, can produce that concurrence of action, that unity of effort, which shall give efficiency to a wise system of education. Let then the voice of the good man mingle with that of the wise in announcing the necessity of speedily adopting such a measure. Instead of one party denouncing another for equivocal political crimes, let all parties unite in attesting their patriotism by their co-operating efforts in so great a cause. Is it a question with any man whether our liberties are secure? Let him know that they depend upon the knowledge of the people, and that this knowledge depends upon a comprehensive and energetic system of education. It is true that some nations have been free without possessing a large portion of illumination, but their freedom has been precarious and accidental, and it has fallen as it rose.

The two things which we are most interested in securing are harmony at home, and respect abroad. By calling into active operation the mental resources of a nation, our political institutions will be rendered more perfect, ideas of justice will be diffused, the advantages of the undisturbed enjoyment of tranquillity and industry will be perceived by everyone, and our mutual dependence on each other will be rendered conspicuous. The great result will be harmony. Discord and strife have always proceeded from, or risen upon, ignorance and passion. When the first has ceased to exist, and the last shall be virtuously directed, we shall be deprived of every source of misunderstanding. The sword would not need a scabbard, were all men enlightened by a conviction of their true interests.

Harmony at home must produce respect abroad. For the era is at hand when America may hold the tables of justice in her hand, and proclaim them to the unresisting observance of the civilized world. Her numbers and her wealth vie with each other in the rapidity of their increase. But the immutable wisdom of her institutions will have a more efficient moral influence, than her physical strength. Possessed of both she cannot fail to assume, without competition, the station assigned her by an overruling power.

Such is the bright prospect of national dignity and happiness, if America give to her youth the advantages of a liberal and just education. On the other hand, should avarice, prejudice, or malice frustrate this great object, and should a declension of knowledge, gradually, but not the less decisively as to a future period, be suffered to triumph, the prospect is gloomy and dreadful. Gigantic power misapplied, towering ambition unsatiated with criminal gratification, avarice trampling poverty underfoot, mark but a few of the dark shades which will, in all probability, envelop our political horizon. On such an event, we must expect the miseries of oppression at home, and conquest abroad.

It may interest the attention, as it certainly will amuse the fancy, to trace the effects of the preceding principles of education on a future age. It has been observed that however virtuous, enlightened, and vigorous our first efforts to aggrandize the human character, it were, notwithstanding, folly to expect the celerity of preternatural agency. A system founded on true principles must gradually and cautiously eradicate error, and substitute truth. The period, will, therefore, be remote before the world is benefited by its complete development.

Let us contemplate the effects of a just system,

I. On the individual citizen.

II. On the United States.

III. On the World.

I. The citizen, enlightened, will be a free man in its truest sense. He will know his rights, and he will understand the rights of others; discerning the connection of his interest with the preservation of these rights, he will as firmly support those of his fellow men as his own. Too well informed to be misled, too virtuous to be corrupted, we shall behold man consistent and inflexible. Not at one moment the child of patriotism, and at another the slave of despotism, we shall see him in principle forever the same. Immutable in his character, inflexible in his honesty, he will feel the dignity of his nature and chearfully obey the claims of duty. He will look upon danger without dismay, so he will feel within himself the power of averting or the faculty of disarming it. . . .

The love of knowledge, which even a moderate portion of information never fails to inspire, would at the same time shut up many sources of misery and open more sources of happiness. The love of wealth would cease to be predominant passion of the heart; other objects would divide the attention, and perhaps challenge and receive a more constant regard.

The acquisition of knowledge is open to all. It injures no one. Its object is disinterested. It delights in distinction only so far as it increases the mass of public good. Here then is an object which all may pursue without the interference of one with another. So far from producing interference, it will constantly tend to destroy it;

for the more men think, the more they will resemble each other, and the more they resemble each other, the stronger will their mutual attachment be.

II. Viewing the effects of such a system on the United States, the first result would be the giving perpetuity to those political principles so closely connected with our present happiness. In addition to these might be expected numerous improvements in our political economy.

By these means government without oppression and protection without danger will exist in their necessary strength.

Politics are acknowledged to be still in their infancy. No circumstance could so rapidly promote the growth of this science as a universal illumination of mind. The minds of millions centering in one point, could not fail to produce the sublimest discoveries. Hence the prospect that our political institutions would quickly mature into plans as perfect as human happiness would require.

If all the genius of a nation could be impelled into active exertion, philosophy, both moral and physical, would soon present a new face. Every new discovery would probably tend to abridge the labor of the body and to allow opportunity, as well as inspire inclination, to cherish reflection. Man would feel himself in possession of two extensive sources of enjoyment, the exercise of the body, and the reflection of the mind; and he would soon find the last as submissive as the first.

This state of things could not fail to elevate the United States far above other nations. Possessed of every source of happiness, under the guardianship of all necessary power, she would soon become a model for the nations of the earth. This leads in the third place to,

III. The consideration of the effects of such a system on the world.

Nation is influenced as powerfully by nation as one individual is influenced by another. Hence no sooner shall any one nation demonstrate by practical illustration the goodness of her political institutions, than other nations will imperceptibly introduce corresponding features into their systems. No truth is more certain than that man will be happy if he can. He only wants a complete conviction of the means, to pursue them with energy and success. This conviction the United States may be destined to flash on the world.

Independent of this necessary effect, other effects will be produced. Many of the most enlightened of our citizens will traverse the globe with the spirit of philosophical research. They will carry with them valuable information and an ardent enthusiasm to diffuse it. Its diffusion will be the era of reform wherever it goes.

But more important, still, will be the example of the most powerful nation on earth, if that example exhibit dignity, humility, and intelligence. Scarcely a century can elapse before the population of America will be equal and her power superior to that of Europe. Should the principles be then established, which have been contemplated, and the connection be demonstrated between human happiness and the peaceable enjoyment of industry and the indulgence of reflection, we may expect to see America too enlightened and virtuous to spread the horrors of war over the face of any country, and too magnanimous and powerful to suffer its existence where she can prevent it. Let us, then, with rapture anticipate the era when the triumph of peace and the prevalence of virtue shall be rendered secure by the diffusion of useful knowledge.

26. Promoting the Arts: An Address to the Society of Artists, Benjamin Henry Latrobe, May 8, 1811

In an Anniversary Oration, Pronounced Before the Society of Artists of the United States, by Appointment of the Society, on the Eighth of May, 1811 [Philadelphia, 1811], Benjamin Henry Latrobe (1764–1820) recognized national prejudices unfavorable to the fine arts in the United States and sought to refute the idea that the arts had no place in a republic. Drawing examples from history, especially of Greece and Rome, he argued that the development of the fine arts was not incompatible with freedom but indeed was beneficial. In appealing for support for American artists, he voiced the hope that "the days of Greece may be revived in the woods of America, and Philadelphia become the Athens of the Western world." In 1803 President Jefferson had appointed the English-born Latrobe, who came to the United States in 1796, surveyor of public buildings. A leading proponent of the Greek Revival in the United States, Latrobe became the most outstanding architect in Jeffersonian America. He was principal architect of the United States Capitol, and his famous Greek Revival Philadelphia city waterworks and Bank of Pennsylvania (to which he *refers in the oration) also contributed to his major influence on the architecture of the young republic. This address is one of the best contemporary statements on the problem of promoting the fine arts in America.*

. . . The custom of delivering an annual oration, or lecture, before the members of the academies of Europe, has generally for its object the instruction of the students in the principles of art, the correction of their taste, and the encouragement of their zeal and industry. In these institutions, supported by the government as essential to its splendour, and upheld by the unanimous opinion of the governed as promoting one of the most rational and interesting sources of their pleasure, it is unnecessary, in an annual oration, to point out the advantages that result from the culture of the fine arts. No argument, no declamation, is so convincing or so eloquent as experience. The indolent, the luxurious, even the vicious rich, while enjoying the pleasure which the works of art afford to them, are innocent; while encouraging and rewarding them, are useful: nor is the most wretched of the poor, less happy than they, while admiring or boasting the monuments of art that adorn his native city, or the church of his village. To the feelings of the Athenian, who walked in the Poikile—of the Englishman who visits Westminster Abbey or St. Paul's—or of the Frenchman, before the Arch of Victory, nothing could be necessary to prove, that the arts have been usefully and honourably employed, in recording the courage, the patriotism, or the virtues of their countrymen.

An easy task, therefore, devolves upon that artist, who is selected to open the course of annual study by a public lecture. Master of the principles and practice of his profession, it is a pleasure to him to exhibit to others the knowledge and the taste that have made him worthy to instruct them.

But at the opening of this infant institution, instruction in the study, or in the practice of any of the fine arts, is less necessary than the labour of proving that these arts have not an injurious, but a beneficent effect upon the morals, and even on the liberties of our country. For we cannot disguise from ourselves, that, far from enjoying the support of the general voice of the people, our national prejudices are unfavourable to the fine arts. Many of our citizens who do not fear that they will enervate our minds and corrupt the simple and republican character of our pursuits and enjoyments, consider the actual state of society as unfit for their introduction: more dread a high grade of perfection in the fine arts as the certain indication of the loss of political liberty, and of the concentration of wealth and power in the hands of a few. Many despise the arts and their professors as useless, as manufacturing neither food nor raiment, nor gathering wealth by the enterprize of foreign commerce; and still more, ignorant of the delight, innocent as it is exquisite, which they afford, seek employment for their idle hours in the gratifications of sense, and the ostentatious display of riches.

Inasfar as these prejudices, the only real obstacles to the triumph of the fine arts, grow out of the political constitution of society in the United States, the attempt to remove them suddenly by argument will be vain. That such obstacles do exist is certain. On the one hand, the subdivision of wealth, resulting from our laws of inheritance, scatters at the commencement of every generation the funds out of which individual citizens might support the fine arts: and the immense territory over which our population is seeking to spread itself, weakens all combined efforts of private citizens by the separation of distance: on the other, the dread of responsibility in the individual representatives of the people, converting all their notions of good government into the single anxiety to avoid expenditure, withholds that degree of public encouragement, which would give example and fashion to individual favour, and establish a *national* love and pride in the fine arts.

But mere prejudices, whether of habit, of ignorance, or of false reasoning, are to be conquered. In our republic, that which arises from an opinion that the perfection of the fine arts is incompatible with freedom,—while it is the most powerful to retard their progress,—is at the same time the most unfounded in *theory*, and the most false in *fact*.

To ancient Greece the civilized world has been indebted for more than two thousand years, for instruction in the fine arts, and for the most perfect and sublime examples of what they are able to produce. But besides this instruction and these examples, we owe to Greece another obligation. The history of Grecian art refutes the vulgar opinion that the arts are incompatible with liberty, by an argument the most irresistible, that of fact upon record.

. . . To enter into a disquisition on that form of government, and on those manners, and laws, which nursed genius wherever it was found among the whole people; which not only gave to the powers of the mind the utmost extent of culture, but to the body all the strength, beauty and grace of which human nature is capable; which held up to exertion every motive that could stimulate, and to excellence every honour that could gratify ambition; would be to compose a dissertation on the history of Greece from her earliest records, to the final loss of her liberties after the age of Philip of Macedon. But to explain the source of her eminence few words are sufficient: *Greece was free*: in Greece every citizen felt himself an important, and thought himself an essential, part of his republic. The only superiority which he was allowed to claim, was that which could be examined by his fellow-citizens, each of whom was his equal and his rival. The education of a Greek soon pointed out, among the various dispositions of his body and mind, that in which he was most likely to attain excellence. The path of glory was equally open to all: precept and example were every where at hand, and reward was as certain as success. The whole mass of energy excited by such a system, could not but produce such effects, as at this distance of time leave it doubtful whether in beholding the mutilated remains of Grecian art, astonishment, or admiration be the predominant sensation. The Apollo of Phidias, the Venus of Praxiteles, the group of Laocoon, are in fact monuments not more of the arts, than of the freedom of Greece; monuments which are not more perfect as examples to artists, than as lessons to statesmen, and as warnings to every republic to guard well the liberty that alone can produce such wonders.

The enthusiasm, which this subject excites, would carry me too far, were I to enter more fully into the proof that in Greece, perfection in the fine arts, freedom in government, and virtue in private life, were cotemporaneous. In the freedom of the Grecian states degenerating into anarchy—in their civil wars disgraced by cruelty and injustice—in their system of slavery—in their private lives, sometimes viciously voluptuous in their most popular leaders, some savagely coarse in their generals and philosophers—in their religion superstitious, intolerant and despotic, ample theme has been found for declamation against this wonderful people. But let those compare their public transactions of war and peace with the acts and system of any other nation, modern or ancient, free or monarchical, who from the comparison look for aid to the political system that they have undertaken to support: all that I ask, and which cannot be denied, is, that Greece was free when the arts flourished, that they were dependent on that freedom, and that freedom derived from them much of her support and permanence.

Greece, indeed, at last, lost her freedom; she lost it when she lost her virtue; she lost it when she prostituted the fine arts to the gratification of vice; when her music which, directed by the poet Tyrtæus, had conducted the Lacedemonians to victory, sounded only to guide the steps of licentiousness; she lost it when her sculpture and painting, instead of immortalizing the forms of her heroes and philosophers, and rendering her gods adorable, became the sycophants of wealth and the slaves of sensuality: then, to use the language of Pliny, not less forcible than true, the *arts ceased* in Greece. For from the reign of Alexander to the extinction of taste in design, and excellence in execution, not a single name is recorded worthy of being placed at the side of those that graced the era of the Grecian republic.

In considering in the same point of view the arts which have decorated the freedom of Rome, or perpetuated the splendor of her monarchy, we have not the same information in detail which Pausanias, Plutarch, and Pliny, together with considerable remains of painting, sculpture, and architecture afford us on the arts of Greece. . . .

Very few and obscure remains, if any, of temples erected in the time of the republic of Rome, record the state of the arts at that period. But to prove from the example of Rome, that the cultivation of the fine arts is by no means incompatible with republican institutions, it is sufficient to know, that they were actually the means of rewarding military and civil merit, and of perpetuating the memory of national transactions, in those times in which the liberty of the Romans is most vaunted. Of the nature of that liberty, and of the character of that people—not as described by their elegant historians and orators, but as exhibited in their conquests, in the use and treatment of their slaves, in their ferocious and bloody amusements, in their brutal enjoyment of the tortures of wild animals tearing each other to pieces, and of gladiators convulsed in the agonies of a dishonorable death, in the attendance of matrons and virgins upon these scenes of horror and crime— nor of their tame submission to the proscriptions of the triumvirs, scenes scarcely equalled, and not surpassed by those of the French revolution, nor of the ease and security in which Tiberius and Nero rioted in blood over the warm corpse of the republic scarcely extinct—of all this, it is not my intention or my business to speak, I merely hint at it, because among the Roman writers, from Cicero downwards, many passages are found, which throw upon the fine arts, introduced more generally into Italy after the conquest and pillage of Corinth by Mummius, the blame of manners softened and corrupted by Greek refinement. Alas! their effect in softening the manners of these polished savages was scarcely perceptible. The prostitution of the arts to gratify vices, in the introduction of which they had no share whatsoever, is too certain. Could that love of truth, that persevering labour, that constant pressing forward of all the faculties of the man towards excellence, that occupation of the whole mind and body by the application and study for which the life of an artist is too short, that contempt of any reward compared with the meed of praise, without which no great artist was ever formed, have prevailed by example, then would cruelty and blood have ceased to be exclusively a Roman amusement.

To refute these calumnies against the arts, it would be sufficient to state what is undeniable, that the buildings and sculpture of the Romans, which are nearest in point of time to the days of the republic, are those of the best taste in design, and of the most exquisite workmanship. For as the monuments of Roman art, during the reigns of the emperors, grow into colossal size and expense, they dwindle into absurdity in the style of their decorations, and the imperfection of their execution, until we arrive at the triumphal arch of the mighty Constantine, a crouded patchwork of parts, pillaged from the trophies of former conquerors, a mixture of the good sculpture of former times, and of the coarsest imitations of his own age.

Respecting these gigantic buildings there is a fact which proves, that even the delusion of a popular government, after it has ceased to exist in reality, is favourable to the promotion of the fine arts. Many of the most splendid of them are monuments erected to the memory of the departed liberty of the people. The largest edifice in the world, erected for the purpose of public amusement, is the Colloseum of Vespasian. In this amphitheatre the Roman people could enjoy their ferocious entertainments at their ease, to the number of more than fifty thousand at once. The theatre of Marcellus is also an enormous pile. The magnificent remains of public baths prove the importance attached to the semblance of popular rights, and the indulgence of popular pleasures, even by the most tyrannical emperors. But when we consider the fifteen or sixteen aqueducts, which once supplied Rome, and of which some still supply the city with water, and others constructed and remaining over the whole empire, all of which were erected and decorated by the best skill of the age, the strict connexion of the interests and enjoyments of the people, and of the cultivation of the arts of design is still more illustrated.

It would be easy to extend the historical evidence, to this point, through more modern times; and to show that the era of the revival of the fine arts, was that of an active republican spirit, and of a very considerable degree of political freedom, which existed in the small commercial communities of Italy. Of this truth, the history of Florence under the merchants, the Medicis, furnishes very prominent evidence.

I have, however, I fear, dwelt on this part of my subject to the fatigue of your patience: but if a conviction can be wrought, and diffused throughout the nation, that the fine arts may indeed be pressed into the service of arbitrary power, and—like mercenary troops, do their duty well while well paid—yet that their home is in the bosom of a republic; then, indeed, the days of Greece may be revived in the woods of America, and Philadelphia become the Athens of the Western world. To produce such a conviction, I have thought it would be more effectual, to set before you the proofs of history, than the less interesting deductions even of the soundest reasoning. And, certainly, if human nature and human powers be at this day what they were from the earliest dawn of art in Greece, to the extinction of the republican spirit in that country;—if the desire of present applause, and of posthumous fame, be still a stronger stimulant to genius than the certainty of wealth;—if talents, wherever scattered in a nation, are more readily and plentifully discovered where they may raise their heads freely and boldly, and employ their power and their activity on subjects of their own choice, than where they must wait the favour of the great, and do the drudgery of adulation,—then is this a soil as congenial to their nature, and as favourable to their growth and perfection, as that of Sparta, Thebes, Delphos, or Athens.

That the wealth and the titles, which arbitrary power has to bestow, will always furnish strong inducements to the cultivation of the fine arts, under monarchical governments, is undeniable. Under a Trajan, an Adrian, a Henry VII, a Charles I and II, a Louis XIV, a Frederic II, or a Napoleon,—monarchs, who, in the excellence of the arts they fostered, and the general encouragement they gave to men of literature and science, sought a considerable portion of their own immortality—the fine arts have flourished with great vigour. Nor ought we to omit mention of the name of George III, by whose patronage our illustrious countryman, West, has become the first historical painter of the age. But in all these instances, and in others which might be added, it has not been owing to the character of the government, but to that of the individual monarch, that the arts have flourished under these reigns.

With the state of the arts in England, and with the influence and power of the British government, we are better acquainted than with that in other states. I would, therefore, ask, what have all the English monarchs, from Henry VII down to the present reign, done for the arts, including the reigns of the two Charles's and of Queen Ann, to whom the fire of London, and the victories of Marlborough, gave so great an opportunity of building churches and palaces? The single name of *Boydell*, an engraver, supported himself, in the outset, by Strahan, a bookseller, eclipses, in consideration of the fine arts, those of all the English monarchs within so long a period: and, without insisting on the accidental circumstance, that the only English coins which do honour to the English mint, are those of the protectorship of Cromwell, it may be truly observed, that in that prosperous and fortunate island, the astonishing progress which the elegant and useful arts have made, is the effect of the spirit of the people—of the very strong tincture of republican principle, which is an essential part of the English constitution, and of the popular institutions and societies, which, as far as their objects extend, are *practically* republican communities.

If then we need not dread the encouragement of the fine arts, as hostile to our best interests, the interests of our morals, and of our liberty, the inquiry, whether the state of society in our country be ripe for their introduction ceases to be of much importance. A propensity to the fine arts is an instinctive property of human nature. To repress it, it is necessary to confine its activity by positive laws, enforced by all the horrors of religious dread. But, where no such restriction prevails, there is no nation so rude, so ignorant, so occupied with the toils and cares of procuring the support of a miserable existence, so harassed by war and rapine, among whom art does not spring up spontaneously, combating the sterility of the soil, and the rigor of the climate, but still struggling and succeeding to exist. The caves of the Hottentot, the deserts of Africa, the rocks of Easter-Island, and the snowy wastes traversed by the Esquimaux and our northern Indians, have their indications of the fine arts; and the club of every savage is carved and painted before it is dyed in the blood of his enemy. Art is a hardy plant. If nursed, tended, and pruned, it will lift its head to heaven, and cover with fragrance and beauty the soil that supports it; but, if neglected, stunted, trodden under foot, it will still live; for its root is planted in the very ground of our own existence. To draw; to imitate the forms around him, is the first delight of the infant; to contemplate and accumulate the productions of art, one of the proudest enjoyments of the polished man; and to be honoured by art with a monument, the last ambition of the dying.

If therefore there exist no prejudice to oppose the growth of art among us, the state of society is always ripe for its introduction. And even where prejudices do exist, as they certainly do among us, the arts themselves, like Hercules in the cradle, will strangle the serpents. Mild, insinuating, of no political party, all they require is a slight introduction to our acquaintance. Received at first with reserve, they will be cherished by the best of our affections, and find patronage from our most legitimate pride. Our vanity will combat our avarice in their behalf; they will sometimes be disgusted and repelled by ignorance and parsimony, but they will be consoled and attracted equally by liberality and ostentation. Their advancement to that footing of security and reward which is their right, will not be rapid, but it will be certain and durable. The taste for the fine arts when it shall become a national taste, will be as permanent as the national language. It will not be a fashion set by a Charles, or a Louis XIV; it will be a law to which the economy of our legislatures will bend, and heroic actions will not go unacknowledged, because a statue or a monument requires an appropriation of money.

. . . the most effectual patronage which in their infancy the fine arts can receive, is the certainty of employment. The enthusiasm

which belongs to genius will do much, but without this inducement to the young who possess superior talents to devote themselves to their cultivation *as a profession*, we shall ever remain mere
occasional and unskilful copyists. When Hippocrates lamented
that to attain perfection in the medical art, life is too short, he
uttered a truth peculiarly applicable to the fine arts. Writers of
the greatest genius have denied the existence of that individual
native predisposition to eminence which is called genius. But
though they fail to prove that education is every thing, and genius is
nothing, it is very certain that he that is most diligent and persevering, will generally be most eminent. Without encouragement therefore, to look forward to the practice of the fine arts for the means
of a competent and honourable enjoyment of the ease and independence which may be procured by trade or agriculture, few, even
of those who feel themselves irresistibly impelled by inclination to
devote themselves to their culture, will follow the natural bent of
their genius.

That subdivision of labour which has been found to produce
such surprising effects in other employments, and which has in
modern times, pervaded every branch of human activity, has separated the professors of the fine arts into distinct classes. The
painters of history, of portraits, of landscape, of cattle, and of sea
pieces, are now distinct persons. The sculptor and the architect,
and the artist, who, by multiplying, perpetuates the works of all the
others, the engraver, have provinces wholly distinct from each
other. This subdivision of the labours of the fine arts is highly
promotive of perfection in detail. Whether it is in other respects
favourable to the formation of great artists, I will not now inquire; but it certainly gives to us, in the actual state of American
society and wealth, the choice of honouring, and patronising those
branches of the fine arts, which we find most conducive to our
pleasures and our wants, and which can most easily attain excellence among us.

I am not of opinion that it would be possible to point out any
set of practicable measures, to be adopted by the general or state
governments, by which the course of the fine arts towards perfection could be promoted among us, so effectual, and so economical,
as the simple system adopted by the Greeks. If meritorious actions
and services rendered to the state, were commemorated by a por-

trait, an historical picture, a bust, a statue, a monument, or a mausoleum, the emulation to excel in the fine arts, would grow out of the emulation to deserve well of the country. The establishment of academies and of schools of instruction in the fine arts, calling for expensive buildings, large endowments and a continual expenditure in maintaining the establishment, would be of little effect without employment of the artists educated in them. Academies should be founded in the encouragement of the works of art. Without the slightest favour from the nation or the state, this society has arisen on the basis of private and individual enterprize, giving to the rising artists of the country the means of support, and paving to them the road to eminence. Affection and pride have asked for portraits, literature for embellishment, and science for elucidation, and we already rival Europe in portraits and in engravings. Commerce has called for beauty in the forms and decorations of her ships, and where in Europe is there a [William] Rush. Let the national legislature honour the hero or statesman of the revolution with busts; and sculptors will not be wanting.—The genius which under exotic influence has given so high a rank to the American pencil of a West, Copley, Trumbull, and Vanderline, would, under domestic patronage, not refuse to inspire the American chisel.— And whence arises it—is it our national ingratitude, our ignorance or our apathy—that those states or municipal bodies, which have endeavoured to erect a memorial to the merits of any of their public men, have confined it to the form of the face or the person; that the majority of the states have not even gone so far, and that the national legislature has absolutely done nothing:—while four American historical painters have attained the highest eminence in Europe, where their talents have been employed in immortalizing the achievements of a lord Heathfield, or of a major Pearson, in the war carried on against us; and where the patriotism of Trumbull, exhibited in his admirable pictures of the death of Warren and of Montgomery, has been obliged to wear the mask of British victory. The annual expenditure which would employ these great artists upon the transactions of our own country, and which would give to them honour and independence, would be as dust in the balance of our public accounts. The national pride, which such records excite, is well worth purchasing at the expense of a few thousand dollars. . . .

But if in painting and sculpture the American public have as yet done nothing for the arts, our necessities and our pride has been more favourable to the advancement of our skill in architecture. It is indeed to be regretted, that instead of adapting our architecture to the age of our society and of our institutions, and exhibiting in our public edifices that republican simplicity which we profess, some of the most magnificent situations in our country and in the world, should be already irrevocably occupied by structures copied from the palaces of the corrupt age of Dioclesian, or the still more absurd and debased taste of Louis the XIV. In this city however it might naturally be expected that the purest taste would prevail. Founded by a man, the beneficent effects of whose wisdom and policy will be enjoyed by a late posterity, and the simplicity of whose manners and principles have descended to a very numerous part of this community as an inheritance, influencing and correcting the character of the whole population, the city is held responsible to the whole union for the purity of her taste in the fine arts. Nor has she altogether set them an unworthy example in her architecture. The beautiful marble with which this neighbourhood abounds, and the excellence of all other building materials, give to Philadelphia great advantages in this branch of the fine arts. The first building in which marble was employed as the principal material of its front, is the Bank of the United States. Although only a copy of a European building of indifferent taste, and very defective in its execution, it is still a bold proof of the spirit of the citizens who erected it, and of the tendency of the community to force, rather than to retard, the advancement of the arts. Only one year after its completion the Bank of Pennsylvania was built. Whatever may have been the success of the architect in devoting his best talents to produce a pure specimen of Grecian simplicity in design, and Grecian permanence in execution, the existence and taste of this building is due, not to the architect, but to a man, unhappily for the fine arts, now no more. Such a building, so different from all that had preceded it in form, arrangement, construction, and character, would not have overcome the dread of innovation, which uninformed prudence always feels, had not the late President of the Pennsylvania Bank, Mr. Samuel M. Fox, united to the purest taste, and extensive knowledge of the subject, an influence of personal character, which inspired implicit confidence in all he approved. If the style of this single building has given to the Philadelphian architecture, even in our plainest brick dwellings, a breadth of effect and a repose vainly sought in other cities, we owe this superiority to the mild but powerful influence of the discriminating taste of this one man. . . .

But if the arts have lost his influence, we have this consolation, that in our institutions there is a wide field for the growth and influence of similar talents and virtues. If they exist they will not remain hidden or powerless. Of this, the supply of this city with water, the bridge of Schuylkill, and many other public works which have risen around us, and are even now springing up in every direction, are the best proofs.

I have already detained you far beyond the right which my feeble powers of instruction or entertainment give me. An attempt to remove the prejudices which oppose the establishment of the fine arts among us, appeared to me the most pressing duty of the orator of the Society of Artists. I have fulfilled but a small part of that duty. If it were necessary to do more, I could call up the spirit of commerce to aid me. I could enlist in the cause of the fine arts—that embellish domestic happiness, that charm leisure, that grace generosity, and honour patriotism—I could enlist in their cause, the demons of cupidity, and of avarice. I could show that though they are instructive, faithful, and amusing friends, they may also be made profitable slaves. I could mention the names of Wedgewood, whose pots and pitchers, and cups and saucers, and plates, shaped and decorated by the fine arts, have thus received a passport into the remotest corners of the globe—of Boydell, whose engraved prints are spread over and ornament the whole surface of the earth—of Bolton, and Watt, and of the smiths and founders of Birmingham, who, true sons of Vulcan, have rendered the fables of Homer, and the visits of the arts and the graces in the forges and furnaces of that sooty god, to assist in the design of the armour of the immortals, not only probable, but true. But I need not proceed further. The presence of this assembly shows that it is unnecessary, and its patronage will be more efficient than the most laboured oration.

To the artists and amateurs who compose this society it must be matter of infinite encouragement to view the effect of their collected talents and industry in the exhibition now opened. The novelty of an exertion to bring together and to arrange the productions of art which cover the walls of the academy, must, necessarily, produce some imperfection, both in the collection and in the arrangement. But without asking for any such allowance, have we not reason to be proud of our infant strength:—that it is considerable:—that among the numerous pictures and drawings, there are many which would not dishonour the walls of the London and Parisian galleries, is certain:—And in this is our superiority; that our strength is our own. It is not hotbedded by imperial and royal patronage, nor even by the nobility of wealth: it is the concentrated force of individual genius and industry, and of the encouragement of private and unproclaimed protection. That this effort of the fine arts may be countenanced by your visits and your approbation, I need not solicit. It is in your power to make your own amusements the foundation of all the eminence to which the most sanguine of us expect to attain; and, as the fair part of this assembly once did in adopting the Grecian dress, to stamp with the sanction of fashion, that which good taste recommends. The success of the exhibition of this year will ensure to you an infinitely superior collection in the next, and not only stimulate the zeal of our artists, but inform them on the best method of accomplishing their object.

In beholding the harmony in which the productions of so many talents are arranged; in considering the general and united effect of all the pictures which cover the walls of the exhibition room, varying as they do in the merit, the manner, the colouring, and the subject of each; I could not help reverting to that moral and social harmony by which the artists of our country might so much improve each other. There is, indeed, in superior genius a gregarious principle, which naturally brings men of similar talents together. Those who are most susceptible of the beauties of truth and of nature, are also the most susceptible of affection. The enthusiast in art, cannot be cold in friendship, nor can any thing contribute more to mutual improvement and excellence, than that mutual esteem and confidence which embellishes the private associations of artists. Each honest advice, each friendly criticism, each communication of knowledge from one artist to another is a step, hand in hand, in the ascent to perfection. As our political independence was achieved by adherence to this motto, let our independence in the arts grow out of the conviction that, *united we stand, divided we fall.*

27. Thomas Jefferson and John Adams on Aristocracy

Jefferson and Adams had served together on the committee to draft the Declaration of Independence; together they had represented the interests of the newly independent nation in Europe, with Jefferson serving as minister to France and Adams as minister to Great Britain. Both men had taken posts in the new government under the Constitution, Adams as vice president and Jefferson as secretary of state. With the formation of the Republican and Federalist parties in the 1790's, Jefferson and Adams became political rivals and contenders for the presidency, which went to Adams in 1796 but to Jefferson in 1800, in a defeat that left Adams so humiliated that he refused to stay in Washington to see his successor inaugurated. After Jefferson's retirement from the presidency, mutual friends succeeded in restoring the former friendship between the two men, and in 1812 they began an exchange of letters which offers one of the most fascinating records in American history. Both Jefferson and Adams were given to speculation in political theory and on the nature of man and society. In the following exchange of views, Jefferson's letter of October 28, 1813, was prompted by questions raised by Adams in earlier letters reviewing the occasion for writing his A Defence of the Constitutions of the Government of the United States, published in three volumes in 1787 to 1788. In this letter, one of his most famous, Jefferson replied with an essay on natural and artificial aristocracy and the form of government that best provided for the elevation of the "good and the wise" into its offices. Adams examined Jefferson's arguments in his reply of November 15, 1813. The texts of both letters are taken from Andrew A. Lipscomb and Albert E. Bergh (eds.), The Writings of Thomas Jefferson (20 vols., Washington, D.C., 1905), XIII, 394–403; XIV, 1–10.

A. *Jefferson to Adams, October 28, 1813*

. . . I agree with you that there is a natural aristocracy among men. The grounds of this are virtue and talents. Formerly, bodily powers gave place among the aristoi. But since the invention of gunpowder has armed the weak as well as the strong with missile death, bodily strength, like beauty, good humor, politeness and other accomplishments, has become but an auxiliary ground of distinction. There is also an artificial aristocracy, founded on wealth and birth, without either virtue or talents; for with these it would belong to the first class. The natural aristocracy I consider as the most precious gift of nature, for the instruction, the trusts, and government of society. And indeed, it would have been inconsistent in creation to have formed man for the social state, and not to have provided virtue and wisdom enough to manage the concerns of the society. May we not even say, that that form of government is the best, which provides the most effectually for a pure selection of these natural aristoi into the offices of government? The artificial aristocracy is a mischievous ingredient in government, and provision should be made to prevent its ascendency. On the question, what is the best provision, you and I differ; but we differ as rational friends, using the free exercise of our own reason, and mutually indulging its errors. You think it best to put the pseudo-aristoi into a separate chamber of legislation, where they may be hindered from doing mischief by their coordinate branches, and where, also, they may be a protection to wealth against the agrarian and plundering enterprises of the majority of the people. I think that to give them power in order to prevent them from doing mischief, is arming them for it, and increasing instead of remedying the evil. For if the co-ordinate branches can arrest their action, so may they that of the co-ordinates. Mischief may be done negatively as well as positively. Of this, a cabal in the Senate of the United States has furnished many proofs. Nor do I believe them necessary to protect the wealthy; because enough of these will find their way into every branch of the legislation, to protect themselves. From fifteen to twenty legislatures of our own, in action for thirty years past, have proved that no fears of an equalization of property are to be apprehended from them. I think the best remedy is exactly that provided by all our constitutions, to leave to the citizens the free election and separation of the aristoi from the pseudo-aristoi, of the wheat from the chaff. In general they will elect the really good and wise. In some instances, wealth may corrupt, and birth blind them; but not in sufficient degree to endanger the society.

It is probable that our difference of opinion may, in some measure, be produced by a difference of character in those among whom we live. From what I have seen of Massachusetts and

Connecticut myself, and still more from what I have heard, and the character given of the former by yourself, who know them so much better, there seems to be in those two States a traditionary reverence for certain families, which has rendered the offices of the government nearly hereditary in those families. I presume that from an early period of your history, members of those families happening to possess virtue and talents, have honestly exercised them for the good of the people, and by their services have endeared their names to them. In coupling Connecticut with you, I mean it politically only, not morally. For having made the Bible the common law of their land, they seem to have modeled their morality on the story of Jacob and Laban. But although this hereditary succession to office with you, may, in some degree, be founded in real family merit, yet in a much higher degree, it has proceeded from your strict alliance of Church and State. These families are canonized in the eyes of the people on common principles, "you tickle me, and I will tickle you." In Virginia we have nothing of this. Our clergy, before the revolution, having been secured against rivalship by fixed salaries, did not give themselves the trouble of acquiring influence over the people. Of wealth, there were great accumulations in particular families, handed down from generation to generation, under the English law of entails. But the only object of ambition for the wealthy was a seat in the King's Council. All their court then was paid to the crown and its creatures; and they Philipized in all collisions between the King and the people. Hence they were unpopular; and that unpopularity continues attached to their names. A Randolph, a Carter, or a Burwell must have great personal superiority over a common competitor to be elected by the people even at this day. At the first session of our legislature after the Declaration of Independence, we passed a law abolishing entails. And this was followed by one abolishing the privilege of primogeniture, and dividing the lands of intestates equally among all their children, or other representatives. These laws, drawn by myself, laid the axe to the foot of pseudo-aristocracy. And had another which I prepared been adopted by the legislature, our work would have been complete. It was a bill for the more general diffusion of learning. This proposed to divide every county into wards of five or six miles square, like your townships; to establish in each ward a free school for reading, writing and common arithmetic; to provide for the annual selection of the best subjects from these schools, who might receive, at the public expense, a higher degree of education at a district school; and from these district schools to select a certain number of the most promising subjects, to be completed at an university, where all the useful sciences should be taught. Worth and genius would thus have been sought out from every condition of life, and completely prepared by education for defeating the competition of wealth and birth for public trusts. My proposition had, for a further object, to impart to these wards those portions of self-government for which they are best qualified, by confiding to them the care of their poor, their roads, police, elections, the nomination of jurors, administration of justice in small cases, elementary exercises of militia; in short, to have made them little republics, with a warden at the head of each, for all those concerns which, being under their eye, they would better manage than the larger republics of the county or State. A general call of ward meetings by their wardens on the same day through the State, would at any time produce the genuine sense of the people on any required point, and would enable the State to act in mass, as your people have so often done, and with so much effect by their town meetings. The law for religious freedom, which made a part of this system, having put down the aristocracy of the clergy, and restored to the citizen the freedom of the mind, and those of entails and descents nurturing an equality of condition among them, this on education would have raised the mass of the people to the high ground of moral respectability necessary to their own safety, and to orderly government; and would have completed the great object of qualifying them to select the veritable aristoi, for the trusts of government, to the exclusion of the pseudalists. . . . Although this law has not yet been acted on but in a small and inefficient degree, it is still considered as before the legislature, with other bills of the revised code, not yet taken up, and I have great hope that some patriotic spirit will, at a favorable moment, call it up, and make it the keystone of the arch of our government.

With respect to aristocracy, we should further consider, that before the establishment of the American States, nothing was known to history but the man of the old world, crowded within limits either small or overcharged, and steeped in the vices which that situation generates. A government adapted to such men would be one thing; but a very different one, that for the man of these

States. Here every one may have land to labor for himself, if he chooses; or, preferring the exercise of any other industry, may exact for it such compensation as not only to afford a comfortable subsistence, but wherewith to provide for a cessation from labor in old age. Every one, by his property, or by his satisfactory situation, is interested in the support of law and order. And such men may safely and advantageously reserve to themselves a wholesome control over their public affairs, and a degree of freedom, which, in the hands of the *canaille* of the cities of Europe, would be instantly perverted to the demolition and destruction of everything public and private. The history of the last twenty-five years of France, and of the last forty years in America, nay of its last two hundred years, proves the truth of both parts of this observation.

But even in Europe a change has sensibly taken place in the mind of man. Science had liberated the ideas of those who read and reflect, and the American example had kindled feelings of right in the people. An insurrection has consequently begun, of science, talents, and courage, against rank and birth, which have fallen into contempt. It has failed in its first effort, because the mobs of the cities, the instrument used for its accomplishment, debased by ignorance, poverty, and vice, could not be restrained to rational action. But the world will recover from the panic of this first catastrophe. Science is progressive, and talents and enterprise on the alert. Resort may be had to the people of the country, a more governable power from their principles and subordination; and rank, and birth, and tinsel-aristocracy will finally shrink into insignificance, even there. This, however, we have no right to meddle with. It suffices for us, if the moral and physical condition of our own citizens qualifies them to select the able and good for the direction of their government, with a recurrence of elections at such short periods as will enable them to displace an unfaithful servant, before the michief he mediates may be irremediable.

I have thus stated my opinion on a point on which we differ, not with a view to controversy, for we are both too old to change opinions which are the result of a long life of inquiry and reflection; but on the suggestions of a former letter of yours, that we ought not to die before we have explained ourselves to each other. We acted in perfect harmony, through a long and perilous contest for our liberty and independence. A constitution has been acquired, which, though neither of us thinks perfect, yet both consider as competent to render our fellow citizens the happiest and the securest on whom the sun has ever shone. If we do not think exactly alike as to its imperfections, it matters little to our country, which, after devoting to it long lives of disinterested labor, we have delivered over to our successors in life, who will be able to take care of it and of themselves. . . .

B. *Adams to Jefferson, November 15, 1813*

. . . We are now explicitly agreed upon one important point, viz., that there is a natural aristocracy among men, the grounds of which are virtue and talents. . . . But though we have agreed in one point, in words, it is not yet certain that we are perfectly agreed in sense. Fashion has introduced an indeterminate use of the word talents. Education, wealth, strength, beauty, stature, birth, marriage, graceful attitudes and motions, gait, air, complexion, physiognomy, are talents, as well as genius, science, and learning. Any one of these talents that in fact commands or influences two votes in society, gives to the man who possesses it the character of an aristocrat, in my sense of the word. Pick up the first hundred men you meet, and make a republic. Every man will have an equal vote; but when deliberations and discussions are opened, it will be found that twenty-five, by their talents, virtues being equal, will be able to carry fifty votes. Every one of these twenty-five is an aristocrat in my sense of the word; whether he obtains his one vote in addition to his own, by his birth, fortune, figure, eloquence, science, learning, craft, cunning, or even his character for good fellowship, and a *bon vivant*.

. . . Your distinction between natural and artificial aristocracy, does not appear to me founded. Birth and wealth are conferred upon some men as imperiously by nature as genius, strength, or beauty. The heir to honors, and riches, and power, has often no more merit in procuring these advantages, than he has in obtaining a handsome face, or an elegant figure. When aristocracies are established by human laws, and honor, wealth and power are made hereditary by municipal laws and political institutions, then I acknowledge artificial aristocracy to commence; but this never commences till corruption in elections become dominant and uncontrollable. But this artificial aristocracy can never last. The everlasting envies, jealousies, rivalries, and quarrels among them; their cruel rapacity upon the poor ignorant people, their followers, compel them to set up Cæsar, a demagogue, to be a monarch, a master; *pour mettre chacun à sa place*. Here you have the origin of all artificial aristocracy, which is the origin of all monarchies. And both artificial aristocracy and monarchy, and civil, military, political, and hierarchical despotism, have all grown out of the natural aristocracy of virtues and talents. We, to be sure, are far remote from this. Many hundred years must roll away before we shall be corrupted. Our pure, virtuous, public-spirited, federative republic will last forever, govern the globe, and introduce the perfection of man; his perfectibility being already proved by Price, Priestley, Condorcet, Rousseau, Diderot, and Godwin. Mischief has been done by the Senate of the United States. I have known and felt more of this mischief, than Washington, Jefferson, and Madison, all together. But this has been all caused by the constitutional power of the Senate, in executive business, which ought to be immediately, totally, and essentially abolished. Your distinction between the aristoi and pseudo aristoi will not help the matter. I would trust one as well as the other with unlimited power. The law wisely refuses an oath as a witness in his own case, to the saint as well as the sinner. No romance would be more amusing than the history of your Virginian and our New England aristocratical families. Yet even in Rhode Island there has been no clergy, no church, and I had almost said no State, and some people say no religion. There has been a constant respect for certain old families. Fifty-seven or fifty-eight years ago, in company with Colonel, Counsellor, Judge, John Chandler, whom I have quoted before, a newspaper was brought in. The old sage asked me to look for the news from Rhode Island, and see how the elections had gone there. I read the list of Wantons, Watsons, Greens, Whipples, Malbones, etc. "I expected as much," said the aged gentleman, "for I have always been of opinion that in the most popular governments, the elections will generally go in favor of the most ancient families." To this day, when any of these tribes—and we may add Ellerys, Channings, Champlins, etc.,—are pleased to fall in with the popular current, they are sure to carry all before them.

You suppose a difference of opinion between you and me on the subject of aristocracy. I can find none. I dislike and detest hereditary honors, offices, emoluments, established by law. So do you. I am for excluding legal, hereditary distinctions from the

United States as long as possible. So are you. I only say that mankind have not yet discovered any remedy against irresistible corruption in elections to offices of great power and profit, but making them hereditary.

But will you say our elections are pure? Be it so, upon the whole; but do you recollect in history a more corrupt election than that of Aaron Burr to be President, or that of De Witt Clinton last year? By corruption here, I mean a sacrifice of every national interest and honor to private and party objects. I see the same spirit in Virginia that you and I see in Rhode Island and the rest of New England. In New York it is a struggle of family feuds—a feudal aristocracy. Pennsylvania is a contest between German, Irish and Old England families. When Germans and Irish unite they give 30,000 majorities. There is virtually a white rose and a red rose, a Cæsar and a Pompey, in every State in this Union, and contests and dissensions will be as lasting. The rivalry of Bourbons and No-ailleses produced the French Revolution, and a similar competition for consideration and influence exists and prevails in every village in the world. Where will terminate the *rabies agri*? The continent will be scattered over with manors much larger than Livingston's, Van Rensselaer's or Philips's; even our Deacon Strong will have a principality among you southern folk. What inequality of talents will be produced by these land jobbers. Where tends the mania of banks? At my table in Philadelphia, I once proposed to you to unite in endeavors to obtain an amendment of the Constitution prohibiting to the separate States the power of creating banks; but giving Congress authority to establish one bank with a branch in each State, the whole limited to ten millions of dollars. Whether this project was wise or unwise, I know not, for I had deliberated little on it then, and have never thought it worth thinking of since. But you spurned the proposition from you with disdain. This system of banks, begotten, brooded and hatched by Duer, Robert and Gouverneur Morris, Hamilton and Washington, I have always considered as a system of national injustice. A sacrifice of public and private interest to a few aristocratical friends and favorites. My scheme could have had no such effect. Verres plundered temples, and robbed a few rich men, but he never made such ravages among private property in general, nor swindled so much out of the pockets of the poor, and middle class of people, as these banks have done. No people but this would have borne the imposition so long. The people of Ireland would not bear Wood's halfpence. What inequalities of talent have been introduced into this country by these aristocratical banks! Our Winthrops, Winslows, Bradfords, Saltonstalls, Quincys, Chandlers, Leonards, Hutchinsons, Olivers, Sewells, etc., are precisely in the situation of your Randolphs, Carters, and Burwells, and Harrisons. Some of them unpopular for the part they took in the late Revolution, but all respected for their names and connections; and whenever they fell in with the popular sentiments are preferred, *ceteri paribus*, to all others. When I was young the *summum bonum* in Massachusetts was to be worth £10,000 sterling, ride in a chariot, be colonel of a regiment of militia, and hold a seat in his Majesty's council. No man's imagination aspired to anything higher beneath the skies. But these plumbs, chariots, colonelships, and counsellorships, are recorded and will never be forgotten. No great accumulations of land were made by our early settlers. . . .

28. An Outsider's View: A Travel Letter, Frances Wright, February, 1820

Frances Wright would later make her home in America and become famous as a radical reformer, but she was a foreign visitor when she wrote the following account during her first trip to the United States from September, 1818, to May, 1820. Twenty-three years old when she began her tour, Miss Wright had already steeped herself in information about America by reading everything she could find, and she had developed an immense enthusiasm for the country. This ardor was strongly reflected in the letters she wrote from the United States and revised for publication in 1821 as a book entitled Views of Society and Manners in America; A Series of Letters from that Country to a Friend in England, During the Years 1818, 1819, and 1820, by an Englishwoman *(London: printed for Longman, Hurst, Rees, Orme, and Brown, 1821). On her second visit to the United States in 1824, Miss Wright was to become better acquainted with the social problems of the new nation and particularly concerned about the problems of slavery and the Negro. Her early account should thus not be appraised as critical history; indeed, a critic for the North American Review in assessing the volume at the time of its publication stated that it was "in fact an eulogium on our country and its character" and could best be viewed by an American "as the model, toward which he should strive to bring his country, rather than as a tablet of actual perfections."*

In the following letter, written near the end of her visit, Miss Wright described the distinctiveness of sections in the United States and optimistically discounted the dangers of the development of sectionalism. Her enthusiasm for the young republic led to exaggeration and inaccuracy of fact, but her writing reveals the excitement she felt about the American republican experiment. This selection is reprinted from the 1821 edition cited above, pp. 374–404.

New York, February, 1820

MY DEAR FRIEND,

Looking to the general plan of the central government, it will be seen with what extreme nicety the different interests of the multitudinous parts of this great confederacy are balanced, or employed as checks one upon the other. In the course of years these interests may be somewhat more distinctly marked than they are at present; some have even thought that they may be more strongly opposed. This appears more than doubtful: but even admitting the supposition, we cannot calculate the probable effects of this without counting for something the gradual strengthening of the national union by the mixture of the people, the marriages and friendships contracted between the inhabitants of the different States, the tide of emigration, which shifts the population of one to the other, the course of prosperity enjoyed under a government more and more endeared as time more and more tries its wisdom, and imparts sanctity to its name. The time was, when none, or but a few of these sacred bonds existed, and still a friendly sympathy was not wanting among the different and uncemented communities scattered along the shores of the Atlantic.

During their colonial existence, the inhabitants of these States had but little intercourse with each other. Vast forests separated often the scanty population of the infant provinces. Varying climate and religion influenced also their customs and character; but still, however, parted by trackless wastes, how little connected soever by the ties of private friendship, they had always two things in common,—language, and a fierce spirit of liberty; which sufficed to bind with a sure though invisible chain all the members of the scattered American family. The strength of this chain has seldom been fully appreciated by the enemies of America: they expected to break it even during the war of the Revolution; and were certain that it would of itself give way when the high-toned sentiment kept alive by a struggle for independence should subside, or when the pressure of common danger being removed, the necessity of cordial co-operation should not be equally apparent: experience has hitherto happily disproved these calculations. The advantages of a vigorous, and the blessings of a beneficient government, directing the energies and presiding over the welfare of the great whole, has been more and more felt and understood, while the influence of just laws, and still more the improved intercourse of the states one with another, have broken down prejudices, and, in a great measure, obliterated distinctions of character among the different quarters of the republic.

The portion of the union that has most generally preserved her ancient moral distinction is New England. The reason may be found in the rigidity of her early religious creed, and in the greater separation of her people from the rest of the nation. Strictly moral, well-educated, industrious, and intelligent, but shrewd, cautious, and, as their neighbours say, at least, peculiarly long-sighted to their interests, the citizens of New England are the Scotch of America. Like them, they are inhabitants of a comparatively poor country, and send forth legions of hardy adventurers to push their fortunes in richer climes: there is this difference, however, that the Scotchman traverses the world, and gathers stores to spend them afterwards in his own barren hills, while the New-Englander carries his penates with him, and plants a colony on the shores of the Ohio, with no less satisfaction than he would have done on those of the Connecticut.

The nursery of back-woodsmen, New England, sends forth thousands, and of course takes in few, so that her citizens are less exposed to the visitation of foreigners, and even to mixture with the people of other states, than is usual with their more southern neighbours. This has, perhaps, its advantages and disadvantages: it preserves to them all the virtues of a simple state of society, but with these also some of its prejudices: it serves to entrench them against luxury, but imparts to them something of a provincial character. Zealously attached to their own institutions, they have sometimes coldly espoused those of the nation. The federal opposition chiefly proceeded from this quarter of the Union.

The political conduct of New England subsequent to the establishment of the federal government sunk her a little for some years in the esteem of the nation. The narrowness of her policy was charged to some peculiar selfishness of character in her people; but their conduct during the revolutionary struggle redeems them from this charge, and leads us to ascribe their errors to refect of judgment rather than to obliquity of principle. Since the war the liberal party, ever numerous, has gained the ascendant; and consequently the eastern states are resuming that place in the national councils which they originally held. It is difficult now to find a *Federalist*, absolutely so called. A certain soreness upon some political topics, a coldness of manner in pronouncing the name of Jefferson, and, I have observed, of *Franklin*, is what may sometimes enable you to detect a *ci-devant* member of the fallen party.

New York and Pennsylvania may perhaps be considered as the most influential states of the Union. The elegant expression lately employed by Mr. Clay, in rendering his tribute to the important services of the latter, may with propriety be applied to both. They are "*the key-stones of the federal arch.*" Their rich and extensive territories seem to comprise all the interests into which the Union is divided. Commerce, agriculture, and manufactures, are all powerfully represented by them on the floor of congress. Their western division has much in common with the Mississippi states, and their eastern with those of the Atlantic. Their population stands conspicuous for national enterprise and enlightened policy, whether as regards the internal arrangement of their own republics, or their share in the federal councils. These powerful states return no less than fifty members to congress, being more than a fourth of the whole body. In proportion as the western states increase, this preponderance will be taken from them; in the mean time, however, it is in no case exerted to the prejudice of the general interests of the Union.

Whether it be from their wealth, or their more central position, affording them the advantage of a free intercourse with the citizens of all the states of the Union, as well as foreigners from all parts of the world, the people of Pennsylvania and New York, but more particularly of the latter, have acquired a liberality of sentiment which imparts dignity to their public measures. They raise extensive funds, not only for the general education of their citizens, (which is equally the case elsewhere,) the founding of libraries, and seminaries of learning, but in the clearing of rivers, making roads and canals, and promoting other works of extensive utility, which might do honor to the richest empires of Europe. The progress of the New York State during the last thirty years is truly astonishing.

Within this period, her population has more than quadrupled, and the value of property more than doubled: she has subdued the forest from Hudson to Erie and the Canadian frontier, and is now perfecting the navigation of all her great waters, and connecting them with each other.

The national revenue being chiefly drawn from the customs, is greatly dependent upon the commercial spirit of New York. Her great sea-port has sometimes furnished one-fourth of the revenue of the United States. The late war of necessity fell very heavily upon her maritime capital. But while her commerce was ruined, she showed no disposition to injure the common cause by separating her interests from those of the confederacy. Her opposition in congress was greatly in the minority to her national support; and, war being once declared, the opposition passed over to the side of the majority. The conduct of Mr. Rufus King, the venerable leader of the federal party in the senate, is worthy of being recorded in the annals of his country. He had opposed the declaration of war simply from an apprehension that the Republic was unequal to cope with her adversary; but finding her determined to brave all hazards rather than submit to degradation, he instantly seceded from his party, pronouncing it to be the duty of every patriot to assist his country with heart and hand in weathering the storm, and volunteered to throw into the treasury part of his private fortune, which he stated to be greater than his necessities.

No state in the Union can point to a longer line of public services than Virginia: she rung the first alarum of the Revolution by the mouth of her Patrick Henry; she led the army of patriots in the person of her Washington; she issued the declaration of independence from the pen of her Jefferson; she bound the first link of the federal union by the hand of her Madison;—she has given to the republic four of the purest patriots and wisest statesmen that ever steered the vessel of a state.

The policy of this mother of the Union has always been peculiarly magnanimous. She set the example to her sister-states in those cessions of territory which have so richly endowed the general government, and out of which have arisen such a host of young republics. The cession made by Virginia comprises the present states of Ohio, Indiana, and Illinois, with the territory of Michigan. For the thousandth part of such an empire as was here bestowed in free gift, men have deluged the earth with blood. We find the liberality of Virginia yet farther evinced in her conduct towards a neighboring state, first peopled by her citizens, and subject to her laws. The manner in which she released Kentucky from her jurisdiction, pointing out the inconveniences arising to her people from their remoteness from the Virginia capital, and encouraging her to erect an independent government, affords a beautiful example of national generosity.

The public spirit of Virginia has invariably been felt in the national councils, and consequently has procured to her a weight of influence more than proportionate to the numerical strength of her representation in congress. There has latterly been a partial hue and cry in the northern division of the Union, on the subject of the Virginia influence. I can only say, in the words of a Vermont farmer, who accidentally closed in conversation with me upon affairs of state, "Whatever be the influence of Virginia, she seems to use it well, for we surely go on very thrivingly; besides that, I see no way in which she could exercise it but by coinciding with the feelings of the majority." The words Virginia influence, you will perceive to mean (so far as they mean any thing) the accident which has drawn from her commonwealth four out of the five presidents who have guided the councils of federal America.

I know nothing which places the national character in a fairer point of view than the issue of the presidential elections. We find local prejudices and even party feelings laid aside, and the people of this multitude of commonwealths fixing their eyes on the most distinguished servant of the state, and rendering the noblest tribute to his virtues that a patriot can receive, or a country can bestow. All the chief magistrates of the republic have been veterans of the Revolution, and distinguished no less for their private virtues than their public services. It was thought that, as Virginia had already given three presidents to the Republic, a strong opposition would have been made to Colonel Monroe. So far from this being the case, no president (Washington excepted) was ever more unanimously chosen; and his name is spoken with respect, and even affection, from Maine to Missouri.

The dignified position taken by Virginia in the national councils, has placed her at the head of the republics of the south; whose policy, it may be remarked, has uniformly been liberal and patriotic; and, on all essential points, in accordance with that of the central and western states. Whatever be the effect of black slavery upon the moral character of the southern population, and that upon *the mass* it must be deadly mischievous there can be no question, it has never been felt in the national senate. Perhaps the arrangement has been prudent, or at least fortunate, which has somewhat tempered the democracy of American government in the south Atlantic states. By the existing constitution of Virginia, and the states south of her, the qualifications required of a representative throw the legislative power into the hands of the more wealthy planters; a race of men no less distinguished for the polish of their manners and education than for liberal sentiments and general philanthropy. They are usually well-travelled in their own country and in Europe, possess enough wealth to be hospitable, and seldom sufficient to be luxurious, and are thus, by education and condition, raised above the degrading influence which the possession of arbitrary power has on the human mind and the human heart. To the slight leaven of aristocracy, therefore, thrown into the institutions of Virginia and the Carolinas, we may, perhaps, attribute, in part, their generous and amiable bearing in the national councils; we must not omit, however, the ameliorating effect produced by the spread of education, and the effect of liberal institutions on the white population generally. Even before the close of the revolutionary war, Mr. Jefferson thought "a change already perceptible;" and we have a substantial proof that the change traced by that philosopher in the character of his fellow-citizens was not imaginary, the first act of the Virginia legislature being the abolition of the slave-trade. May she now set an example to her neighbouring states, as she then did to the world, by combating steadfastly the difficulties which her own fears or selfish interests may throw in the way of emancipation!

But the quarter of the Republic to which the eye of a stranger turns with most curiosity, is the vast region to the west of the Alleghanies. The character of these republics is necessarily as unique as their position, and their influence is already powerful upon the floor of congress.

In glancing at their geographical position, the foreigner might hastily be led to consider them as growing rivals rather than friendly supporters of the Atlantic states. It will be found, however, that they are at present powerful cementers of the union, and that the feelings and interests are such as to draw together the north and south divisions of the confederacy.

The new canals will probably draw off the produce of the western counties of New York to the Atlantic; still, however, a portion will find its way down the western waters, as their navigation shall be perfected from Erie to New Orleans. At all events, this route will continue to be preferred by the western counties of Pennsylvania, shortly destined to be the seat, if they are not so already, of flourishing manufactures. The advance made in this branch of industry, during the last war, and for some years previously, has received some checks since the peace, but appears likely soon to proceed with redoubled energy.

It may be worth observing, that there is something in the character of the American population, as well as in the diverse products of the soil, which seems favorable to the growth of manufactures. I do not allude merely to their mechanical ingenuity, which has shown itself in so many important inventions and improvements in ship-building, bridges, steam-boat-navigation, implements of husbandry and machinery of all kinds, but to that proud feeling of independence, which disinclines them from many species of labor resorted to by Europeans. There are some farther peculiarities in the condition and character of the scattered population of the west, which rendered the birth of manufactures simultaneous with that of agriculture. In planting himself in the bosom of the wilderness, the settler is often entirely dependant upon his own industry for every article of food and raiment. While he wields the axe, and turns up the soil, his wife plies the needle and the spinning-wheel, and his children draw sugar from the maple, and work at the loom. The finely-watered state of Ohio affords so easy an egress for its internal produce, that could a sure market have been found, it seems little likely that it would have attempted for many years any great establishments of domestic manufactures. But the policy of foreign countries threw so many checks in the way of the agriculturist, and so completely suspended commerce, that the new stimulus given to human industry was felt in the most remote corners of the union.

The instantaneous effect produced by the commercial regulations of Europe, it seems almost impossible to credit; cotton-mills and fulling-mills, distilleries, and manufactories of every description, sprung, as it were, out of the earth; in city, town, village, and even on the forested shores of the western waters. The young Ohio, for instance, which had existed but eight years, in 1811 poured down the western waters woollen, flaxen, and cotton goods, of admirable but coarse texture, spirituous liquors, sugars, &c., to the value of two millions of dollars.

The wonderful aptitude of the Americans for labour of every species, however removed, seemingly, from their accustomed habits, is easily explained, if we consider, first, the mental energy inspired by their free institutions, and, secondly, their general and practical education. An American youth is usually trained to hit a mark with the certainty of an old English cross-bowman; to swim with that dexterity which procured for the young Franklin in London the name of the *American aquatic*; to handle a musket like a soldier, the mechanic's tools like a carpenter, the husband-man's like a farmer, and, not very unfrequently, the needle and scissars like a village taylor. I have taken Ohio as an instance; but the people of the western region universally were in the habit of making in their own families the cotton and woollen garments in which they were clad. This prepared them for that new direction of national industry which the policy of foreign countries rendered indispensable.

The ports being again thrown open by the peace, many of the young manufactures began to decline; many, however, have kept their place from their intrinsic excellence, (more especially the coarse cotton and woollen fabrics,) in spite of the imprudent trade which has glutted the market with foreign goods, and ended by ruining half the fortunes of the great commercial cities. Things seem now to be finding their level; and the citizens are discovering that mercantile speculation is a ruinous game, when the raw produce of the country is not taken in kind for the wrought fabrics of Europe: perhaps Europe may find this a losing game, too; but of this I am not learned enough to speak.

The inhabitants of the west have seen with peculiar dissatisfaction the decay of their manufacturing establishments. It is not only that they have been driven back upon agriculture, without finding a sufficient market for their produce; but (what you may perhaps smile at) those simple but proud republicans are by no means pleased to see their good homespun forsaken by their daughters for the muslin and silks of France and the Indies. Many make a positive resistance to so unbecoming a dereliction of principle and good taste, and hold staunchly to the practice of clothing every member of their family in articles of domestic manufacture. Many gentlemen of property are in the habit of making, on their own estates, every single article of clothing and household furniture: young women of cultivated education, and elegant accomplishments, are found dressed in plain cotton garments, and men presiding in the senate-house of their country in woollen clothes, woven and fashioned by the hands of their own domestics, or even by those of their children.

The reviving ascendancy of the manufacturing over the commercial interest creates a strong community of feeling between the northern and western sections of the Union. Pittsburg, the young Manchester of the United States, must always have the character of a western city, and its maritime port be New Orleans. Corinth was not more truly the eye of Greece than is Pittsburg of America. Pennsylvania, in which it stands, uniting perfectly the characters of an Atlantic and a western state, is truly the key-stone of the federal arch.

But if the new states are thus linked with the north, they have also some feelings in common with the south, and thus, drawing two ways, seem to consolidate that confederacy which Europeans have sometimes prophesied they would break. In the first place, Kentucky and Tenessee, the oldest members of this young family, have not only been peopled from Virginia and the Carolinas, but originally made part of those states. Generously released from their jurisdiction, they still retain a marked affection for their parents; and have, too, a community of evil with them, as well as of origin, in the form of black slavery. It is not unlikely, that the mixture of slave-holding and non-slave-holding states to the west of the Alleghanies, helps to balance the interests between the northern and southern sections of the Union on the floor of congress.

I must here refute a strange assertion, which I have seen in I know not how many foreign journals, namely, that the United States' government is chargeable with the diffusion of black slavery. Every act that this government has ever passed regarding it has tended to its suppression; but the extent and nature of its jurisdiction are probably misunderstood by those who charge upon it the black slavery of Kentucky or Louisiana; and they must be ignorant of its acts who omit to ascribe to it the merit of having saved from this curse every republic which has grown up under its jurisdiction.

When first torn from the British empire, we have seen that every corner of the then peopled America was smitten with this plague. Now not one half is, although by the acquisition of Louisiana an immense foreign addition has been made to the evil. It was not until the adoption of the federal constitution, that the congress possessed any power to legislate upon the subject of the slave-trade. The abolition laws passed before that period were passed by the states in their individual capacity, and could not be enforced beyond their own respective territories. The powers vested by the new constitution in the general government enabled it to enforce the cessation of the trade throughout the Union, but gave it no control over the domestic slavery wherever existing. The emancipation already effected in eight of the thirteen original states has been effected in each by the acts of its own legislature.

There are at present twenty-two republics in the confederacy; of these, twelve have been rendered free to black and white; the remaining ten continue to be more or less defaced by negro-slavery. Of these five are old states, and the other five either parted from these or formed out of the acquired territory of French Louisiana. Thus,—Kentucky was raised into an independent state by mutual agreement between herself and Virginia, of which she originally formed a part. Tenessee, by mutual agreement between herself and Carolina, to which she was originally attached. Mississippi was surrender to the general government by Georgia, to be raised when old enough into an independent state; but with a stipulation that to the citizens of Georgia should be continued the privilege of migrating into it with their slaves. Louisiana proper, formed out of a small portion of the vast territory ceded under that name, came into the possession of the United States with the united evils of black slavery in its most hideous form, and the slave-trade prosecuted with relentless barbarity. The latter crime was instantly arrested; and, under the improving influence of mild laws and mental instruction, the horrors of slavery have been greatly alleviated.

In all these cases the federal government has been powerless to effect the eradication of slavery. It has, however, been all powerful to prevent its introduction in such territories as have been placed under its control.

Ohio was the first state formed from the commencement upon American principles. It was planted by the hand of congress, in the vast region ceded by Virginia to the north-west of the river Ohio. In the formation of a new state out of the national waste lands, its government is entrusted to the congress of the United States, who mark its boundaries, nominate its public officers and defray the expenses of its government, until its population amounts to sixty thousand souls; when it is entitled to summon a convention, establish its own constitution, enter upon the administration and expenses of its own government, and take its place in the confederacy as a independent republic.

In 1787, the congress passed an act, establishing a temporary government for the infant population settled on the lands of Ohio; and the government then established has served as the model of that of all the territories that have since been formed in the vacant wilderness. The act then passed contained a clause which operated upon the whole national territory to the north-west of the Ohio. By this, "slavery and involuntary servitude" was positively excluded from this region, by a law of the general government. Ohio, Indiana, Illinois, and Michigan, have already sprung up in the bosom of this desert; the three first independent states, and the latter about to pass from her days of tutelage to assume the same character.

It is deserving of observation, that for the passing of this law a unanimous vote of the states was necessary, according to the old articles of confederation then in force. By a unanimous vote it was passed; not a dissentient voice being raised by Virginia, who had ceded the territory in question, nor by the other states of the south, who thus voluntarily deprived their slave-holding citizens of the right of migrating into it.

Thus saved from the disgraceful and ruinous contagion of African servitude, this young family of republics have started in their career with a vigor and a purity of character that has not an equal in the history of the world. Ohio, which twenty-five years since was a vacant wilderness, now contains half a million of inhabitants, and returns six representatives to the national congress. In the other and younger members of the western family, the ratio of encrease is similar. It is curious to consider, that the adventurous settler is yet alive, who felled the first tree to the west of the Alleghanies. The log-hut of Daniel Boon is now on the wild shores of the Missouri, a host of firmly established republics stretching betwixt him and the habitation of his boyhood.

It is plain that in the course of a few generations, the most populous and powerful division of the American family will be watered by the Mississippi, not the Atlantic. From the character of their infancy we may prophesy, that the growing preponderance of the western republics will redound to the national honor, and will draw more closely the social league, which binds together the great American family.

Bred up under the eye, and fostered by the care of the federal government, they have attached themselves to the national institutions with a devotion of feeling unknown in the older parts of the Republic. Their patriotism has all the ardor, and their policy all the ingenuousness of youth. I have already had occasion to observe upon the enthusiasm with which they asserted the liberties and honor of their country during the last war. Their spirit throughout that contest was truly chivalrous. The anecdotes recorded not only of the valor, but of the romantic generosity of the western army of volunteers, might grace the noblest page of the revolutionary history. Nor have the people of the west shown themselves less generous in the senate than the field. In the hall of the representatives, they are invariably on the side of what is most honorable and high-minded. Even should they err, you feel that you would rather err with them than be wise with more long-headed or more cold-hearted politicians.

In considering America generally, one finds a character in her foreign to Europe,—something which there would be accounted visionary; a liberality of sentiment, and a nationality of feeling, not founded upon the mere accident of birth, but upon the appreciation of that civil liberty to which she owes all her greatness and happiness. It is to be expected, however, that in the democracies of the west, these distinctions will be yet more peculiarly marked.

It seems to be a vulgar belief in Europe, that the American wilderness is usually settled by the worst members of the community. The friend I write to is well aware that it is generally by the best. The love of liberty, which the emigrant bears with him from the shores of the Connecticut, the Hudson, or Potomac, is exalted and refined in the calm and seclusion of nature's primeval woods, and boundless prairies. Some reckless spirits, spurning all law and social order, must doubtless mingle with the more virtuous crowd; but these rarely settle down as farmers. They start ahead of the advanced guard of civilisation, and form a wandering troop of hunters, approximating in life and, sometimes, in character to the Indians, their associates. At other times they assume the occupation of shepherds, driving on their cattle from pasture to pasture, according as fancy leads them on from one fair prairie to another still fairer, or according as the approaching tide of population threatens to encroach upon their solitude and their wild dominion. . . .

I have given but a rude sketch of the great divisions of this republic: a subject of this kind admits not of much precision; or, at any rate, my pencil is not skilled enough to handle it ably. I wish you to observe, however, that the birth of the new states has tended to consolidate the union; and that their growing importance is likely to be felt in the same manner; contrary to the calculations of long-sighted politicians, who foretold that as the integral parts of this great political structure should strengthen and multiply, the cement which held them together would crumble away; and that as the interests of the extended community should become more various, it would be distracted with more party animosities.

The fact is, that every sapient prophecy with regard to America has been disproved. We were forewarned that she was too free, and her liberty has proved her security; too peaceable, and she has been found sufficient for her defence; too large, and her size has insured her union. These numerous republics, scattered through so wide a range of territory, embracing all the climates, and containing all the various products of the earth, seem destined, in the course of years, to form a world within themselves, independent alike of the treasures and the industry of all the other sections of the globe. Each year they are learning, more and more, to look to each other for all the various articles of food and raiment; while the third great human necessity,—defence, they have been from infancy practised to furnish in common. The bonds of union, indeed, are more numerous and intimate than can be easily conceived by foreigners. A people who have bled together for liberty, who equally appreciate and equally enjoy that liberty which their own blood or that of their fathers has purchased; who feel, too, that the liberty which they love has found her last asylum on their shores; such a people are bound together by ties of amity and citizenship far beyond what is usual in national communities.

harper ⚡ torchbooks

HUMANITIES AND SOCIAL SCIENCES

American Studies: General

LOUIS D. BRANDEIS: Other People's Money, and How the Bankers Use It ‡   TB/3081

HENRY STEELE COMMAGER, Ed.: The Struggle for Racial Equality   TB/1300

CARL N. DEGLER, Ed.: Pivotal Interpretations of American History   Vol. I   TB/1240;   Vol. II   TB/1241

A. S. EISENSTADT, Ed.: The Craft of American History: Recent Essays in American Historical Writing
       Vol. I   TB/1255;   Vol. II   TB/1256

CHARLOTTE P. GILMAN: Women and Economics. ‡ Ed. by Carl N. Degler with an Introduction   TB/3073

MARCUS LEE HANSEN: The Atlantic Migration: 1607-1860.   TB/1052

JOHN HIGHAM, Ed.: The Reconstruction of American History△   TB/1068

ROBERT H. JACKSON: The Supreme Court in the American System of Government   TB/1106

LEONARD W. LEVY, Ed.: American Constitutional Law   TB/1285

LEONARD W. LEVY, Ed.: Judicial Review and the Supreme Court   TB/1296

LEONARD W. LEVY: The Law of the Commonwealth and Chief Justice Shaw   TB/1309

HENRY F. MAY: Protestant Churches and Industrial America   TB/1334

RICHARD B. MORRIS: Fair Trial: Fourteen Who Stood Accused, from Anne Hutchinson to Alger Hiss. New Preface by the Author   TB/1335

RALPH BARTON PERRY: Puritanism and Democracy   TB/1138

American Studies: Colonial

BERNARD BAILYN: The New England Merchants in the Seventeenth Century   TB/1149

JOSEPH CHARLES: The Origins of the American Party System   TB/1049

HENRY STEELE COMMAGER & ELMO GIORDANETTI, Eds.: Was America a Mistake? An Eighteenth Century Controversy   TB/1329

CHARLES GIBSON: Spain in America †   TB/3077

LAWRENCE HENRY GIPSON: The Coming of the Revolution: 1763-1775. † Illus.   TB/3007

PERRY MILLER & T. H. JOHNSON, Eds.: The Puritans: A Sourcebook   Vol. I   TB/1093;   Vol. II   TB/1094

EDMUND S. MORGAN, Ed.: The Diary of Michael Wigglesworth, 1653-1657   TB/1228

EDMUND S. MORGAN: The Puritan Family   TB/1227

RICHARD B. MORRIS: Government and Labor in Early America   TB/1244

WALLACE NOTESTEIN: The English People on the Eve of Colonization: 1603-1630. † Illus.   TB/3006

JOHN P. ROCHE: Origins of American Political Thought: Selected Readings   TB/1301

JOHN SMITH: Captain John Smith's America: Selections from His Writings   TB/3078

American Studies: From the Revolution to 1860

MAX BELOFF: The Debate on the American Revolution: 1761-1783   TB/1225

RAY A. BILLINGTON: The Far Western Frontier: 1830-1860. † Illus.   TB/3012

GEORGE DANGERFIELD: The Awakening of American Nationalism: 1815-1828. † Illus.   TB/3061

WILLIAM W. FREEHLING, Ed.: The Nullification Era: A Documentary Record ‡   TB/3079

JOHN C. MILLER: Alexander Hamilton and the Growth of the New Nation   TB/3057

RICHARD B. MORRIS, Ed.: The Era of the American Revolution   TB/1180

R. B. NYE: The Cultural Life of the New Nation: 1776-1801. † Illus.   TB/3026

A. F. TYLER: Freedom's Ferment   TB/1074

LOUIS B. WRIGHT: Culture on the Moving Frontier   TB/1053

American Studies: Since the Civil War

MAX BELOFF, Ed.: The Debate on the American Revolution, 1761-1783: A Sourcebook   TB/1225

W. R. BROCK: An American Crisis: Congress and Reconstruction, 1865-67 ° △   TB/1283

A. RUSSELL BUCHANAN: The United States and World War II. † Illus.   Vol. I   TB/3044;   Vol. II   TB/3045

EDMUND BURKE: On the American Revolution. † Edited by Elliot Robert Barkan   TB/3068

THOMAS C. COCHRAN & WILLIAM MILLER: The Age of Enterprise: A Social History of Industrial America   TB/1054

WHITNEY R. CROSS: The Burned-Over District: The Social and Intellectual History of Enthusiastic Religion in Western New York, 1800-1850   TB/1242

FOSTER RHEA DULLES: America's Rise to World Power: 1898-1954. † Illus.   TB/3021

W. A. DUNNING: Reconstruction, Political and Economic: 1865-1877   TB/1073

HAROLD U. FAULKNER: Politics, Reform and Expansion: 1890-1900. † Illus.   TB/3020

FRANCIS GRIERSON: The Valley of Shadows   TB/1246

SIDNEY HOOK: Reason, Social Myths, and Democracy   TB/1237

WILLIAM E. LEUCHTENBURG: Franklin D. Roosevelt and the New Deal: 1932-1940. † Illus.   TB/3025

JAMES MADISON: The Forging of American Federalism. Edited by Saul K. Padover   TB/1226

ARTHUR MANN: Yankee Reformers in the Urban Age   TB/1247

GEORGE E. MOWRY: The Era of Theodore Roosevelt and the Birth of Modern America: 1900-1912 †   TB/3022

R. B. NYE: Midwestern Progressive Politics   TB/1202

JAMES PARTON: The Presidency of Andrew Jackson, From Vol. III of the Life of Andrew Jackson ‡   TB/3080

---

† The New American Nation Series, edited by Henry Steele Commager and Richard B. Morris.

‡ American Perspectives series, edited by Bernard Wishy and William E. Leuchtenburg.

* The Rise of Modern Europe series, edited by William L. Langer.

** History of Europe series, edited by J. H. Plumb.

¶ Researches in the Social, Cultural and Behavioral Sciences, edited by Benjamin Nelson.

§ The Library of Religion and Culture, edited by Benjamin Nelson.

Σ Harper Modern Science Series, edited by James R. Newman.

° Not for sale in Canada.

△ Not for sale in the U. K.

3